THE REMARKABLE LIFE
OF REED PEGGRAM

THE REMARKABLE LIFE
OF REED PEGGRAM

THE MAN WHO STARED DOWN
WORLD WAR II IN THE NAME OF LOVE

ETHELENE WHITMIRE

Viking

VIKING
An imprint of Penguin Random House LLC
1745 Broadway, New York, NY 10019
penguinrandomhouse.com

Grateful acknowledgment is made to Debra Farrar-Parkman for permission
to reprint the excerpts of the personal letters of Reed Peggram, which
have been approved solely for use in this book.

Image credits may be found on page 291.

Designed by Christina Nguyen

LIBRARY OF CONGRESS CONTROL NUMBER: 2025029890
ISBN 9780593654194 (hardcover)
ISBN 9780593654200 (ebook)

Printed in the United States of America
1st Printing

The authorized representative in the EU for product safety and compliance is
Penguin Random House Ireland, Morrison Chambers, 32 Nassau Street,
Dublin D02 YH68, Ireland, https://eu-contact.penguin.ie.

TO LAURA REED,

for taking a chance to start a new life in the North
to give her family a chance for a better future

Contents

THE REMARKABLE LIFE
OF REED PEGGRAM

Prologue

On Saturday, August 20, 1938, twenty-four-year-old Reed Peggram boarded SS *Veendam* of the Holland America Line set to sail from Hoboken, New Jersey. The steamship, one of the largest in its fleet, was headed toward Rotterdam, Netherlands, but Reed's final destination was Paris. A doctoral student in comparative literature at Harvard University, Reed was traveling on the prestigious Rosenwald Fellowship to study at the Sorbonne, a fellowship that had been given to literary and cultural luminaries like Zora Neale Hurston, Langston Hughes, and W. E. B. Du Bois before him.

Although no photographs exist of him walking up the gangplank, there's no doubt that he was dressed in a suit and tie. Reed was a dapper dresser, fastidious about his appearance, and in photographs he had an erect carriage and a penetrating gaze that belied his humble beginnings. He was slim and average in height, dark brown and handsome with dark hair and eyes and full lips that easily curved up on one side in a playful smile.

Besides his intended intellectual pursuits, he had something else on his mind: this journey was his chance to become a proper gentleman. He already read the right books, attended the theater, opera, and symphonies, and went to art museums. He spoke French fluently—his Harvard professor said "comparable to a native born Frenchman"—and knew German and Spanish too. He had wowed in the halls of America's finest universities, had found a network of like-minded intellectuals, but he longed for the experience that he knew would shape his worldview and make him into the person he felt destined to be—the experience of traveling abroad. The fact that he was African American was no hindrance to his aspirations. Reed didn't see himself as others sometimes did. In fact, he already knew how to wield his considerable charm, sharp wit, and good looks to great effect. Beyond the cultural and academic significance such a trip would offer, Reed carried personal ambitions too. Travel to Europe would mean the chance for sexual freedom as a queer man in spaces that might be more open and where no one knew him, and indeed he carried with him letters of introduction to meet like-minded men on the continent. He also hoped to find love. He was a romantic, he wrote poetry, and it was no accident that the thesis he intended to finish in Paris was on decadence in nineteenth-century French literature—a movement that prized extravagance and lushness of language, embraced aesthetic hedonism, and was uninterested in conventional societal expectations. And he would fall deeply in love with a Danish man named Arne—but it would be his downfall.

As Reed boarded the ship to cross the Atlantic Ocean, the US State Department was already urging American citizens to leave Europe. The continent was on edge about another possible great war breaking out. But Reed ignored this call—he had waited much of his life to go to Paris. His undergraduate thesis was about the novels of Gustave Flaubert, *Madame Bovary* and *A Sentimental Education*; he'd spent years studying the French language and listening to the music of Debussy. He finally had the funds and an opportunity to live in Paris and study at the Sorbonne and the national library of France. He would not let the threat of war deter him.

SEVENTY-EIGHT YEARS AFTER REED first arrived in Europe, I gave a keynote address in September 2016, "The African American Presence in Denmark in the 20th Century," at the University of Copenhagen during a symposium about Denmark and African American culture.

I'd first visited Copenhagen for two months in 2010 on a whim. At the time, I was watching a lot of Danish films and wanted to live abroad while revising my first book. So I decided to go to Copenhagen. While there, I fell in love with the friendly people and with the city—a beautiful blend of old architecture, brightly colored exteriors, and cobblestoned streets, mixed with interiors that reflected cool, modern Scandinavian design.

The apartment where I originally lived was in the Christianshavn section of Copenhagen, where canals flow throughout, earning it the nickname of "Little Amsterdam." From the rooftop, I could see the iconic Church of Our Saviour with its winding exterior staircase. I loved the café culture with candles lit throughout the day during all seasons to create *hygge*—coziness. I returned multiple times before I came back to Copenhagen in an official capacity as a Fulbright Scholar and gave the talk that would direct my research for years to come.

The symposium was at the Søndre Campus of the university on the outskirts of Copenhagen in the Amager section of the city, and was sponsored by the US embassy in Denmark in support of my Fulbright assignment. This campus's modern buildings with lots of ongoing construction stood in contrast to the historical campus in the city center, founded in 1479. The seminar room was stark—not Danish design minimalism with blond woods, but plain white with industrial, functional furniture. My colleague Martyn joked that the department's space resembled a prison with the main floor opening up to offices on tiers like cells.

Several students from the course I was teaching, "Introduction to African American Women," were in the audience, as were many of my friends, both Black and white, including the widows of jazz legend Dexter Gordon and journalist Skip Malone, subjects in my project about African Americans in Denmark. Two of my African American friends, Furaha and Cherene, English professors in the United States, were visiting, and Cherene was also presenting at the event.

For forty-five minutes, I spoke about African Americans who visited, studied, performed, and lived in Denmark during the twentieth century: Booker T. Washington, Ella Fitzgerald, Ben Webster, and Billie Holiday; educators, writers, painters, singers, jazz musicians, diplomats, Black Panthers, and many other African Americans, both famous and obscure, had had significant experiences in Denmark. The presentation ended to applause, and I prepared for the question and answer session that was to come next.

I got a few questions about why African Americans' experiences were overwhelmingly positive. Did they form communities in Copenhagen? What impact did their presence have on the Danes? Then a young African American graduate student from Boston, whom I'd invited to the event, Teju Adisa-Farrar, raised her hand. I'd met Teju through Denise, a mutual acquaintance, who'd virtually introduced us when she'd realized we'd both be in Copenhagen at the same time. Denise probably thought it would be good to connect Teju with another African American person in this Nordic nation—I could even tell Teju where to get her dreadlocks groomed because I had them too. But I couldn't have anticipated the words that came out of her mouth. With a voice as clear as a bell, she announced that Reed Peggram, one of the focal points of my talk, had been her great-uncle.

Although Teju had never met Reed because he died before she was born, she recognized the photograph I'd used during my presentation, having seen it in her home growing up. She wanted me to know—she wanted everyone in that lecture hall to know—that there was more to Reed's story than met the eye. I also wanted to know more. Of all the people I'd discussed during my presentation, Reed was one of the most intriguing. He was a brilliant scholar who attended some of the oldest and most prestigious educational institutions in the United States and in France. He was one of few African Americans to graduate from the Boston Latin School in 1931 and one of a handful of African Americans to attend Harvard University in the 1930s, where, I later learned, he fell in love with the future famous composer Leonard Bernstein.

A few days later, Teju came to my office at the university. As we spoke, I realized what an incredible coincidence this was. Teju's family is quite small—about fifteen members in the whole world. Her father, Dr. Tarik Farrar, was extremely close to his uncle Reed. He'd also attended Harvard and became a university professor—the career Reed desired but never attained.

As a historian, I had struck gold. I knew that meeting Teju—and eventually her aunt and father—would give me access to a man whose experiences fascinated me. I came into possession of copies of a treasure trove of approximately two hundred letters that Reed wrote between 1936 and 1945 detailing his experiences, who he met, and what he thought. Reed's grandmother Laura had saved the letters he sent to her when he lived in New York while studying at Columbia University and letters he sent from Paris, Copenhagen, and Florence before and during World War II. I would eventually travel to the places where he lived and visited in the United States, France, Denmark, and Italy; I would stay in the two hotels where he resided during the 1938–39 academic year in Paris. I saw his library card from the Shakespeare and Company bookstore in Paris and knew every book he checked out. I collected a large number of primary sources, including photographs of Reed from his educational institutions and the Danish and Italian national archives.

LIKE REED, I AM also the child of two blue-collar workers, and although we lived comfortably, circumstances never allowed them to have abundant material success. My father grew up under Jim Crow in South Carolina and ultimately migrated to New

Jersey. He only had the opportunity to achieve an eighth-grade education, even though he'd wanted to stay in school. Although I did not attend elite Ivy League universities like Reed, I did attend public universities—first Rutgers and then the University of Michigan for my doctorate—something that my father was proud of. I was able to become a college professor—at the University of California–Los Angeles (UCLA) and the University of Wisconsin–Madison. Reed and I both came from humble backgrounds. We both had the same dream to become a college professor. In this way, Reed's story—his survival—was personal.

So much of Reed's story is exceptional: at the time, it was rare for even wealthy African Americans to have achieved so much, and yet he came from very humble beginnings. What he had done was unheard of for the time. I had no doubt that at least part of his success had to do with his charisma, which more than one Harvard intellectual had noted. Unlike many successful African Americans during the first half of the twentieth century, he was dark-skinned, obviously Black. He did not have a chance to pass as white, even if he'd wanted to. In high school and college yearbook photographs, he was clearly identifiable as the lone African American in any group, including the Phi Beta Kappa photo at Harvard—a fact that made me feel a sense of kinship with him since I, too, often worked and was educated in predominantly white spaces.

But Reed's life is also a window into how many exceptional stories have been lost to history, reinforcing a narrative that this kind of captivating, exhilarating life, one devoted to dignity, beauty, and passion, could not exist for a young, poor Black man like Reed. I have made it my mission to do recovery work about

African Americans, rescuing them from obscurity. Growing up, I learned very little African American history beyond information about the same figures—Dr. Martin Luther King Jr., Rosa Parks, and Malcolm X. It was easy to think, unconsciously, that it was rare for African Americans to do something worthy of note.

I want to show a richer portrait of African Americans beyond the myth that so many of us are poor, uneducated, and limited in our interests, dreams, and aspirations, which was the dominant narrative I had been told. I want to hear stories of people who persevered in the face of racism and legal segregation even when those forces tried to crush their opportunities and ambitions.

When I first came across Reed's story, I had been researching a new project about African Americans in twentieth-century Denmark. Luckily, major historical Black newspapers are now digitized, so I could search all of them simultaneously from my laptop or from my desktop in my campus office overlooking Lake Mendota in Madison, Wisconsin. The headlines about Reed were provocative: "Negro Escapes German Camp in Italy," "Two Scholars Flee Concentration Camp," and "Boy Friends Scorn Bombs, Come Out OK."

War correspondent Max Johnson, writing for the African American newspapers the Cleveland *Call and Post*, the New York *Amsterdam News*, and the Baltimore *Afro-American*, called Reed's and Arne's story "a modern version of Damon and Pythias," the Greek legend about two friends who were willing to sacrifice their own lives for the sake of the other, concluding, "If Peggram's story proves to be correct, it will undoubtedly become one of the greatest human-interest stories yet revealed in this war."

The deeper I delved into the life of Reed Peggram, the more

I realized that this wasn't just a human-interest story. In many ways, Reed's story mirrors the larger narrative about African American individuals during and after World War II. The conflict became a pivotal turning point in the civil rights movement and in the lives of the nine hundred thousand African American soldiers who served on the ground, on ships, and, as with the Tuskegee Airmen, as pilots in the skies. The African American press and organizations like the National Association for the Advancement of Colored People (NAACP) waged a "Double V" campaign. They wanted to achieve victory against Fascism abroad during World War II and victory over racism in the United States. There was a movement afoot to no longer accept treatment as second-class citizens. They were transformed and wanted opportunities for advancement and to fight discrimination and segregation.

After the war, Isaac Woodard, a veteran, was in uniform when police attacked him—blinding him—for asking to use the bathroom at a bus depot shortly after he returned from fighting valiantly overseas. The judge who presided over the trial of the law enforcement officer who blinded Woodard was so outraged by the not-guilty verdict that he went on a crusade that culminated in a landmark civil rights case led by Thurgood Marshall, representing the NAACP, and to the eventual *Brown v. Board of Education* case that ended the "separate but equal" legal decision of *Plessy v. Ferguson*. The furor over the blinding of Isaac Woodard was just one of many reasons that President Truman eventually ended segregation in the military in 1948.

After World War II, African American men were given only bad options, their fate not entirely under their control. They were tasked with discovering how to make their way out of impossible situations, even when that meant something as simple as just surviving. While we've heard some of the stories about how veterans did so after the war, what's missing from these narratives is an understanding of how civilians—everyday people—did the same thing. Even before the war ended.

While there are many World War II books about spies, code breakers, and resistance fighters, few titles share the stories of civilians living in Europe on the eve of the war and during the occupation, being imprisoned in a camp, and surviving. There are even fewer stories of African Americans, much less a queer African American scholar who went to Europe for a one-year fellowship and ended up staying for seven years—nearly the entire war in Europe. Telling Reed's story sheds light on experiences particular to a person—but also to a nation—that have for too long remained underexplored. Reed yearned for a better life, filled with intellectual pursuits, international travel, beauty, art, music, and love. He wanted to escape from the stereotype of what it meant to be an African American in the United States. He believed that his magnetism and intelligence could overcome racial prejudice, and he believed he could find love despite anti-homosexual laws and beliefs.

Reed wrote to his mother that "my trip to Europe has been one of the most unusual. If I ever get out of all of this alive, I won't have to write novels. I can simply write books about myself and my adventures." While he was never able to write that book, his story was not lost. This is one of those books.

ONE

"An Unusually Fine Representative of His Race"

R eed's maternal grandmother, Laura Reed, born just four years after the end of slavery in 1869 in Dinwiddie, Virginia, felt validated in her decision to move to Boston in 1895. Laura was one of eight children; her father was a laborer and later a farmer, and her mother kept house. Their family was described as mulatto—a mixture of Black and white ancestry—though they would have been treated undoubtedly as Black in post–Civil War America. Although many of the 1890 census records were either lost or severely damaged in a disastrous fire, we know she married John Reed on May 4, 1892, when she was twenty-three years old. John, like Laura, was from Dinwiddie. By the following August, her husband was dead of unknown causes at age twenty-three. Laura was now a single parent to an infant daughter. Although she lived in a thriving community of African Americans where some held elected office in the Virginia Senate and House of Representatives, worked as lawyers, and had the opportunity to obtain a postsecondary education at the Virginia Normal and Collegiate Institute established in 1883 for the Black population, she nevertheless wanted to leave for the promise of more prospects in the North, or possibly she was looking for a new adventure.

Twenty-five-year-old Laura migrated to the North most likely by train from Virginia with probable stops in Washington, D.C.; Baltimore; Wilmington, Delaware; Philadelphia; New Haven, Connecticut; and Providence, Rhode Island, until she reached her final destination—Boston. A relative was retiring and suggested her as a replacement for a janitorial job in the Boston public schools. She traveled with her young daughter, Mamie, who had been renamed Mary after a white schoolteacher told her Mamie wasn't a "real name." Laura yearned for a better life for herself and, more important, for her child, hoping to escape legal segregation, and for more educational and occupational opportunities available in the North. With only a third-grade education, she had limited job prospects; consequently, she wanted her daughter to obtain a higher degree of education.

Laura migrated nearly two decades before the beginning of the mass exodus of African Americans that is now known as the Great Migration, which took place between 1915 and 1975. When Laura arrived in Boston, a large number of African American organizations run by women throughout the United States had gathered there for the First National Conference of the Colored Women of America in order to create a national organization for African American women. Josephine St. Pierre Ruffin, an activist and editor, organized the conference, and guest speakers included Anna Julia Cooper, an author, educator, and activist. At the Sorbonne, Cooper became one of the first African American women to receive a Ph.D. Their focus was on uplifting less fortunate African American women by providing financial, moral, and spiritual guidance.

It is unlikely that Laura attended this event, because the conference participants were from the elite classes, including Margaret Murray Washington, the third wife of twice-widowed Booker T. Washington, and Helen Pitts Douglass, the widow of Frederick Douglass. But Laura would've believed in their message of uplifting the race—with a focus on women. A few years later, by 1900, she settled at 110 Hemenway Street with her daughter, Mary, and her sixteen-year-old sister Elizabeth Harvey, who had followed in her footsteps migrating north. Their neighbors included Black families, most also from Virginia, and white people, many of whom were foreign-born, hailing from England, Scotland, Canada, Ireland, and Germany. They primarily toiled in the service industries, with occupations including laundress, cook, seamstress, florist, bartender, salesman, housekeeper, hotel waiter, and hotel clerk. Laura worked as a "janitoress" at a local school and took on additional work cleaning homes for wealthy Dorchester families. Elizabeth, despite her young age, worked as a domestic, possibly cooking, cleaning, and doing laundry in private homes. Laura hoped to save her daughter from such a fate and dreamed of owning her own home one day.

By 1910, when Mary was nineteen, they had moved to 281 Hancock Street and Elizabeth no longer lived with the family, but Laura took in a lodger, William Smith, a forty-year-old African American porter for the railroad. It was common for families, especially African American households, to take in lodgers to help with the rent. In this new neighborhood, the majority of their neighbors were white and born in Massachusetts, with a smaller number of immigrants from England and Ireland. Their occupations were blue collar: teamster, bricklayer, laundress, painter, blacksmith, driver, and grave digger. Laura continued working as a janitor and cleaning houses on the side.

Mary graduated from Girls' High School—perhaps among the first in her family to reach this educational achievement. Laura must've been proud and felt validated in her decision to move north.

It is not known how Mary met Reed's father, Harvey, but in March 1914, twenty-three-year-old Mary wed twenty-five-year-old Harvey Thomas Peggram. They may have bonded over having family ties in Virginia: Harvey was from Petersburg, in Dinwiddie County, mere miles from where Laura had grown up. Harvey's surname was an unusual one, and evidence suggests that he can trace his roots back to the white Pegrams (with one *g*) of Petersburg and Dinwiddie County. John Pegram was a Virginia state senator and a major general in the Virginia state militia in the War of 1812, and served in Congress in the US House of Representatives. He was also a "planter"—a more genteel name for an enslaver, usually denoting a more privileged status. The enslaved African American people, whose names were not recorded, were most likely Harvey's ancestors. As was the custom of the census takers, they did not name the enslaved people on the schedule, noting only their gender and age ranges. It is possible that the formerly enslaved took the surname Pegram and changed it to Peggram post-emancipation.

Harvey's maternal grandparents—Reed's great-grandparents—

were Amanda and Joseph Briggs, born around 1831 and 1828, respectively, during slavery. But Joseph was not enslaved. At the time of their marriage, they lived in Norfolk, Virginia, where Joseph worked as a carpenter in construction in 1850. He eventually moved his family to Petersburg, home of one of the largest populations of free Black people in the state of Virginia. These roots suggest that Harvey came from a community where education and activism were embedded in the fabric of his birthplace.

A few months after their wedding, Mary gave birth to the only child born from this marriage, Reed Edwin, on July 26, 1914. On that day, the local newspaper, the *Boston Sunday Globe*, reported that the Boston Red Sox baseball team won thanks to a triple in the ninth inning by left fielder George Edward "Duffy" Lewis and his single in the eleventh. Another headline on the front page was more ominous: "Armies Mobilize for Great European War." World War I, or the Great War as it was called before there was a World War II, was about to commence after the assassination of Archduke Franz Ferdinand in Sarajevo. Although the war officially began two days after Reed's birth, the United States did not immediately enter the battle and struggled to remain neutral despite sympathy with Britain and France and their support of the Allies.

Mary's new family lived at 281 Hancock Street with Laura. During the ensuing years, Harvey worked variously as an instructor, a card writer, and a stenographer to support his young family. But Harvey was really a dreamer and a performer who traveled around the East Coast reciting poetry and acting in churches. In May 1917, he successfully staged a short play in Pittston, Pennsylvania, in St. Mark's A.M.E. Church. A review enthused, "The professor showed great ability in handling the playette, his impersonation of the Jew, Italian, Irishman and Negro being perfect. He held his audience in laughter for almost two hours and the affair was much enjoyed." He performed with a soprano soloist and an accompanist. Harvey did not have a doctorate, but sometimes the honorific of professor was conferred on a member of the African American community as a sign of respect for a person's intellect. Harvey had graduated from Peabody High School and attended the Hampton Institute, later Hampton University, a Black institution in Virginia that in 1907 was primarily a trade school and offered elementary- and secondary-level curriculum. But for an African American born in 1891, attending such an institution indicated someone who had aspirations and took their education seriously. Other evidence of Harvey's striving was his membership in the Boston Negro Business League, the local chapter of the National Negro Business League presided over at that time by Booker T. Washington. The organization's objective was "to promote the commercial and financial development of the Negro" to advance the race. They brainstormed business ideas while encouraging members to own their own businesses, taught them about marketing, and provided a meeting place for like-minded individuals. The 16th Convention of the National Negro Business League was held in Boston in August 1915. The members attended business sessions and presentations about "Raising Poultry for Market" and "My Department Store." Women also presented at sessions including "How I Have Carried on the Ice Cream Manufacturing Business Established by My Mother and Father." The program had ads for various businesses including real estate agents, grocery stores, stenographer services, piano lessons, and a bookstore that sold race books. Attendees could take trolley trips to historic sites in Boston including the Paul Revere House and a trip down Boston Harbor on the steamer *The City of Boston*. The convention ended with a reception with ham, chicken and lobster salads, potatoes, peach fritters, and pound cake.

The United States entered the Great War on April 6, 1917, when President Woodrow Wilson declared war on Germany after repeated submarine attacks on passenger and merchant ships, including the *Lusitania* in 1915, resulting in a great loss of American lives.

Harvey was inducted into the US Army on November 6, 1917. He boldly declared on his draft card that he was an artist—an unusual occupation for an African American man at the beginning of the twentieth century. He eventually went to training camp, Camp Lee, but didn't think much of the hierarchical nature of the armed forces. Weeks after the United States entered the war in 1917, Camp Lee was established as a mobilization and training camp to prepare men to go to France and Germany. In various documents, Harvey listed his mother as his next of kin, perhaps indicating that Harvey and his wife, Mary, were no longer together.

The following year, Harvey published a poem in the March 9, 1918, edition of the *Richmond Planet* newspaper in Virginia entitled "'Who Is That Man?' or 'The Lieutenant.'" It was attributed to Harvey Thomas Peggram, but underneath his name it said, "Mr. Peggram writes under the name of Peggy, the artist."

Who is that man who's very straight,
Who's on the job soon after eight,
Who, if you breathe without prevention
Yells to you, "You're at Attention?"
THE LIEUTENANT

Who is the man with eyes so keen,
Who when he visits the latrine
And finds the fellows by the score,
Puts them all out of the door?
THE LIEUTENANT

Who is the man with uniform nice
Who catches fellows shooting dice;
And tho they're frightened to be sure
He simply bellows, "As you were!"
THE LIEUTENANT

Who is the man with leggins leather;
Who walks as tho he were a feather,
And when he meets you on the street
Looks you over from head to feet?
THE LIEUTENANT

Who is that man who, all the time—
Whether rain, hail, storm or shine—
Seldom with the soldiers jokes,
But never forgets his fancy smokes?
THE LIEUTENANT

Who is that man with pretty shoes;
Who frequently reads the "Daily News,"
And while He's in the trolley car,
Still smokes his twenty five cent cigar?
    THE LIEUTENANT

Who is he who, when going along
If he sees you're getting in wrong
Will bellow to you, "Now cut that out"
And have you make the face about?
    THE LIEUTENANT

Who is that man who you can see
Every morning at reveille;
And who, if you go "drooping round"
Will cut you off from going to town?
    THE LIEUTENANT

Who is that man, who after all
Is not necessarily tall;
Who's fond of popularity
And, really has authority?
    THE LIEUTENANT

He seemed to be mocking this authority figure in the poem, likely based upon his experiences in the army. No other published poems were located under his real name or his pseudonym, but the poem's contemptuous tone suggests a rebellious streak that sometimes held his dignity dearer than his safety.

In early 1918, while a trooper at Camp Lee, Harvey traveled approximately twenty-five miles to Richmond, boarded a street-car, and sat down. At some point the conductor told him to move farther in the back to make room for white passengers. Harvey protested that there were plenty of seats in the front for the white people to sit and refused to move. He was arrested and taken to a police station. Harvey called the office of the *Richmond Planet* and the editor, John Mitchell Jr., paid one hundred dollars to bail Harvey out. Justice H. A. Maurice listened to Harvey's explanation and sent him back to the military base.

Segregated streetcars in Richmond had a long history. Fourteen years before Harvey's incident, African American citizens boycotted the streetcars in 1904 over a court decision to reverse forty years of integration on Richmond streetcars. The new legislation gave the streetcar companies the option of segregating the streetcars—leaving the decision up to the conductor, who was almost always a white man. The conductor would also be able to arrest noncompliant citizens. There wouldn't be official signs dividing the streetcar, but white passengers would sit up front and African Americans in the back, and they would have to continue moving back as more white passengers entered. Not surprisingly, the African American community protested. John Mitchell Jr. was one of the people leading the charge to boycott the streetcars, writing numerous articles in the newspaper. The subsequent boycott eventually bankrupted the company running the streetcars, but was ultimately defeated when a new company took over and a 1906 legislation strengthened the segregation order. Mitchell, born enslaved, became the editor of the *Richmond Planet* in 1884 and had a reputation as "the fighting editor," which might have been enough for the judge to decide he did not want to take up a battle against Harvey.

After he completed training, Harvey's ship, SS *Suwanee*, departed from Newport News, Virginia, on May 15, 1918, for France. Harvey was a private in the Medical Unit as part of the Veterinary Corps in the National Army, responsible for taking care of animals. The army found it was often easier to use horses than vehicles to traverse the rough and muddy terrain in France for a variety of tasks, including transporting equipment, artillery, and supplies, and as ambulance services. Harvey was honorably discharged on March 7, 1919, and his military service officially ended on September 9 of that year. He was discharged 100 percent disabled. There were no indications that he suffered any physical injuries; this was likely in reference to his mental disability.

Once back in the United States, Harvey did not return to live with Mary and Reed. Although Mary was torn about whether she should take him back, Laura was adamant that Mary should leave him.

Harvey was eventually diagnosed with dementia praecox, or what was commonly known as schizophrenia, and was hospitalized on January 7, 1920, at Central State Hospital, formerly the Central Lunatic Asylum for Colored Insane, in Petersburg, Virginia. He was twenty-eight years old, his occupation listed as a "paid writer." Although he had fled the South for the better prospects in the North, Harvey ended up back where he started in his hometown. Mary filed for divorce on November 26, 1920, on the grounds of desertion and was given custody of six-year-old Reed when the divorce was granted on May 27, 1921.

Mary had more education than her mother and supposedly better occupational prospects, but in many respects, she had repeated her mother's life under different circumstances, now without a husband and with a young child in her care. She became a day worker, doing laundry and cleaning houses. Laura, who always wanted more for Mary, was heartbroken. African American women working in private homes were often vulnerable to sexual harassment and assaults from the fathers and sometimes the teenage sons. Additionally, the jobs were frequently humiliating. Housekeepers were regularly asked to enter residences through the back doors, occasionally they were not allowed to use the bathrooms during their working hours, and they were consistently told to use honorifics such as "Sir," "Miss," and "Mister" to address the adults and sometimes the children, while they were called only by their first name. Although Reed was young, he no doubt observed both his mother and grandmother return home weary after an exhausting day spent doing physical labor. Surely he overheard them describe degrading experiences, demeaning treatment like cleaning floors on their hands and knees, and the disgusting work cleaning bodily fluids in bathrooms, in bedding, and in clothes. Like his grandmother, Reed dreamed of a different future for himself.

Laura sometimes brought her grandson, a cute, well-mannered, dark-skinned child, along as she cleaned private homes. She worked for Harriet Browne and her three schoolteacher daughters C. Margaret, Ruth, and Hattie, and for Frank L. Clapp, a civil engineer who later married Ruth. Reed noted the trappings of the Clapp and Browne families—their books, music, and art. He possibly heard their discussions about their international travels, attending the theater, the opera, and symphonies. Perhaps they gave Laura and Reed their discarded books and records. It was in these homes that the seed of hope first grew in Reed about living a better life than his mother and grandmother did. Although the Clapps and Brownes were white, Reed thought if he was successful academically and dressed and carried himself with the same comportment as these two distinguished families, he could overcome the barrier of his race and modest origins. He began to take on his grandmother's yearning. Reed, too, noted the Brownes' condescension, and it fueled his desire to show them he was just as good as their family.

In hopes of escaping her fate as a cleaning woman and a single parent, Mary married Phillip Hutchinson Farrar, a man sixteen years her senior who had lost both of his legs in a train accident, moving to Bayonne, New Jersey, to be with him. Unlike Mary, Phillip only had a sixth-grade education. It seemed like an unlikely match, but Phillip was a hard worker and provided for his family as a laborer for an oil company despite his disability. Like her first husband, Phillip was a war veteran, but of the Spanish-American War, having served from April to August 1898. But most important, Mary no longer worked cleaning other people's homes.

Unfortunately, Phillip did not become a second father to Reed. He did not get along with his stepson, who loved classical music, wrote poetry, and preferred reading books to playing sports. Phillip doted on his two biological sons with Mary: Phillip Hutchinson Farrar Jr., born on May 30, 1925, and Vincent Harvell Farrar, born on November 8, 1926, when Reed was a preteen. After living with them for two years, Reed left his mother's new family in New Jersey and returned to Dorchester to live with his grandmother. He enrolled in Edward Everett Elementary School. In a photograph in his student record, he smiled while looking quite debonair in a suit and tie, with hair parted in the middle and trimmed neatly on the sides, in a style he would carry through young adulthood. His eyes twinkled and his look was a knowing one with an impish grin. Reed graduated from the eighth grade from Edward Everett Elementary in 1927.

While Reed continued observing the Clapps, Frank L. Clapp observed both Reed and Laura too. Clapp, acquainted with Reed since birth, noticed how bright he was. Perhaps with Laura's gentle urgings, Clapp used his connections to help Reed gain admittance into the Boston Latin School in 1927. The school was located in an imposing building with four columns framing the front entrance on Avenue Louis Pasteur. Founded in 1635, it is the oldest public school in the United States. Alumni include multiple Harvard University presidents, governors of the state of Massachusetts, and five signers of the Declaration of Independence, including John Hancock. Famous alumni include Benjamin Franklin, Samuel Adams, Paul Revere, and Ralph Waldo Emerson. Very few African Americans attended the Boston Latin School. Parker Bailey, Class of 1877, was the first African American graduate—over two hundred years after it was founded. Students completed an examination and obtained a letter of recommendation from their middle school headmaster in order to be admitted. After World War I, a total of seven African Americans had graduated from Boston Latin School by the 1920s.

Reed thrived there. If his race was a hindrance to his progress, he did not let it show. He had an aptitude—and indeed a passion—for foreign languages. He studied German, French, and Latin, while also participating in the Literary Club and as the business manager for the Dramatic Club.

He observed his classmates' mannerisms. He listened quietly as they discussed their vacations traveling abroad and their leisure-time activities. Despite being African American, he felt like he fit into this world, and it helped him to dream of a different future. It is little wonder that Reed would flourish the most when imagining himself in other places and as other people. For him, it was a matter of survival. He made a little money during high school by tutoring in French and Latin and delivering newspapers.

After Reed had lived with his grandmother for several years, Laura petitioned for legal guardianship of him in 1929. Harvey was listed as "an insane person" and was informed of the proceedings and served a citation via registered mail. Mary signed a form giving her "assent to the granting of the foregoing petition." Guardianship would allow Laura to have more control over Reed's finances and medical care if anything should happen to him. She had been able to save the extraordinary sum of approximately $2,500—around $45,000 in today's dollars—from the $40 a month Reed received from the US Veterans' Bureau based upon his father's disability after serving in the Great War. These funds would help pay for his future college tuition and expenses, including for books, clothing, and glasses.

Reed was one of very few African Americans in his graduating class of 262 students, ranking in the first quarter of the Class of 1931. He received several awards, including "Of Conduct

Above Criticism," "Of Perfection in Attendance," and "Exemplary Conduct and Fidelity"—an award selected by the teachers. Reed also obtained honors on his College Entrance Examinations Board exams in elementary Latin, elementary French, elementary German, and advanced Latin. He received the Modern Prize during his first three years, which was equivalent to the honor roll. Besides studying foreign languages, he took courses in English, ancient history, American history, algebra, geometry, and physics.

Reed applied to college during his senior year. He would be the first in his family to attend a nontechnical trade institution of higher learning, and he wanted to attend the most elite institution of higher learning in the country—Harvard. During this time, Boston Latin School served as a feeder school to Harvard, with a disproportionate number of their graduates enrolling there. Reed benefited from this connection. There was no place to indicate race on his application because almost everyone who applied was white. Because a photograph was attached to his application, there is no doubt that Harvard was aware that Reed was an African American. The writers of his letters of recommendation took care to mention that he was a gentleman as well as noting other positive behavioral aspects of his personality— the discussion of his intellect seemed to be an afterthought.

Frank L. Clapp wrote a two-paragraph letter of recommendation when Reed applied to Harvard, almost equally about Laura as it was about Reed. He began by noting, "His grandmother, a colored woman, has worked in my family and that of my wife's for over 30 years." Clapp praised Laura for purchasing her own home at 1 Sumner Court and said, "She is a woman of limited education but fine character and great common sense and good judgment." In contrast to Laura, Clapp inherited his home from his family, which traced their origins back to one of the earliest English settlers in America. Of Reed, Clapp told Harvard, "He is a very fair student and attentive to his studies. Enjoys publicity and is fond of approbation. I know of no instance where he was dishonorable or dishonest," and he noted that he did not exert himself physically in athletics. Laura also wrote a letter on Reed's behalf and said her grandson "is a quiet, studious type but somewhat nervous too. He has generally been very conscientious in what he does."

Laura's home at 1 Sumner Court in the Dorchester section of Boston was surrounded by white neighbors all born in Massachusetts except for Laura and one other family, from Italy. There were a mix of middle-class and professional occupations on the block, including an office manager, an inspector for the fire department, a schoolteacher, a clerical worker, a truck driver, a freight handler, a helper, a medical doctor, a longshoreman, a couple of people who worked in the steel industry, a salesman, a cashier, and the Italian neighbor, who owned a fruit stand.

As would be evident throughout his academic career, Reed's accolades were repeatedly couched in terms of his skin color. Boston Latin School headmaster Joseph L. Powers informed Harvard that Reed was "an unusually fine representative of his race (colored)." A teacher, L. O. Glover, wrote:

He is a good scholar; perfect in conduct; popular with his school-mates; thoroughly competent and reliable, so that he has been Room Treasurer in the school banking system for the past four years. His father is not living and he is supported by his grandmother, who is custodian of a Boston school.

Reed told both Boston Latin School and Harvard that his father was dead. Perhaps he lied to eliminate the shame of appearing to be fatherless and to remove the stigma of mental illness from his personal narrative. And didn't it sound better to say that your father died valiantly serving overseas during the Great War? In reality, in 1931, Harvey was still a patient at Central State Mental Hospital.

Reed, excited about the prospect of graduating from the Boston Latin School and going to Harvard, imagined all of the future opportunities afforded to men who attended. He focused on reinventing himself as a scholar. But his race was not forgotten as he enrolled in Harvard.

TWO

Harvard University

Reed was one of a thousand members of Harvard's Class of 1935, its 296th. New student orientation activities took place between Friday, September 25, and Monday, September 28, 1931. *The Harvard Crimson* reported that they were the first class to take possession of the Yard, the historic central part of the campus that included a church, administrative offices for the president and deans, and now twelve dormitories to house the freshmen, who were required to live on campus. Freshmen's lives centered around the Union, which contained dining halls, common rooms, and a library. Reed registered for his courses in Memorial Hall.

After selecting his courses, Reed joined the new students for a buffet-style dinner in the Union and later for an informal gathering in the Living Room section of the building. He would've listened to remarks from President A. Lawrence Lowell—who was responsible for negative policies that impacted both queer and African American students at Harvard. In May 1920, a little over a decade before Reed matriculated, Cyril Wilcox, a freshman at Harvard, had died by suicide after being suspended for alleged homosexual activity. Cyril's brother enlisted Harvard administrators' help to find the students who he believed had "led his brother astray."

Harvard thus created a secret court to interrogate students as to their sexual orientation and, as a result, expelled many suspected of homosexuality or of fraternizing with homosexual men in the community. A few of the students who were suspected of homosexual activity also committed suicide. Harvard's Appointment Office played a pivotal role in elongating this persecution by including a letter in the students' files of recommendation that encouraged potential employers to request a secret file— apparently an offer that no prospective employer turned down— to inform them of information not found in the students' academic records. One letter followed a graduate for decades after he left Harvard. Although this court was supposed to be secret, no doubt queer students at Harvard, like Reed, heard whispers about it and feared being found out.

The secret courts were far from the only oppressive measures that Harvard enacted in those days. In 1922, President Lowell forbade African American students from living in the dorms despite the rule requiring freshmen to reside on campus. He thought students from the South would not want to live and dine with African Americans. Among those excluded was Roscoe Conkling Bruce Jr., who was the grandson of the second African

American senator in US history, Blanche K. Bruce. The other five banned students had equally prestigious pedigrees.

High-profile African American figures condemned Lowell, including Harvard alumni W. E. B. Du Bois and journalist William Monroe Trotter. James Weldon Johnson, representing the NAACP, also joined the fight. In 1923, Harvard's Board of Overseers reversed Lowell's decision. However, despite the rejection of the old policy, African American students were strongly encouraged to live off campus until the 1950s. The messaging was clear: even if Harvard had accepted them, they would never *really* be accepted. Reed did not live on campus during his freshman year. Nonetheless, he spent a lot of time on campus and very little time at home in Dorchester.

Throughout the new student orientation, students listened to speeches including ones from the dean of Harvard College, A. Chester Hanford, and the dean of freshmen, Delmar Leighton. At 9 a.m. on Saturday morning, the freshmen and other new students gathered in the New Lecture Hall to hear speeches by the assistant librarian of Harvard College, W. B. Briggs, an associate professor of history and literature, who was also a master of the Kirkland House, a dorm, and they would also hear again from the dean of freshmen. The rest of the day was devoted to meeting with faculty advisers. Reed was assigned to a twenty-nine-year-old professor, George Zipf, a linguist known for creating "Zipf's law" recognizing that a few words are used most often. Zipf received an A.B., M.A., and Ph.D. from Harvard, and studied in Germany at the University of Bonn and the University of Berlin. Students also took language examinations on this day—Reed most likely took French and German. Later that night there was another informal gathering held in a dining hall in the Union where students could listen to the director of athletics and a football coach, and a student who was the captain of the football team would speak about "Athletic and Physical Training at Harvard." Afterward, students were shown films of athletic events. Given his lack of interest in sports, it's unlikely Reed would have attended that meeting.

The next day, Sunday morning, at 11 a.m., a reverend, the dean of the Theological School, preached a special sermon for new students in Sanders Theatre. On Monday night at 7:30 p.m. in the Phillips Brooks House, students could attend a reception for new students and meet with various leaders of extracurricular student organizations, including the Glee Club, the *Crimson* newspaper, the *Lampoon*, and Instrumental Clubs. Reed eventually joined the German and poetry clubs. There was music and refreshments were served. These speeches indoctrinated the young students to begin thinking of themselves as Harvard men and to remind them that they were entering into an elite community that would bestow a prestige that would follow them long after they left these hallowed grounds. If Reed looked around him, he would've seen a sea of white faces: something he was used to after his experiences at Boston Latin School. But perhaps he felt that he had overcome this "disadvantage" and had made it.

Founded in 1636, Harvard College had no official policy barring African Americans from enrolling—that is, if they had the grades, the funds, and the inclination to apply and an "acceptable demeanor," and as long as they remained low in numbers. Other Ivy League institutions, including Yale and Princeton, remained segregated until after World War II. Between 1870 and 1941, Harvard enrolled approximately 165 African American students—a rate of about two or three per year.

It was not easy being an African American student at Harvard. The first was admitted in 1847 but died of tuberculosis before the academic year began. It would take nearly two more decades before Harvard admitted another one, Richard T. Greener, in 1865. Before Greener, the only African Americans at Harvard were enslaved people, as well as those later working at the institution as janitors, waiters, or servants accompanying white Southern students for low wages. Greener had to repeat his freshman year due to supposedly poor academic preparation, although he thought he was judged unfairly by some faculty due to racism. After his initial rough start, he settled in and became involved in the social life at Harvard. He joined a theater club and served as the vice president of a secret society. It took him five years to complete his degree, but he graduated as a member of the Class of 1870. Greener's biographer stated that, upon commencement, he received "a white man's education," which meant his career options were limited as an African American. However, he became a librarian at the University of South Carolina and obtained his law degree while there during the Reconstruction era. Afterward, he taught at the historically Black institution Howard University, eventually becoming the dean of its law school. Later, he was appointed as the US consul in Russia.

Many of the early African American students at Harvard had both fond recollections and searing criticisms of their time there. W. E. B. Du Bois, author of *The Souls of Black Folk*, received an A.B. in 1890 and a Ph.D. in 1895—the first African American to receive that advanced degree from Harvard. Du Bois famously said he was "in Harvard, but not of it." After being mistaken for a waiter at a reception, he concluded that it was better to focus on his studies and consort with his own—other African Americans in Boston—than to interact with white students and have negative experiences.

Ambivalence best captured the divided feelings of African American students. They were cognizant of the supposed opportunities afforded to them by a Harvard education, while aware of the limitations they faced because of their race and the sting of some insults that they had to bear. One student, in descriptions of his time there reminiscent of Reed's experiences, said he was "never regarded in absence of the black factor."

Philosopher and future Harlem Renaissance figure Alain Locke also went to Harvard, but took a different view of his fellow African American students. He received an A.B. in 1908 and a Ph.D. in 1918. His biographer Jeffrey C. Stewart said that Locke was "icily distant" from his fellow African American students at Harvard. They frequently invited him to social events and he would write to his mother using derogatory terms to refer to them. He even planned to not acknowledge them if he was walking with white people, believing that white faculty and students had better contacts. He was dismayed to see African American students choosing to have their own separate table in a cafeteria.

Stewart speculated that since Locke was queer, he wanted to avoid pressure to engage in heterosexual activities, including attending dances with African American women. Locke chose to focus on his studies and was elected to Phi Beta Kappa in

1907. He later obtained a Rhodes Scholarship to Oxford. But as with Greener, Locke's career options were limited because of his race, despite his level of educational attainment. Indeed, he spent most of his academic career at Howard University, in Washington, D.C., which, given his earlier stance on fraternizing with African American people, must have vexed him.

A decade before Reed received a master's degree, Harlem Renaissance poet Countee Cullen was awarded a master's degree in English from Harvard in 1926. Cullen only spent nine months at Harvard, but he enjoyed his time in Cambridge. He was already a member of the national Black fraternity Alpha Phi Alpha and spent most of his time congregating with other African American students.

Reed was by no means in the racial majority while at Harvard, but still, there were a few more Black students than at his Boston high school. He must have likewise felt a sense of comfort in the other students who shared his intellectual interests.

Although Harvard did not warmly welcome African American or queer students, it was the best institution in the nation, and Reed was determined to succeed there despite all possible impediments. When he arrived at Harvard in the fall of 1931, Lowell was still the university's president, and although he retired halfway through Reed's college career, his policies and ideas would linger far longer at the institution.

Reed was determined to become a French professor and an accomplished linguist. This ambition must have seemed like a far cry from cleaning people's houses like his grandmother and mother did. The job also spoke to him because of the automatic status awarded to a professor. He must have believed that with status comes protection, and as a young, African American queer man with no financial safety net, that was undoubtedly appealing.

Reed moved relatively easily through the world of his white, male peers. Since his time at the Boston Latin School, he had learned to watch how they dressed, how they behaved, what issues they discussed and how they discussed them, what they read, what concerts they attended, as well as what they listened to. He used his natural charm to assimilate to the person they wanted him to be. As a result he seemed comfortable around them despite the disparities in their race and economic backgrounds.

Reed held somewhat similar views of the other African American students as Locke, whose own desire to succeed in a white world caused him to betray core aspects of his identity. Additionally, Reed's grandmother, Laura, urged him to be careful with associating with *certain types* of African Americans for fear that he would be looked down upon by association. It is notable, however, that she did not give the same warning about avoiding certain types of whites.

Reed enrolled in four courses his first academic year. The first was "German 1a. Prose and Poetry," which involved translation, reading, and writing. Not surprisingly, he took French 3, designed for students who had a reading knowledge of French and the principles of its grammar but lacked opportunities to speak the language. He took "History—European History from the Fall of the Roman Empire to the Present," which met on Mondays, Wednesdays, and Fridays. Finally, Reed took an unlikely course, "Biology—Life and Its Environment," not having expressed an interest in a career in the sciences. It was a heavy load, requiring students to write reports and complete several hours of work in a laboratory each week. The course met on Tuesdays and Thursdays for lectures and sometimes on Saturday "at the pleasure of the instructor." Reed was in classes five days a week and perhaps on some Saturdays too.

One student whom Reed grew close to was Cyril Leo Toumanoff. Perhaps they met in the European history course that they both had during their first year. Reed and Cyril had a lot in common. Both lost a parent during their childhood, although Harvey was "lost" under different circumstances. Cyril's mother, Elisabeth Zdanoff, was murdered in 1917 in Russia by the Bolsheviks during the October Revolution, when Cyril was just four. Both were primarily raised by their maternal grandmothers, who doted on them. Both came from a modest background but under different circumstances. Cyril's father, Leo Constantine Toumanoff, was a general in the Russian army and fled the country in 1920. But now he was an immigrant working as a librarian at Harvard's Baker Library serving the business school, making $1,500 a year. He said it was just enough to support himself. Cyril, concerned about how he would be able to fund his Harvard education, applied for funds from Harvard through the Committee on Scholarships and Other Aids for Undergraduates and received $700 from the Russian Students Fund in New York. However, his arrogance rubbed some the wrong way—one recommender, a lecturer, concluded that while Cyril should get funds, he suggested "not too much, however, for I fear he is inclined to think that assistance is his just due." Cyril received the Price Greenleaf scholarship from Harvard for $500 for his freshman year, requiring him to work as a monitor or clerk for up to four hours a week.

They shared an interest in foreign languages. Cyril spoke both Russian and French, having lived in Russia and France. Extraordinarily, when he arrived in the United States in 1929 at age fifteen, two years before he entered Harvard, he did not speak English. He mastered the language and excelled in his studies at the Lenox School in Lenox, Massachusetts, completing four years of schoolwork in two years.

Other similarities included their extracurricular interests. Cyril's recommender noted, "His interests and tastes run strongly along artistic lines . . . and his appreciation of beauty in all its forms would be marked in an adult, and is far above anything I have ever known before in a boy." Another letter writer remarked, "The boy seems to have a background of real culture and refinement far beyond that of almost any American boy I know." Like Reed, Cyril was uninterested in sports.

Cyril had another trait in common with Reed—arrogance— although Reed was either able to mask this trait or others were unable to conceive of an African American's ability to be arrogant when they were often considered second-class citizens. No one mentioned it in Reed's letters of recommendation. Shortly after Cyril's arrival on campus, he submitted a "Correction in Form of Name" document asking that his name be changed from Cyril Leo Toumanoff to Prince Cyril Leo Toumanoff. His father told him he was a Georgian prince of Armenian descent. His former headmaster previously said:

His chief weakness seems to be an inability to forget that princely titles are not as important in America as they are in Russia, with the result that at times he is imbued with an undue sense of his own importance.

He also wrote that Cyril "suffers from a rather egocentric view of things. He looks on life more as an opportunity for self-development than of usefulness to others." A Harvard lecturer had more favorable things to say about Cyril's personality and intelligence, and another found him to be charming.

Cyril's father submitted a letter on his behalf to Harvard, offering interesting insights into his thoughts about his only child. He said:

> Isolation from actual life, feminine influence, and the fact that he was being spoiled resulted in his being utterly unpractical. . . . Being ignorant of men and life he measures things by their external appearance. Frequently good appearance and refined manners form for him the criterion for judging people. This fact results in the forming of unhappy acquaintances and in the falling under undesirable influence.

But perhaps one of the most salient aspects of their friendship was Cyril's romantic relationship with a man, Olgerd Paris Michael Vincent Sherbowitz-Wetzor, nicknamed "Olgy," a college professor nearly twenty years older than Cyril. Reed called Cyril and Olgy "the kittens," and the two would serve as a model for Reed about the possibility of a long-standing same-sex relationship. Olgy was born on March 31, 1896, in Nice, France, but was of Polish descent. He taught Russian history, Polish history, and medieval Slavic history and lectured at Harvard University, where he most likely met Cyril and Reed. Cyril and Olgy described their relationship as "cousins" in various documents, including in Harvard records, a convenient and common cover.

Cyril encountered difficulties and was placed on academic probation after a psychiatric illness during the spring 1932 term of his freshman year and was described as "a very high strung unstable Russian boy who has been in emotional difficulties all year." He did not return to campus following the April recess after receiving a warning in March about his academic progress when he failed to take exams in his courses. Reed meanwhile successfully breezed through his first academic year at Harvard.

In his next year at Harvard, Reed dove headlong into German language, literature, and history; he topped off his French fluency by taking a composition course where he learned to write and speak with ease, and a French literature course conducted entirely in French. He took philosophy and psychology, which interested him, though nothing so much as his passion for languages.

Reed enrolled in several French courses, including "French Literature in the Eighteenth Century" and a graduate-school-level French course, during his junior year. He expanded his language studies to include a basic introductory course in Spanish grammar, reading, and composition and one called "Modern Spanish Novels and Plays." He took another philosophy course—"The Function of Reason and an Introduction to Social Psychology," taught by

Assistant Professor Gordon Allport, author of the groundbreaking 1954 book *The Nature of Prejudice.*

During this time, the fall 1933 semester, a new student named Montfort Schley Variell (called Monty) arrived on campus. He and Reed shared an interest in music, they both studied French and German, and were both members of the German Club. According to Reed's family, they may have had a romantic relationship too. Photographs show a strikingly attractive young white man with dark hair and full lips. Monty studied at an American school in Munich, Germany, and graduated from the prestigious Phillips Exeter Academy. His assessment from his high school in his Harvard application began with, "A slender, handsome boy with a very intelligent and sensitive face."

Monty planned to major in Romance languages, and his father wanted him to pursue a diplomatic career, but his intended vocation was music—specifically, he planned to be a concert pianist. He and Reed shared this passion. Reed often played the piano as a hobby and was drawn again and again to those with whom he could share music.

But unlike Reed, Monty came from an illustrious family. His father, Dr. Arthur Davis Variell, was a leprosy expert decorated by Syria, Portugal, France, and Spain for his work with Great War refugees. His maternal grandfather, Admiral Winfield Scott Schley, was a hero of the Spanish-American War. At Harvard, where he was expected to follow in his family's footsteps, Monty must have felt like an outsider. His astronomy professor, upon reporting that Monty was earning a grade of D at midterm, concluded, "I am afraid that Mr. Variell is not very intelligent."

But there is another reason Monty might have felt like an outsider: on his Harvard application, Monty's father wrote that his son avoided alcohol and tobacco and had had "too few associations with girls." The suggestion being that Harvard could make a gentleman out of his son—a heterosexual gentleman. Yet when he came to Harvard, he met Reed, forming a strong bond.

In the meantime, Reed's father, Harvey, was sent to the Veterans Administration Hospital in Tuskegee, Alabama, part of the Tuskegee Institute, arriving on September 1, 1933. After close to thirteen years at Central State Mental Hospital in Virginia, he moved to an institution with an entirely African American staff. While it was segregated just like Central State Mental Hospital, this crucial difference would result in better treatment for him as an African American patient. The Veterans Administration Hospital was also in a new building that cost $272,000 (nearly $5.7 million in 2024). *The Chicago Defender* reported that the modern building was three stories and large enough to accommodate 350 veterans from across the United States. During Harvey's time in these two institutions, there was no indication that he was in contact with Reed through letters or visits. Reed meanwhile seemed unaware of his father's exact whereabouts.

Unlike his wealthy friends and classmates, Reed was constantly seeking ways to pay for his education at Harvard, frequently applying for scholarships. In 1934, he finally admitted a lie: his father was not dead. He wrote a letter to the assistant director of the World War Orphan Committee, an organization that provided educational assistance to the children of men from Massachusetts who died serving the United States during the Great War. Reed conceded that this description did not apply to him.

My father was disabled in the World War. I have never had any definite facts as to whether he is dead or not, but a slight allowance is offered my grandmother, who is my guardian, by the U. S. Veteran's Bureau. It does not necessarily provide for my education.

But he argued, "Theoretically speaking, one is just as badly off by the permanent disability of one's father as one would be by his decease, although I do not pretend to seek the same compensation." He also explained that his mother had remarried and could not offer him financial support because her new husband, whom he pointedly referred to as "Mr. Farrar," only made enough to support his immediate family.

For his final undergraduate year, Reed actively pursued obtaining an on-campus residence, believing it would give him opportunities to connect with other students and form associations that could benefit him in the future. It would also give him more privacy for his romantic adventures, far from Laura's prying eyes, and better prospects to meet potential romantic partners. Reed contacted Dean Hanford in a May 20, 1934, letter asking to be put on a waiting list for a suite or an expensive room in either Claverly Hall or Little Hall if one became available later for a reduced price. It is unknown if he was successful in securing a room, given Harvard's unofficial policy of discouraging African American students from living on campus, but nevertheless, Reed spent a lot of time listening to records on a phonograph in Monty's dorm room.

He enrolled in a French composition course and another on "French Literature in the Seventeenth Century." He also took a contemporary English literature course and continued his interest in psychology by taking a course called "Aesthetics." Instead of continuing to study German, Reed enrolled in two courses in the Spanish Department: "Spanish Literature of the Sixteenth and Seventeenth Centuries" with a focus on Cervantes, and "Spanish Drama in the Golden Age."

Reed excelled academically at Harvard, often making the dean's list, and was inducted into the Phi Beta Kappa honor society during his senior year. It must have irked his white classmates to know that he'd done better than them. Yet if Reed faced any reprisals for his success, he did not write about them, or not to Laura, the most frequent recipient of his letters.

As he considered his post-baccalaureate future, Reed applied for a Rhodes Scholarship and looked like a promising candidate. He longed to live abroad in Europe, where he would have a chance to become exposed to a different culture and continue to reinvent himself as a proper, sophisticated gentleman. He asked A. Chester Hanford for a recommendation for a studentship at Trinity College in Cambridge. Hanford agreed.

"He is one of the highest scholars in his class," wrote Hanford. "Last November he was elected to membership in Phi Beta Kappa. He is a thorough gentleman." Hanford shared a copy of the letter with Reed, who promptly thanked him. Reed must have been elated at this hearty praise from such a powerful man. But there was another letter Reed did not see.

"I wish to supplement my letter of May 29th to you about Mr. Reed Peggram by stating that he is a negro," Hanford wrote in his second, secret letter. "It seemed to me that you should know that fact." Hanford continued, "He is, however, the most able colored student I have ever known and is most highly regarded by his instructors and classmates. I do not remember any one else of his race who has in recent years been elected to Phi Beta Kappa." Finally, Hanford wrote, "He is a young man of good manners and gets along very well with his white classmates." This last statement was no doubt meant to convey that Reed wouldn't make any waves at Trinity, a very white institution.

Tutor Andrew Sydenham Farrar Gow replied with gratitude: "Thank you for your testimonial and letter about Reed Peggram," he said. "I should like to thank you however for telling me that Peggram is a Negro. I should certainly have been somewhat taken aback if I had admitted a man with such a name unwarned." Although Gow insisted this information would have no bearing on whether Reed was awarded the prestigious scholarship, Reed did not get it. Perhaps this rejection saved him from the humiliation and isolation that fellow Harvard graduate Alain Locke faced as the first African American Rhodes Scholar. Locke was miserable during his time at Oxford, facing racial prejudice, most notably from fellow American students, and he did not finish his degree while there.

Reed's academic record placed him on the dean's list and in what was called the First Group of scholarship holders. Because he achieved this distinction, he was given a memento from Harvard, a book from among books of the world's literature. The letter informing Reed of this honor stated that "you will find that possession of a Detur gives one a certain bond with many eminent men of the nineteenth and the twentieth centuries." Students used to participate in a ceremony during commencement. However, now the presentation of the book was considered unceremonious, and Reed was instructed to stop by Hanford's office at 4 University Hall to pick up his unidentified book.

As Reed prepared for the next phase of his career or education, he asked his professors to write letters for his placement file in the Appointment Office. While Reed's "secret" file never discussed his sexual orientation, it did discuss his race at length. Surely administrators did not indicate that other students were white. Did they discuss how the white students dressed, or their personality, or comportment? But in Reed's case, all of this information was offered to potential employers.

Psychology professor Gordon Allport wrote that Reed was "a gentlemanly and well-appearing colored boy." By now it must have felt unremarkable that, in these circles, he would always be described in term of his race. Even his freshman adviser, Zipf, had a difficult time describing him without mentioning his race and his class background. Zipf wrote, "Peggram has an enthusiastic buoyant personality which will make him an ideal teacher." And, "Peggram (colored) has a very alert mind and a very high intelligence, he also has an unusual amount of intellectual curiosity." But, perhaps to lessen the blow of being "colored," Zipf assured future prospective employers, "He is a perfect gentlemen; he came to tea at our house with several of his friends and I was amazed at his urbanity and social poise (for after all he comes from very humble parents)." And, using language that was common during this time period, Zipf said, "I understand that he is well-liked and much respected by class-mates, including those not of his race." In other words, Reed was welcomed by white people and got along with them. Interestingly, Zipf concluded, "He accepts very neatly his social position and is neither obsequious nor presumptious [*sic*] nor bitter." Another letter writer, psychology professor Dr. Hadley Cantril, wrote, "He is facile in his expression, attractive in his personality, and has made a good adjustment in college for a negro. I could recommend him very highly for a teaching position where his race would not interfere with the requirements." Professor A. F. Whittem wrote a one-sentence recommendation but was able to squeeze in information about Reed's race: "Peggram is a courteous colored lad of good appearance who has done excellent work in French & Spanish."

In 1935, Reed graduated from Harvard magna cum laude, with a degree in Romance languages and literatures. He completed a fifty-eight-page thesis for honors in French literature, titled "A Comparison of the Personal Element in *Madame Bovary* and *L'Éducation sentimentale*," dedicating it to his tutor, Marcel Auguste Françon, an expert in sixteenth-century French literature. Reed began with a quote from Henry James: "Impersonal as he wished his work to be, it was his strange fortune to be the most expressive, the most vociferous, the most spontaneous of men." Part of his two-page preface stated, "It is customary to regard Gustave Flaubert as an objective and impersonal writer, who conquered the lyrical exuberance that lay at the bottom of his nature by dominating his imagination and insisting upon a philosophy of impassivity." In his appendix, Reed anticipated criticism for not focusing on Flaubert's life, stating, "I have consciously avoided presenting elements that might be by nature sleep-provoking." He had adopted the cheeky mode of presentation common to those with privilege. He was enjoying himself.

Reed became the first person in his family to receive a bachelor's degree—and it was from the most prestigious institution in the

United States. It is unknown if his mother and two younger brothers traveled from New Jersey to help him and his grandmother celebrate this incredible achievement by attending Harvard's elaborate weeklong commencement ceremonies. Harvard celebrated the Class of 1935 with festivities beginning on Saturday, June 15, with a sermon conducted in the Memorial Church. There was a dance on Monday, and Class Day was on Wednesday, beginning with exercises of unspecified nature followed by a lunch buffet. Then the Class of 1935 members joined previous classes in a parade culminating in the stadium where a Confetti Battle and other events took place, followed by a Harvard-versus-Yale baseball game. That night, the Glee Club performed in front of the squash courts, followed by humorous entertainment. Finally, there was a dance until one o'clock in the morning for students, friends, and returning alumni. Commencement took place on Thursday, June 20, at eleven o'clock in Harvard Yard. Graduates would be "admitted into the fellowship of educated men."

That summer, Reed turned twenty-one years old, and Laura's legal guardianship ended after six years. But their bond would be unbreakable and intertwined.

After not getting the Rhodes Scholarship, Reed decided to remain at Harvard for another year and study for a master's degree in comparative literature. The Great Depression was still ongoing by the time the Class of 1935 was graduating, and it was difficult to find employment. Many of Reed's classmates applied to graduate school to ride out the economic slump.

Reed enrolled in "Studies in the French Drama of the Nineteenth Century," conducted entirely in French. He took "Comparative Literature: Its Aims and Methods" and two additional courses in the same department, "Studies in the Literature of the Renaissance, with Special Reference to England and the Romantic Movement in European Literature," and a course simply titled "Reading and Research."

Because he lived with Laura during most of his time at Harvard, Reed did not write letters to her. This means there is much about his experiences there that we will never know. But during the 1935–36 academic year, another African American man, John Hope Franklin, enrolled in Harvard University's history program, also seeking a master's degree. He would later become one of the United States' most eminent historians. He recounted his time at Harvard in his autobiography, *Mirror to America*. Born in Oklahoma, he received his bachelor's degree at the Black institution Fisk University. He boarded off campus with three other African Americans—two Harvard students and a Great War veteran. His experiences and worldview were very different from Reed's, having grown up around almost entirely Black communities and educational institutions. Franklin and other African American students at Harvard sought solace in nearby Roxbury, where the African American community welcomed them. A couple, Fisk alumni, invited Franklin into their home for Thanksgiving and Christmas. African American Harvard students often ate fried chicken dinners at Estelle's, a Roxbury restaurant. When Franklin and a female companion attempted to eat in a restaurant in Cambridge, they were ignored and not served. Reed was lucky to have his grandmother nearby to welcome him with a home-cooked meal.

Franklin noted the small number of other African American graduate students at Harvard—including one in comparative literature, Reed. He recalled, "I had extensive contact with students who never showed the slightest condescension toward me." But he noted:

> [A] day, and often an hour, didn't go by without my feeling the color of my skin—in the reactions of white Cambridge, the behavior of my fellow students, the attitudes real and imagined struck by professors.

He mentioned a professor who told a "darky" joke during a class lecture. His fellow students didn't laugh, but Franklin wondered if the silence was due to his presence.

Franklin recalled that he experienced "sheer loneliness" during his early days at Harvard after coming from Fisk University, where it was much easier to socialize. He joined a few organizations on campus to ease his feelings of isolation and witnessed a troubling incident where a student was not allowed to run for an office because he was Jewish. Around the same time, Franklin heard that a doctoral committee had failed another student and insisted he spend four more years studying because he did not "look like" a Harvard Ph.D.

At the end of the academic year, Reed earned a master's degree. He wanted to study for a Ph.D. at Harvard, but he reluctantly ended up at Columbia University in New York City after failing to gain admittance into a doctoral program at Harvard for an unknown reason—after having graduated Phi Beta Kappa for his bachelor's and completing a master's degree at the institution, all the while being praised as an individual with exemplary intelligence, grades, and demeanor. Many African Americans had difficulty getting accepted into Ph.D. programs. For example, while Percy Julian received a master's in chemistry from Harvard in 1923, he had to go to the University of Vienna in Austria in order to obtain a doctorate in chemistry because he was not accepted into the Ph.D. program at Harvard. He could not get a teaching assistantship needed to complete his doctorate because Harvard believed white students would not accept instruction from an African American.

During this period, African Americans who completed an undergraduate degree, most often at Black institutions in the South, and who wanted to pursue additional professional and graduate degrees—like John Hope Franklin—had very few options. The Black institutions often did not have graduate programs, and these students were not accepted into their own state institutions. They could receive so-called segregation scholarships to attend white, Northern universities. Their graduate experiences were often characterized by court battles, loneliness, and discrimination inside the institution by racist professors, administrators, and fellow students, and outside they struggled to find housing and places to eat after making the often treacherous journey from the South to the North by car or on segregated trains.

Harvard's records are silent about why Reed was not accepted into a Ph.D. program despite his stellar academic record. Reed considered his time at Columbia as a temporary leave of absence from Harvard.

THREE

Columbia University

n the fall of 1936, Reed took the steamer *Providence* from Boston to New York City to begin his new life at Columbia University. He was now a twenty-two-year-old doctoral student in English and comparative literature with a $500 Graduate Residence Scholarship. This was his first time living away from Boston, other than the brief, unhappy stint with his mother and her new husband in Bayonne, New Jersey.

He was assigned room 1231 in John Jay Hall, a fifteen-story dorm at Columbia University. The building was named after the founding father and first chief justice of the US Supreme Court, who was a 1764 graduate. It was designed by the architects from the prestigious firm McKim, Mead & White, one of whom, Charles Follen McKim, had also designed the main branch of the Boston Public Library at Copley Square that Reed loved so much.

In the Morningside Heights section of New York City, Reed felt like he was living in an exclusive part of the city. It was almost like having his own apartment. The room was larger than he expected, with enough space to house his books and a chiffonier, a closet, a desk, a trash can, a rug, two chairs, an overhead light, a desk lamp, two mirrors, and a medicine desk. If he received a message in the downstairs office, he would get a buzz. One of his favorite activities became using the elevators. On his first day he said, "I have been on it at least two dozen times and it is not six o'clock yet."

Laura continued supporting his lifestyle in New York City through funds from her tenants. Reed was able to purchase shoes and a fashionable three-piece suit, and was able to replace glasses he broke—he obliquely referred to the incident—manipulating her to send the funds without explicitly asking for them. He mentioned dropping his glasses in an October 7 letter, and an October 13 letter began, "Thank you so much for your lovely letter last week and the assistance on my glasses."

Missing his grandmother, he wrote more than a dozen letters to her during his first semester at Columbia. He often inquired about her health, the Boston weather, Boston politics, her tenants—including one he referred to as Lady Astor. He described the weather in New York City, his meals, the people he met and his activities in his new city, the food in the dorms (not good), but the meals were a part of his scholarship. He spent a good portion of time discussing his laundry case—something college students used to send dirty clothes back home. Sometimes he asked Laura to include a book from his home library when she returned the case with his freshly washed clothing. She sometimes included a surprise snack. He told her not to worry about him, that the "bid-dies," whom he described as "nice old Irish ladies," made sure he was comfortable. Later, he told her that in New York City the women were called "maids" and not "biddies." As someone who likely had not had much opportunity to travel, his grandmother would have relished in these small details.

When the maids did heavy cleaning, which included polish-ing the floors and cleaning the rugs and curtains, African Amer-ican men assisted them. Reed frequently noted the occupations of the African Americans he encountered—often they held ser-vice jobs. The subtext was clear: if he wanted his fate to be dif-ferent, he'd have to do what few people in his position had been given the opportunity to accomplish.

That belief was threatened when he searched for a job off campus at a bookstore during the spring semester. Reed hoped to get a job ordering books and helping customers to select reading material to purchase. He was hopeful that as a doctoral student in English and comparative literature at Columbia University with a bachelor's and master's degree from Harvard, he would be hired. But he expected that he would only be offered a job doing menial labor. It was an irony Reed must have noted, that after all his education and all his achievements, after how hard he worked to dress and talk like he belonged, he had a deep-seated fear that no matter what he did, he would never be able to transcend his race.

He developed a routine at Columbia, getting up between eight and eight-thirty in the morning in order to make it to break-fast by nine. And he began making friends, including a fellow graduate student and John Jay Hall resident, Newton Stephen

Arnold, from Wichita, Kansas, and a recent Class of 1936 graduate of the University of Kansas. Blond and blue-eyed Newton was two years younger than Reed and bigger and taller at six foot three inches and 185 pounds, compared to Reed's height of five foot and ten inches and about 140 pounds. They made quite the pair. Newton also received a Graduate Residence Scholarship and studied Germanic languages. The two became fast friends and shared a dream of studying abroad in Europe.

Despite his initial reluctance to attend Columbia University, Reed enjoyed living in New York City—even though for him it didn't measure up to Harvard or Boston. He concluded during his first week, "People here look decidedly uninteresting and I have determined to pay them little attention." Later he wrote, "People here are not as brilliant as at Harvard, and most of them think that I am a terrible snob, but I can see that they really envy me." He also wondered how people knew he had been to Harvard. He speculated that "perhaps one can tell by looking at me."

He enrolled in his seminar in Comparative Literature 1. He also studied under the direction of Professor Paul Hazard, a visiting scholar at Columbia from France in the fall of 1936. Reed studied comparative literature, English, and multiple semesters of French, bolstering his dream of going to live in Paris one day. He studied for his thesis under Professor Fernand Baldensperger, a Germanist who helped to develop the comparative literature discipline in both the United States and in France. Reed had taken one of his classes at Harvard. Reed visited Harvard's campus during the winter break to make a case for his application to a doctoral program.

When Reed returned to Columbia University for the second

semester, he moved to a bigger room, number 1238, in John Jay Hall. While there, he received a rather mysterious message asking him to return a phone call. No name was attached to the message. Reed called and a woman answered stating that the young man who expected his call was currently away. She wouldn't tell Reed who it was but told him to call back later. Reed called again, but the mystery caller still wasn't in. Now angry, Reed left a message telling the mystery person to return the call before 6 p.m. Around 5:30 p.m. he received another phone call. It was Monty, his Harvard friend, who was in New York City for the weekend and wanted to take Reed out for dinner. They dined and caught up on their various activities. Monty was looking forward to seeing Reed back at Harvard the next year—Monty planned to attend graduate school there and hoped Reed would be admitted to the doctoral program in comparative literature. They separated at 9 p.m. so that Monty could see his girl friend (two words in Reed's letter).

Despite his initial lack of enthusiasm for both Columbia and New York City, Reed found a church where he attended mass, visited museums, and went to the symphony and the opera wearing a tuxedo he brought with him for special occasions. He teased Laura when she told him she had watched the movie *Maytime*, a musical love story with operatic songs, recalling how she used to refuse to listen when he played opera on the radio while living with her.

On Friday, April 2, 1937, Reed entered Carnegie Hall, a Neo–Italian Renaissance building located on Seventh Avenue and 57th Street, in time for a scheduled 8:30 p.m. concert. He had a ticket to see the contralto Marian Anderson perform, accompanied by pianist Kosti Vehanen. Anderson sang selections from Monteverdi, Handel, Bach, and Schubert, including the highlight "Ave Maria," before a packed audience that included people standing in the back. The delighted audience enthusiastically applauded and cheered her performance. Reed was proud to hear one of his own people perform on the stage of this majestic hall in front of a multiracial audience. He thought Anderson was "one of the greatest singers in our race." He noted, "She had been abroad until last year, and sang with great success in almost every European country. She can sing in several languages, and she included only four spirituals on the program." Reed would remember and talk about this performance for decades.

Reed made the most of his time in New York City, partaking in its cultural offerings. He went to the theater and saw three one-act plays. He usually told Laura he was given a ticket, perhaps trying to explain how he could afford these outings.

Despite his resentment about not being at Harvard, Reed was determined to make the most of his experience at Columbia. He wrote for a French publication, *Chimere*, at the university and contributed an article, "Nouvelle letter persane," a satire in imitation of Montesquieu. Laura shared the article with her employer, Miss Browne, when she cleaned her home, no doubt bragging about the success of her grandson at an Ivy League institution. Reed was amused that Miss Browne wanted to look up the references mentioned in the article because she did not realize it was a satire. For example, the city of "Krenwoy" was an anagram for New York. He told Laura that it "showed she didn't understand it." The satire made fun of Columbia University—confirming that Reed still looked at his education there with a bit of disdain.

He also wrote a book review of François Mauriac's *Les Anges noirs* for *Chimere*.

Besides Monty, Reed remained in contact with other friends back at Harvard, including Cyril and Olgy, a.k.a. "the kittens." He was thrilled when Olgy became a full professor at Georgetown University, a promotion that came with an increased salary. Reed thought, "Perhaps we shall have our little summer home together after all, as they promised." Olgy told Reed that he was glad for his raise and that he could help him financially until he could support himself.

Reed was so committed to leaving Columbia, and assured that he would be accepted at Harvard, that he did not apply for a fellowship at Columbia for the following academic year, stating, "Frankly, this goddam place is so awful in comparison to Harvard that I would rather not go to any college next year than be here." He crowed, "Of course I am a big success here, but the people bore me. I don't feel as if I am learning anything at all," except from professors at Columbia who had gone to Harvard like Baldensperger. He admitted, "I am prejudiced." He thought the students did not measure up and he was not having an exchange of ideas with brilliant students like he had at Harvard, even as he acknowledged that many students there seemed to like it.

He looked forward to attending a party on a boat where he was going to meet a young African American man who was the secretary for Roland Hayes, the noted African American singer who performed to great acclaim across the United States and Europe. However, although Reed thought the man was nice, he didn't find him to be very interesting. He was more impressed with the other people he met at the party, where the crew spoke both English and German. He also met an actor who gave him a ticket to his show.

During the party, Reed encountered a woman, dressed in men's attire, sitting alone reading a book. Curious, Reed ventured closer so that he could read the title and made a cheeky remark about the popularity of the book. Amused, she replied that she was in fact the author. She introduced herself as Jan Gay and remarked, "Well, it kept me for three years." Perhaps she was reading her 1932 book *On Going Naked*, which made her a leader in the nudism movement. Reed was relieved that she wasn't angry, and she thought he was funny. He felt that they would become good friends, and they made plans to meet the following week.

Gay was a pseudonym of thirty-five-year-old Helen Reitman, an author who wrote a series of children's books illustrated by Eleanor Byrnes, who used the pseudonym Zhenya Gay. Jan Gay also studied homosexuality, establishing the Committee for the Study of Sex Variants in 1935 and interviewing homosexual men and women, creating case studies for each person.

Reed was inspired by Jan Gay's stories of travels to South America and Europe. He considered taking time off from his studies during the next year, hoping to work and save money so that he could finally make it to Europe. A German artist friend also offered to pay his way to Europe. Reed dreamed of meeting a millionaire who could finance his trip. His mother told him he needed to worry about how he would get back to the United States in case of a war. Reed was sure, as an American citizen, that the State Department would readily assist him.

A few weeks after Reed met Jan Gay at the boat party, they

met up again and chatted during a walk by the river. Reed shared his uncertainty about pursuing a Ph.D. because he was really interested in writing. She encouraged him to get as much education as possible even if he had to go broke doing it. But Reed was restless and still wished that he could have traveled instead of spending the year at Columbia. He wanted to have some life experiences. Before they parted, Jan promised to take him dancing in the future.

Jan Gay visited Reed at John Jay Hall at the end of May. Because she was a woman, she was not allowed in his room, so Reed met her in the lounge downstairs. She brought a friend, a young Black man from Haiti, an artist who also worked for the government. The man didn't speak English, so the three of them conversed in French. Reed asked some of his friends from Columbia to join them and Jan invited a man, about seventy-six years old, a father figure to her, who lived nearby. He had loaned her $20,000, which no doubt intrigued Reed, but he was not charmed by the man and found him to be boring. The man from Haiti told Reed that he would love living there and thought he could get a job teaching French literature and English. The cost of living was low, and Reed envisioned writing on the side and visiting the United States during the summer. And if he became a citizen, he could avoid being drafted into the next war. Perhaps he was thinking about his father's fate? Reed considered, "I would rather go there than to the South, of course, as negroes in Haiti are regular aristocrats." He figured he could live in a hotel for about $60 a month and round-trip fare was a little over $100. Reed was restless. He wondered if Cyril and Olgy would support his trip to Haiti.

However, when he shared his plan with Jan, she told him that he would not like living in Haiti. She said it was a nice place to visit but "there is not nearly so much culture there as the natives pretend. Most of the people live in huts and work on farms, and there is only one civilized city in the whole island." Reed thought, "I must confess, all the people I have met from Haiti so far have been well educated." He was torn and didn't know who he could believe.

Reed continued encountering interesting people, including a man named Jimmie Thomas from France. In spite of his earlier feelings, he was starting to feel sorry about leaving New York now that he was finally meeting people he found stimulating. Jimmie's father was an African American married to a French woman. Jimmie performed in theater, movies, and concerts and worked in the movie industry, where he made a handsome living. But he was now interested in studying for the ministry—much to Reed's dismay. Jimmie claimed it was his calling, but Reed was skeptical and thought it was a passing fancy. Jimmie planned to return to France that summer and invited Reed to visit— unless his parents came to the United States to visit him. Reed no doubt hoped that they would remain in France so that he could visit. Jimmie told Reed that he would love living in France, which echoed what his white friends had been telling him. Reed was intrigued by Jimmie's offer to live with his family in France.

Reed thought, "Colored people in France get along so beautifully that I know I would enjoy myself." And "I am sure that I would like the atmosphere very much." He recalled, "When I was graduated from college, I thought surely I would get a fellowship to go abroad; but that failing, I gave it up for a while." He was still

unaware, and had no way of knowing, how the dean had sabotaged his chances by including the second, secret letter detailing
his race. Instead, Reed considered it a failure on his part.

Reed thought, "Certainly, a colored gentleman—when really
a gentleman like myself—has a hard time in this country; and I
would be silly to stay here if I could do better somewhere else."
Perhaps he was reflecting on his lack of opportunities to teach in
the types of educational institutions that had in fact educated
him. Did he know that Harvard's Appointment Office would
never send his credentials to other Ivy League universities? Or
was it evident because he had never had a faculty member who
looked like him?

Later, when Reed called Jimmie Thomas, a woman with an
accent answered his phone. Reed suspected it was his mother
visiting from France, and he hoped to meet her. But later, Reed
ended his friendship with Jimmie when he did not show up for a
meeting and didn't telephone or send a telegram. Reed was furi-
ous at his rudeness. That path to France was now closed.

Reed finally heard back from Harvard. He was admitted into
a Ph.D. program and offered a $400 scholarship. Insulted, he
considered not accepting it. He felt like he merited more, because he knew that other students were offered scholarships
worth $1,000. Despite his displeasure at the amount of the
scholarship, he still took some petty joy in it, telling his grandmother, "I wish I could have seen the expression on Miss
Browne's face when you told her about my success on the scholarship."

He calculated that he still needed to come up with an additional $200 for living expenses. He hoped to find a summer job

or to do some secretarial work for Olgy and Cyril—most likely typing up their academic work or selling some of his stories to journals. He also considered taking the teachers' examination in Boston in order to get a summer job or contacting the tutoring bureau to see if he could do some translation work. He thought that if he could earn $25 for several weeks during the summer that he could support himself during the next academic year. He also was confident that he could earn a prize at Harvard next June to obtain additional funds.

Meanwhile, his classes finished at the end of May, but because Columbia continued serving meals to the students until the first week of June, Reed declared, "I'll be damned if I go home until I have had my money's worth." He was also allowed to stay in his dorm room, but his usual dining room was closed and the students on scholarship were allowed to eat in the Faculty Club. Reed preferred this dining experience because the food was better and "polite colored waiters" gave them "fingerbowls and offer you a newspaper to read at breakfast." He thought, "If the rest of the year had been like this, I would have found it much pleasanter." After the dorms closed, he would make his way to Boston by either train or boat and considered getting a large crate to transport all of his books, using suitcases for his heavy clothes and sending his light clothes in his laundry case. He planned to live at Sumner Court with Laura and Nona Whitehead, Laura's younger widowed sister, unless he had a better offer.

As he packed to leave New York City, he was still waiting to hear from Cyril and Olgy about a possible secretarial job for the summer. He also considered asking Olgy for $300 for the next year, despite earlier stating that he needed less money for living expenses. He knew he was being bold but thought, "Well, there's no harm in asking. Doesn't the Bible say, 'Ask, and it shall be granted'?"

He also hoped to move in with Cyril and Olgy later in the summer. He was increasingly frustrated with their lack of commitment to giving him a secretarial job. He lamented:

> I must say, the kittens never answer that part of the letter when I ask them about the work they promised me for the summer. I have mentioned it in every letter for the past month, and they have continued to ignore it except when they have said, "Everything will be all right." That is very vague, but it may mean something. And then after Olgy got his advancement, he spoke of himself as the providing little pig. That is pleasing too.

Reed was wistful about leaving New York City but stated, "Even if Columbia offers me nothing at all in the way of culture, and being in New York has cost a lot of money, I shall always be glad I came here merely for the privilege of having met Miss Jan Gay. She is really wonderful." He had spent the previous day with Jan drinking vodka. She planned to rent a home in western Massachusetts for the summer and invited him to spend a few days there. He told Cyril and Olgy that they would all like each other.

When his residential fellowship ended, Reed left New York City to return to Boston and an uncertain summer and future at Harvard, in Haiti, or maybe even in Europe.

FOUR

Harvard Redux:
"This Regrettable Incident"

R eed was thrilled to be back at Harvard University in the fall of 1937. During this time, he became enamored with an undergraduate entering his junior year named Leonard Bernstein. The future *On the Waterfront* and *West Side Story* composer had the same dark good looks and musical talent as Reed's friend Monty, who had graduated a few months earlier. Even before Leonard arrived at Harvard, it was possible Reed knew of him, for Leonard had also graduated from the Boston Latin School.

A simmering friendship came to a boil—for Reed, at least—when they spent time in a dimly lit music room in one of the residential colleges, sitting next to one another listening to a quartet play Beethoven. Leonard closed his eyes as the soaring piano compositions of Debussy were played, including "Cloches à travers les feuilles." Reed was in "ecstasy and agony at once," sitting so close, but dared not to touch him "for fear of breaking the spell of such exquisite beauty." Debussy's music lacked harmonies and was considered atonal, but to Reed it was mesmerizing.

Reed wrote a series of love letters to Leonard, including his own poems and references to T. S. Eliot, Rachmaninoff, Eros and Psyche, Diaghilev's treatment of Nijinsky, and the speech of Aristophanes in the *Symposium*. Reed felt he was a strong writer and could best express himself that way. He signed the letters "Devotedly, Reed" and "To Leonard in deepest affection Reed." He began one letter with, "Thank you for letting me spend those few hours with you tonight. They were very beautiful." He opened another letter with, "Leonard, Dearest, An experience as beautiful as that of Saturday night should be seconded however imperfectly."

Reed attached a poem he'd written a while earlier, he said, as an appendix to the remarks in his letter. He said, "I think it sums up quite adequately just what happened to me." The letter was typed, and the poem was handwritten, signed "To Leonard from Reed October 19, 1937."

> Loving. And if it might be expressed simply,
> Without confusion. There will be no need
> For repetition. And repetition.
> Nor is it a question of the body only.
> Sometimes almost without the body.
> And expression is difficult.
>
> Just to see you has been enough.
> And to touch your hand is consummation.
> Whether in a room, without the music.

> Or in the open, surrounded by satyrs.
> Whether in a room without all this
> Or with all this, and it is still enough.
>
> Elusive. Emotion is always elusive
> Out of revenge, protecting Beauty.
> And Beauty is light, covering darkness.
> If there were darkness and no light
> Or if there were darkness and no beauty
> There could be Beauty
> Because love
> And there could be Beauty
> Because love
> And there shall be light and Beauty and love.

Leonard Bernstein, who was deeply conflicted about his sexuality, told Reed that he found his letters to be repulsive. This stunned Reed, who believed that Leonard felt the same way about him. Reed replied, feeling misled:

> Thank you for letting me know as soon as you did. But why, oh why, did you wait even this long—especially after my gropings and hesitations in trying to discover whether it were really true? Why did you lead me to believe that I was not mistaken—or were you unable to comprehend until recently.

Given Leonard's response, Reed said, "I have suffered a nervous shock and a feeling of inward desolation every time I have thought of you this afternoon."

And he knew a friendship between them was no longer possible.

> The gods have conspired against us. . . . A casual acquaintanceship . . . may or may not persist. But friendship, no; for you have released in me great wells of emotion that would do physical as well as mental damage to me if kept in a "suspended" state, inflamed continually by your presence and forcibly checked in their expression by your difference in temperament.

Crushed, Reed asked Leonard to "destroy all my letters and any other material that I have sent or given you during this regrettable incident," hoping their relationship could somehow return to the pre–October 16 letter, and urging that the flirtation and Reed's feelings not deter Leonard's presence in their mutual social life. "I am writing this note especially to deter you in case you had any intention of withdrawing from the group at Sprague's." He wanted Leonard to continue attending the salon because "all of us are counting upon your presence quite regularly, as you know, and I hope you will not disappoint us."

He included a second poem with a letter adopting the persona of an old woman who was lonely:

MY NEW HOUSE

My new house had a garden in front
(Flocks and geraniums bordered by hyacinths),
And I lived alone, waiting for guests.

And indeed, there are always tourists in summer,
And no one else could have had such a throng
In the garden as I did.
I was the host, and called from the door
To my guests, who stopped in the yard near the threshold
And I was lonely, because they did not come in.

Fertile ground produces in summer,
And weeds luxuriate faster than hyacinths,
Spreading exultantly leaves through the flower-beds.
Mine was no luxury.
Nobody wanted a house with no garden,
And weeds are too common. Shrill voices
Screeched in my half-open windows.
Malicious rocks bounced over my carpet.
I was the host, and wept at the door
(My plants were afterwards buried in flower-pots).

Then there came tramps,
Those who looked down upon houses with gardens
(Although I was host, and received at the door).
And after the visiting and the laughter
And after the hospitality, there were no handshakes.
And I was still lonely, even when they came again.

Now I am old,
An old woman, wrapped in my shawl,
Sitting by the fireplace, rubbing my cat.
My house is an old house, but I do not mourn.

I cannot weep where there are no tears

And I cannot laugh where there is no laughter.

Despite being rebuffed by Leonard, Reed was happy that his friend Monty was still at Harvard after graduating in the spring with a bachelor's degree. Monty remained for the next two years studying for a master's degree in music in the Graduate School of Arts and Sciences.

Reed decided to concentrate on his own studies. While pursuing his doctorate in comparative literature, he enrolled in courses in Romantic philology, three comparative literature courses, and two in English. Besides studying for his doctorate, he wanted to publish some of his creative writing and critical pieces in a non-academic journal. He also wanted to pursue getting a fellowship to fund a year studying abroad in France for his dissertation research—living in Paris was one of his dreams.

Reed contacted John Lehmann, the editor of *New Writing*, a literary journal published in a book format. Lehmann founded the journal in 1936 and published authors including Christopher Isherwood, W. H. Auden, and Stephen Spender. Reed explained that a Mr. Delius Giese, whom he had met while living in New York, suggested he submit his short story to the publication. Reed wrote:

I have a short story entitled Pocket Muse which I should like for you to consider. I cannot promise that I am necessarily a Leftist, but I am in sympathy with the general attitude of your contributors. After all, it is as hard to deny that the contemporary scene is "an old bitch gone in the teeth" as it is to understand how Mr. Mussolini (as Kung-Fu-Tse) can rejuvenate the "botched civilization."

I have followed with special interest literary trends in England, and at Harvard (B.A. '35, M.A. '36) studied under Prof. Theodore Spencer, whose intimate association with Dr. I.A. Richards and Mr. T.S. Eliot was of valuable assistance to me. Right now I am a prospective candidate for a PH.D in Comparative Literature.

My publications to date are not numerous, and are best passed over in silence. While I notice that most of your contributors are well-known, I hope you will not reject my work on these grounds, provided you find it of satisfactory quality. New Writing, as far as I can see, is exactly the sort of publication in which I would most prefer to express myself.

Reed did not describe the short story in this somewhat bizarre letter. Nevertheless, Lehmann requested to see the manuscript and Reed submitted it on October 14, 1937, writing:

I have written this story largely to present the college intellectual as I have known him on the northeastern coast of the U.S. Some one [*sic*] has said that it is a virtue in a writer for his point to be missed, and while I know that I am running the dangerous risk of committing hybris by saying so, I suggest that there may be several interpretations possible for Pocket Muse. As author, I prefer to stress the connection between Russell Merton and Master Edward Knowell, expressed in the title, which takes away somewhat the over-emphasis upon contemporaneity (although I do not pretend to subscribe to the Ben Jonson theory of humours). If I did care to moralize, I would ask, rather than suggest, what age will finally offer a solution for these problem children. Perhaps none, when they make such excellent subjects for this tragi-comedy of human existence.

Reed felt he was languishing in America and that it was important to have experience living abroad to become the type of distinguished gentleman he longed to be, and he began seeking funds from organizations to make his dream of living abroad come true. He felt that he would be a success as an African American in a different country than his own. He was in contact with his friend from Columbia University, Newton, who shared his dream of studying in Europe for their respective doctorates.

In November 1937, Reed contacted the Rosenwald Foundation, which had established a fund in 1917 to support African American scholars and artists through fellowships. They initially told him that they did not support study abroad at that time. Reed wouldn't give up so easily; he mentioned the case of his friend William Harrison, who also studied at Harvard, and who used his fellowship to conduct research in Cambridge, England. He also cited his two previous degrees and his current enrollment in a Ph.D. program in comparative literature at Harvard, arguing that he had discovered that documents crucial to the completion of his dissertation were in France and that he was fluent in French. He mentioned his need for financial assistance and his strong academic record, including receiving a Phi Beta Kappa key from Harvard College and other academic honors. His dissertation, entitled "The Notion of Decadence in Nineteenth Century Literature," would be supervised by Dr. Fernand Baldensperger, whom he had studied under at Columbia University. In his Statement of Plan of Work, Reed described his research, inspired by a seminar he had attended at Harvard University. He wanted to study the nineteenth century, he said,

> to see what were the aims and literary ideals of the writers of that period, having become convinced that "decadence" in its true sense had little application here, just as "romantic" does not necessarily mean "propensity to fall in love." The subject offered enormous possibilities, as the question is one to be tackled not only from its nineteenth century phase but in its relation to literature as a whole.

Professor Baldensperger wrote a letter of recommendation, and, in a continuing pattern, he mentioned Reed's race in a more obtuse way. He wrote:

> This young man has great linguistic abilities, a rare sense for literary appreciation. Whether some emotive aspects of his personality, a liking for the more subtle and dreamy aspects of poetry, for example, is due to individual or to "racial" reasons, is difficult to ascertain.

Paul Hazard, a professor at the Collège de France, who taught Reed during the fall 1936 semester at Columbia, also wrote a favorable recommendation (in French but translated by someone at Harvard) that omitted a mention of his race. Lawrence S. Mayo, an assistant dean at Harvard University's Graduate School of Arts and Sciences, confirmed Reed's previous bachelor's degree (but neglected to mention his master's) and verified his current enrollment and strong academic record in a letter of recommendation. He also stated, "He has an attractive personality, and his courtesy is above criticism."

Although Reed mentioned in his application that he had conducted "considerable creative writing," he said he had not made "serious efforts to have any of these things published." But Reed did write to John Lehmann again on January 5, 1938, thanking him for considering his short story for *New Writing*, although it was ultimately rejected. Not giving up, Reed asked:

> I wonder would you be at all interested in another short story, which is now in preparation, for a future issue of "New Writing"? I have not yet titled it, but I would be very glad to submit it upon its completion.

Reed also corresponded with Dorothy Norman about a new journal she began editing and publishing in 1938, originally called *The American Quarterly* and later renamed *Twice a Year: A Book of Literature, the Arts, and Civil Liberties*. Norman was a writer, photographer, and supporter of Planned Parenthood, the National Urban League, and the American Civil Liberties Union. Reed wrote to her about contributing poems and prose for publication in her journal. He introduced himself as a graduate student at Harvard studying comparative literature and mentioned that he was working on a critical essay about André Gide, the famous French writer who was also queer. She replied on January 18, 1938:

> Of course I would like to see your work, and I should be particularly interested in a piece on Gide. I am interested in both critical work as well as stories and poetry. Just so that the material comes out of direct experience and is alive. Otherwise there are no limitations.

To his delight, Reed received both a John Harvard Fellowship and the Rosenwald Fellowship to attend the Sorbonne and to conduct research at the Bibliothèque Nationale. The fellowships must have seemed like a lifeline. The Rosenwald Fellowship came with an initial payment of $500 and $100 on the first of every month, for a total of $1,500. Reed asked for an advance of the first month because he planned to sail to France in August. He was informed that he could receive the full amount of the fellowship before he left because it would make exchanging money easier—an offer he hadn't known was possible.

Reed did not submit anything for several months to *Twice a Year*, but contacted Dorothy Norman again in July 1938, asking if he could still send her some pieces to review, and he mentioned the Gide essay, warning her that it was currently over eight thousand words. He sent her some pieces but not the Gide essay. She politely replied on August 5, 1938, "Thank you so much for the enclosed. Although I fear we cannot use the things you have sent, I should still like to see the piece on Gide. Do send it along if you still care to do so. I should like to see it."

Reed sent an update on his accomplishments for a report on the activities of the Class of 1935.

Harvard College, Class of 1935, The Triennial Report, 1938

After a year at Columbia (1936–1937), I returned to Harvard to complete the requirements for a Ph.D. Very much interested in Comparative Literature as a back-ground for creative writing and as a discipline for nature criticism. Preparing a dissertation, scribbling small bits (scholarly and otherwise) from time to time, and looking forward to a year in Europe, with subsequent breaking into print.

The fellowship was the perfect excuse to leave Cambridge behind and any bitter memories of his unrequited infatuation with Leonard Bernstein. Here was an opportunity for Reed to go to a place where no one would know that his mother and grandmother were cleaning ladies and that his father was in a mental institution. He was a man with two Harvard degrees working on his third, could speak French fluently, and loved to discuss literature, art, and music. Here was his chance to follow in the footsteps of his Boston Latin School and Harvard classmates who regaled him with tales of their overseas adventures. He did not seem to dwell on his status as African American being an impediment. He imagined returning to the United States and being able to begin conversations at dinner parties with, "When I was in Paris . . ."

FIVE

Bon Voyage

After a tearful farewell with friends and family, Reed boarded a ship from Boston to New York City that sailed along the Cape Cod Canal. During the trip, his ship got caught in a "vivid" electrical storm. The sky was filled with dark, towering clouds occasionally disrupted by jagged lines of lightning and rumbling, booming thunder. The change in the atmosphere caused a tingling sensation on his skin. Instead of being scared, he stayed on deck for two hours until after midnight, appreciating the stunning beauty. He fearlessly recalled, "I liked the flashes and the crashes very much."

The next morning, his Columbia University friend Newton picked him up at the dock. They were sailing to Europe together. Reed wanted to rent a room at Columbia, but they claimed to not have any available rooms. Reed said cryptically, "I can't say I really blame them after the way I carried on there at New Year."

Instead, he checked into the King's Crown Hotel on 420 West 116th Street in Morningside Heights for two dollars a night. To his delight, the hotel had a private bath, where he soaked for a half hour and used their stationery to dash off a letter to his mother, Mary. This was his first stay in a hotel, but he imagined that he would patronize more of them once he got to Europe. He was surprised to not have a problem getting a hotel room as an African American and hoped to have the same experience in Germany, where he would have to spend the night on his way to Poland to visit a friend. He also planned to live in a hotel upon his arrival in Paris. The King's Crown was very accommodating, even allowing him to check out late because his ship did not sail until midnight.

That evening Reed met friends for dinner at a French restaurant. He joined his friend Newton, Hugh (Newton's friend from Kansas), and Jan Gay, who borrowed a car that she struggled to drive. Newton helped her start the car after she had a taxi push it, thinking the battery was dead, only to realize that she hadn't turned on the ignition. They had a madcap last night tooling around New York City and Gay "nearly ran down several people and almost wrecked the car."

Making good on her earlier promise to take Reed dancing, Jan took him to the Savoy Ballroom in Harlem at 596 Lenox Avenue between 140th and 141st Streets. The sign glowed and lit up the avenue. The ballroom could hold two thousand patrons, but often more people squeezed in. There was always a line down the block of people waiting to gain entrance. They entered on the ground floor and took one of the two marble staircases to the second floor where the ten-thousand-square-foot ballroom covered the entire space. The décor was glamorous and classy. Chandeliers hung from the ceiling. Reed described it as "modernistic" and

gaudy, and not at all "colored" looking, except for the people, who are as colored as you can find anywhere. There are two orchestras which alternate. On the dance floor you find some of the wierdest [*sic*] dances performed that you will ever see. In fact, most people who go there go to watch the dancing rather than to dance themselves.

Couples did the wildcat and the Lindy hop. Reed soaked it all in. "When they played Flat-Foot Floojie I thought they would go mad. It was wilder than a revival meeting." The song, actually entitled "Flat Foot Floogie (with a Floy Floy)," was one of the major hits of 1938 written by Slim Gaillard, Slam Stewart, and Bud Green, with Gaillard and Stewart performing as Slim & Slam. Most of the lyrics were nonsense, repeating the title. "Floogie" was originally "floozy"—a reference that proved to be too racy. The floor bobbed under Reed's feet from all of the people dancing.

The next evening, despite the late hour, a large group of friends showed up to see Reed set sail, including Jan and Hugh, who was masquerading as Reed for the sake of Newton's father, who did not approve of his son sharing a berth with Reed. Newton's father, Morris, owned a car dealership back home and did not like that his son had befriended Reed—perhaps because of his race, or perhaps because Morris, with only an eighth-grade education, resented this African American scholar.

Reed received a few telegrams from family members, and a

book from his friend Harold. He was joining a long list of African American expatriates in Paris that included painter Henry Ossawa Tanner in the nineteenth century and writer Langston Hughes, nightclub owner and singer Bricktop, performer Josephine Baker, jazz musician and soldier James Reese Europe in the early twentieth century, and writers Richard Wright and James Baldwin, who would arrive after Reed's journey. There was something magical about Paris, an anticipated captivating charm that drew African Americans because of its reputation for embracing them.

Newton and Reed walked up the gangplank of SS *Veendam* of the Holland America Line on August 20, 1938. If Reed worried about being segregated on the ship like other African Americans had been before him, he didn't mention it in his letters home. Formerly enslaved abolitionist Frederick Douglass described his transatlantic crossing experience where he was forced to stay in third-class accommodations and was almost thrown overboard after giving an antislavery speech. Principal of the Tuskegee Institute Booker T. Washington recalled, "I had just a little fear that we would not be treated civilly by some of the passengers." He said his fear was based on how others had been treated—most likely referencing Douglass. Reed, however, found the other passengers, primarily German and Dutch, to be "terribly friendly." In his usual sardonic way, he lamented, "I only wish I were more interested in them."

The ship had three classes: cabin, tourist, and third, where Reed and Newton shared cabin 376, which had both hot and cold running water. Of course, Reed thought the most interesting people were in third class since other passengers often went down to visit them.

Newton and Reed sat on deck chairs with their typewriters and curious passengers looked over their shoulders to see how their machines worked. Reed assumed and hoped that most of them could not read English because he thought they would be shocked by the content of some of the letters that he was writing.

The ship had a lounge with comfortable chairs in which to read or to write letters. Reed used the stationery to write letters to his family but later admitted that there was no need for numerous letters since every day followed the same itinerary. There was also a smoking room where a brochure suggested "a rendezvous before or after meals where you can linger to discuss light and frothy things as you plan your European trip." There was a gym, a pool, and a college orchestra. There was teatime in a café and a dining room for meals. The brochure mentioned that there were often college students on board, like Reed, but the people featured looked white. Entertainment included masquerade balls, treasure hunts, and a library. Reed did not say if he participated in any of these activities, but there is no doubt that he used the library and enjoyed listening to the orchestra.

The trip was smooth sailing with warm weather. They had large quantities of food to choose from at mealtimes and opportunities for leisure activities including movies and various games played on the deck such as shuffleboard, Ping-Pong, or tennis. Despite the numerous events, Reed grew bored with the daily repetition of seeing the same people and same unchanging Atlantic Ocean every day. During the approximately weeklong journey he developed a routine with Newton: they woke up between eight and nine and ate breakfast; drank beef tea at eleven and then ate lunch at twelve-thirty and had tea at four o'clock; at five-thirty they scheduled a bath of heated salt water that prevented the soap from foaming, followed by dinner at six-thirty, and they usually ended the night by listening to music or watching a movie. Occasionally, Reed played the piano and sang German songs with the Germans on board.

As novel as the passage must have been, Reed looked ahead to a new life in Europe: a reinvention as a refined, sophisticated gentleman.

He would begin his new life in Paris.

SIX

A Distinguished Scholar in Paris

Reed had finally arrived at his destination—Paris. He had longed to live there for as long as he could remember. From his taxi, he might have seen the Louvre, Notre-Dame, and the Seine on his way to his hotel. He was dismayed, though, to discover that the hotel he selected, the Hôtel de Seine, located at 52 rue de Seine, was not in fact on the Seine, sending Laura a postcard upon arrival: "The first picture shows the front, the second shows the reception hall. The view of the river has absolutely nothing to do with the hotel, as you would have to walk five minutes to see it, but it makes a good advertisement."

Reed did not live in the Montmartre section of Paris where many African American expatriates resided and made no mention of attending jazz clubs even though the legendary nightclub Chez Bricktop, managed by Ada "Bricktop" Smith, was still operating when he first arrived in the city. Langston Hughes got a job there as a busboy when he turned up in Paris in 1924. Instead, Reed's hotel was located in the 6th arrondissement, also known as Saint-Germain-des-Prés. The arrondissement, half of the size of New York City's Central Park, measures two square kilometers, or three-quarters of a square mile. Thomas Jefferson and Sally Hemings lived in that section, as did Benjamin Franklin. It was considered the heart of the literary quarter of Paris. Authors F. Scott Fitzgerald, Ernest Hemingway, and Gertrude Stein were residents. Jean-Paul Sartre and Simone de Beauvoir patronized the café Les Deux Magots and Café de Flore next door, which Picasso liked. Later, James Baldwin and Richard Wright would frequent these too. Although these cafés were a very short walk from Reed's hotel, he did not mention spending his days writing in any cafés. He preferred to write in his hotel room. Perhaps he selected this neighborhood because it was a fifteen-minute walk to the Sorbonne where he enrolled in classes, and a ten-minute walk to the Bibliothèque Nationale de France where he studied, and a short walk to the American Express office where he picked up his mail.

He educated Mary and Laura about hotel living in Paris and how having hot water and heat from a radiator was considered a luxury and that few hotel residents took baths because of the extra expense, of twenty cents. He was not allowed to use the wash bowls after 10 p.m., and, most important, he was not permitted to type after that hour. Despite the rules, he liked hotel living because he thought French hotels were both very nice and inexpensive. He said, "I personally prefer being here [in a hotel] than in a private family because my life is more of my own." He could decide when and where he wanted to eat, unlike in a private home where he would have had to bend to the family's schedule. Reed found a restaurant where he could eat for twenty-five cents per meal if he agreed to eat ten meals there. Every meal came with soup, meat, vegetables, dessert, and wine. Some restaurants included bread and a napkin in the price, while they were often extra in other European countries. He drank more wine than ever before, but he assured Laura:

> I don't mean what you think: I mean that in France people drink wine with their meals instead of water. . . . French people think it is very vulgar to get drunk, and they look down upon any body [*sic*] who drinks too much, although everybody drinks a bit.

He liked the two women who ran the hotel, but he really wanted a hotel run by a man, for an untold reason. His room cost twelve dollars a month, and for that price he got both hot and cold running water, heat from a radiator, telephone service (he could get messages from the proprietors and use the phone to return calls), and electricity. Evidently these amenities were quite fancy, according to his friends. Despite his comfort, he was also looking for a furnished apartment to rent because it afforded more privacy and fewer rules. But he grew to like this hotel and moved to another room that was warmer and had a mantel where he could stack his books. The only thing he lacked was a radio. He loved listening to the radio or records on a phonograph—he often visited people who offered this source of entertainment—but never seemed to have his own. He declined to spend the extra thirty cents the hotel would charge for the electricity used by the radio, and hoped instead to find a friend like Monty, in whose dorm he used to listen to records at Harvard. Reed befriended the landlady's son, a medical student who played the piano. They chatted and Reed borrowed books from him. He hoped they would invite him downstairs to listen to their radio. He said, "I have already impressed them with the fact that I like concerts very much and that I cannot afford to go as much as I would like." Trying to use his charm, he said, "I have also praised France as a very wonderful country, and I think that should get me somewhere."

The women running the hotel reminded him of Laura because they got upset not knowing when he would return when he got phone calls, and they often mixed up the names of the people who called—just like she did.

During his first week in Paris, Reed was able to figure out how to navigate his way around town, and wasted no time making connections. He even obtained an opera ticket from a woman whose husband couldn't attend. The ticket was in a prime orchestra seat, and although it was free, Reed had to tip the usher five cents, but he figured it was still cheaper than the cost of the ticket. He also lamented having to tip the toilet attendant; Reed joked that it would be a great job for Laura to get when she retired because of all the money she would make every day from the men who had to pay her for the privilege of urinating. He handwrote in the margin of the typewritten letter that he was just joking.

Reed also ran into an African American acquaintance, Frank Snowden, and his wife, Elaine, in Paris on their way back to the

United States from their trip to Italy. Frank, a professor of Blacks in antiquity with a faculty appointment at the historically Black institution Spelman, was a little older than Reed but was also a graduate of Boston Latin School, which fueled his interest in the classics, where he learned Latin and Greek. Frank also attended Harvard, where he received a bachelor's (Class of 1932) and master's degree in classical philology (Class of 1933). The Snowdens were only reluctantly returning to the United States after having had a wonderful time in Europe. Reed noted that Paris used to be filled with Americans but most had returned home.

After dropping off his steamer trunks, Reed left Paris on Monday, September 5, catching a train through Germany on his way to Warsaw to see his friend whom he called "the Count." Reed felt that the people in Germany were kind to him, including even Hitler's police officers—what he called the Nazis—most likely pleased, he thought, that he could speak German. He was able to engage people in conversation while there. Reed fared better than his friend Newton, who was beaten in Munich when he did not show the proper respect to a speech being given by Hitler. When people in the crowd saw him refuse to applaud they followed him, punching him in the face and breaking his glasses. Newton reported his assault to the police, but discovered that they were not sympathetic—they expected everyone to cheer for Hitler, including foreigners. Reed thought that Newton should've played along—that's what he did while in Germany. They eventually met up in Warsaw.

The Count was Antoni Sobański, a queer writer who was part of Poland's artistic community. His parents really were a count and a countess who lived in a mansion. Reed met Sobański, also known as Toni, through their mutual friend Clarence and discovered to his delight that Toni was generous about sharing his money with others. The Count was "eloquent, humorous, ironic, witty and cultivated," a glamorous figure with friends who were diplomats, academics, and bohemian characters he met during his travels to Berlin, Vienna, London, Paris, and Petersburg. He was also a highly respected writer, having published essays and newspaper articles—most famously his writings noting the rise of the Third Reich in Germany. Like Reed, Toni was a linguist and spoke five or six languages. Toni treated them like royalty, paying for all of their meals, which included guinea fowl, partridge, and mushrooms. They drank vodka. The Count's valet laundered Reed's clothes, pressed them, shined his shoes, drew his baths—his first since leaving the ship—and even opened doors for Reed. Toni threw a party for his guests that included Polish nobility. Reed felt that he was very popular because there was only one other colored person, of undetermined origin, in Warsaw. The other person was not American, because Reed said he didn't encounter any. He liked that people turned to look at him on the street. He cherished the attention for the most part but complained about a Polish woman who he said made a pass at him at a nightclub. She didn't speak English and Reed didn't understand her Polish, but he was sure that she was fascinated by his color and wanted to bed him.

He felt lucky that most of Toni's friends spoke some French or German so he could communicate with them. During his stay in Warsaw, he noted that while Toni knew lots of important people and that he was from nobility, he didn't boast or make a big deal about it. Reed did observe Toni kissing ladies' hands in public. He said it was a custom of people in his social class, but that he never did it outside of Poland. Reed told him that Cyril and Olgy, whom he called "the Prince and the Professor," did it in America. Toni, who knew them, said they must be "tiresome people."

Reed did not note any rising tensions in Poland about a possible impending war. Perhaps he was distracted by all of the social engagements or did not want to dwell on any unpleasantness while he was living his dream. He left Poland on Thursday, September 15. He was sad to leave and hoped to see Toni when he visited Paris in the future. Reed was also glad that he had a chance to see other parts of Europe "while there is still some left to see." He traveled once again through Germany. He befriended a man from Sweden on the train. They were able to converse in English, French, and German. Reed encouraged him to book a room in his hotel in Paris. Reed took the time to see a movie while in Berlin. The whole return trip took two days and he arrived in Paris on Saturday, September 17.

After two days in Paris, Reed headed to London on Monday, September 19, for a weeklong visit, armed with letters of introduction from Jan Gay. He planned to meet English poet Stephen Spender and Reginald Foresythe, a pianist, bandleader, arranger, composer, and songwriter. Spender, born in London in 1909, also wrote novels, essays, and dramas, but it was his poetry and his future publication *The Still Centre* that established him as a leading figure. Foresythe, born in London in 1907, was called "mysterious, most adventurous." He specialized in combining classical and jazz music and was known for his hit "Dodging a Divorcee." He was also queer and biracial—the son of a white mother and Black father. Foresythe had moved to the United States in 1930 to focus on jazz and had great success. Duke Ellington allowed him to live in his apartment in New York City—much to his chagrin. Foresythe damaged the apartment due to drunkenness and brawled in local bars before eventually returning to England. Reed also made plans to meet his friend William Harrison, who was now a journalist for the *Boston Chronicle* newspaper founded by him and other Caribbean men.

Reed had a knack for making friends quite easily. He had befriended an Englishman on the *Veendam* who invited him to stay with him in London. Perhaps the gentleman was the physics lecturer from the University of London whom Reed thought was the most interesting person on the ship. However, their wires got crossed and it took two days for Reed to connect with him. Meanwhile, Reed stayed with a Jewish man, a German refugee he also met on the ship, but who was not living in very nice accommodations. The landlord charged Reed a dollar per night for the bed linens and was upset when he requested meat with his breakfast, but Reed didn't care. He wanted to get his money's worth. She also charged five cents for hot water.

Luckily, Reed eventually found his English friend and took him up on his offer, sleeping on a cot in his one-bedroom apartment. He took a daily bath, drank his alcohol, listened to the radio, read his books, and ate breakfast with him—consisting of cornflakes, toast with marmalade, bacon, and coffee—for no charge. The man refused to take Reed's money. This friend took Reed around in his car to see his friends and to a dance where Reed was propositioned by a woman. He declared, "What a sensation it creates to be an American—and a colored one at that."

But, he revealed, his real reason for going to London was to meet with writers and show them his work.

He noticed that people in London were buying gas masks and being told to "hide in the safest part of the house when the bombs fall. The safest part, for some strange reason, is usually the bathroom."

Reed met Stephen Spender, but if he saw Reginald Foresythe, he did not mention it. His trip to London didn't go unnoticed and made the pages of African American newspapers back home in the United States. Rudolph Dunbar, the London correspondent for the Associated Negro Press, had a column, "European Comments," published in the New York *Amsterdam News* and replicated in other newspapers. Dunbar lamented that he was not in town to greet Reed and another African American on his way to London—Langston Hughes. Dunbar mused, "If they make the right contacts," both Reed and Langston "will serve a useful purpose in breaking down some of the prejudice against our race." Reed's friend Newton sent him a clipping from the Kansas City Black newspaper, *The Call*. Reed crowed to Laura, "You see that your little brown boy is becoming quite famous, getting mentioned beside Langston Hughes."

Reed returned to a Paris on edge. Europe was on the brink of World War II and most foreigners were departing. Just as he arrived, the US State Department strongly encouraged Americans to leave Europe. Despite the war clouds gathering, Reed declared, "I shall stick it out until the bombs fall on my hotel." He was determined to remain as long as he could; after all, he had been waiting for this opportunity to study and live abroad for years. He observed, "In Paris they were actually digging holes in the streets for people to get into if there was an air raid, and gas masks were to be given out by the government to all the population." Despite these ominous signs, Reed chose to ignore them because this was simply not the Paris that he envisioned.

Janet Flanner, writing a column for *The New Yorker,* described the mood in Paris in 1938:

> Unlike London, which made elaborate preparations for air raids, Paris during the week of anxiety offered its citizens nothing but sand to extinguish incendiary bombs, the advice that all inhabitants should dive into their coal cellars when the sirens screamed, and plans to scatter the population throughout the countryside.

She estimated that there were about fourteen thousand Americans remaining in Paris. And:

> For their protection and evacuation, the American Embassy had in readiness stocks of food, gasoline, fleets of motorcars, and shipping arrangements which included temporarily parking refugees in Madeira. Two cruisers waited to take off American nationals at Brest.

On September 29 and 30, 1938, Neville Chamberlain and Édouard Daladier, the prime ministers of Britain and France respectively, along with Adolf Hitler and Benito Mussolini representing

Germany and Italy, met in Munich to reach an agreement that would allow Germany to annex part of Czechoslovakia, hoping to prevent another world war from happening and to maintain peace. Reed was optimistic. He thought, "I guess we will have peace for a little longer." He mused, "I am really so glad that there is going to be peace, for I would have hated for Europe to go to War just as I got here, when I had been wanting to come for so long."

Despite everything going on, Reed was ready to socialize. He had letters of introduction from Toni for several of his friends in Paris. He hoped to meet them, "provided Europe is not at war by that time. It may well be that I shall be hiding in cellars to keep from getting hit by bombs." This could not have been very reassuring for Laura to read. He then said that even a war would not make him return to the United States: only running out of money would make him go back.

When Reed went to the American embassy to receive permission to use the Bibliothèque Nationale de France for his academic reading, they told him to return to the United States at once. He refused, knowing that it was only a request and that they could not force him to go. He ignored this portentous warning while pondering, "But I must say, I really wondered just how I was going to be able to dodge all the bombs when they started throwing them."

Returning to his hotel, Reed finally unpacked his trunk after living out of a suitcase for a month. The women running his hotel were so kind that they even visited his new friend from Sweden in the hospital after a bout of appendicitis. His prodigious letter writing annoyed the women running the hotel because he consumed a lot of paper and envelopes. He planned to buy his own envelopes soon—or better yet, he asked Laura to send him some when she next sent a large package. He marveled at the low cost of grooming in Paris too. "A French haircut is something wonderful. Shampoo, tonic, and general treatment all for forty five cents. And almost every shop has hair dressing. I really did not need to bring so much with me." Reed noted, "Almost everything that I need I can find here. I really packed as if I was going to a desert island." He could easily purchase typewriter ribbons, brushes and polish for his shoes, and a cigarette lighter. His friend Newton also thought the same thing, because "he packed a dozen typewriter ribbons." Reed signed off, "Cheerio," noting, "As they say in England (even on busses and telephones)."

Reed said that it was easier to meet people in England and Poland than in France. He mused, "But perhaps they could afford to be generous in Warsaw and London because they knew I was leaving so soon, and here in Paris I make the mistake of telling them that I am going to stay all winter." He was surprised that he had not met more people in France, although he had been invited to several dinners and stayed overnight twice away from the hotel—like he often did in Boston and Cambridge— lamenting that "whereas in Poland and England I felt that at any moment I was about to find that rich interested person I have always been looking for who would say to me that he was going to take me in hand." Reed had hoped to make important connections by attending Harvard, but none of his friends, including "the kittens," had helped him in the way he desired. He was looking for a patron or a benefactor who would provide him with financial support while he focused on his writing.

One thing that disappointed Reed was the number of British and Americans in France. To his dismay, he heard quite a bit of English being spoken on the streets of Paris. But he did befriend an American living in Paris, Dr. Beryl Orris, born in Rock Island, Illinois, around 1913. It's not known how they met. Orris studied psychiatry in institutions in Berlin and Vienna and studied with Sigmund Freud and Havelock Ellis. He was a pudgy, balding man who dressed in suits with a handkerchief in the pocket and a bow tie. On a chain he wore armless glasses that he held up to his eyes for a more scholarly look. He made money by giving lectures on a variety of topics.

Another American that Reed befriended in Paris was a fellow Rosenwald scholar, Howard Swanson, who was writing a symphony and studying with the legendary teacher Nadia Boulanger in Paris. Boulanger, a French woman, had led the Boston Symphony the previous year. Howard joked with Reed that when he gave her a fifty-dollar bill to pay for five lessons, Boulanger said, "I really hate to take money from my good pupils," as she was putting the money in her pocketbook. Howard was working on "Variations on a Negro Theme" to be performed in Cleveland, Ohio.

They both hoped to get their fellowships renewed for another year. Like Reed, Howard came from a modest background. Born in Atlanta, he migrated to Cleveland with his family. His father died when he was a teenager, and as the oldest child, he went to work at the post office to support his family. Recognizing his musical talent, his teachers urged him to devote more time to school, so Howard switched to the night shift. When he realized that he could not spend the required time practicing to excel as a performer, he decided to focus on composing.

Reed surprisingly conveyed little envy about Howard's living arrangements in Paris. Howard lived in a four-room apartment near Reed's hotel with a grand piano and his own private bathroom. Howard told Reed that "whatever happens to him later, he will always be able to look back upon his year in Paris as a time he lived like a king." Howard even had silk pajamas and a cleaning woman so that he could devote all of his time to composing.

Despite his new exciting life in Paris, Reed stayed in touch with his other American friends. Cyril enrolled in a doctoral program in the School of Foreign Service at Georgetown University where his boyfriend Olgy was now a professor and they lived together as "cousins."

Reed also entertained visiting American friends. He said, "I have created a second Harvard right here in Paris" by meeting so many people from Boston. He even met three Americans who remembered him from the Boston Symphony, although Reed did not remember them at all. Perhaps he stood out as one of few African Americans in the audience. He got lots of letters from people in the United States who were making their way to Paris, and he felt like a "reception committee." He was flattered to be so popular.

After getting permission to conduct research at the Bibliothèque Nationale, Reed turned to the matter of leisure reading and became a member of the lending library at Shakespeare and Company. He made the pilgrimage to 12 rue de l'Odéon to the bookstore that was within a five-minute walk from his hotel, following in the footsteps of other expatriates like Ernest Hemingway, F. Scott Fitzgerald, James Joyce, and Ezra Pound, and met the legendary proprietor, Sylvia Beach. Beach, an American, founded the bookstore in 1919, and it sold English-language literature, a counterpart to the nearby French-language bookstore of her girlfriend, Adrienne Monnier. For a small subscription fee, students like Reed, studying at the University of Paris, who often could not afford to purchase books, could borrow and read contemporary books and literary journals in English. He signed up in September 1938 for a six-month membership with which he could borrow one item at a time for the student rate of seventy francs, with a fifty-franc deposit. He checked out his first book on September 26. It was an anomaly since it was not fiction but the biography of Hart Crane, a queer poet who died by suicide in 1932.

He checked out *Mr. Norris Changes Trains* by Christopher Isherwood on October 10, and returned it the next day. An indication that he read it and liked it is the fact that he checked out a second book by Isherwood on October 11, *Sally Bowles*. He devoured the books. Reed likely enjoyed the sense of adventure experienced by the young narrator, who encounters a mysterious Mr. Norris and an equally mysterious Sally Bowles during his travels in Berlin.

Reed's borrowing practices had clear patterns. He mainly borrowed literature by American and British authors—the core of the collection. The remaining literature included plays from Sweden (Strindberg), *The Guermantes Way* from France (Marcel Proust), and one from Germany (Thomas Mann).

A rare exception to his fiction tastes besides Crane's biography was *Journey to a War* by W. H. Auden and Christopher Isherwood, a travel narrative set in China. The settings of the other books were, not surprisingly, mainly England and the United

States, a few set in Germany, and in one instance Tahiti—Somerset Maugham's *The Moon and Sixpence*—and the Black Sea region, Sparta, and Greece in Scottish author Naomi Mitchinson's *The Corn King and the Spring Queen*, the only book he read by a woman writer. The novels were about adultery, prisoners of the Great War, and a fictionalized account of the life of Paul Gauguin. But a common theme was a man on an adventure—a topic that encompasses the campus novels *Of Time and the River: A Legend of Man's Hunger in His Youth* by Thomas Wolfe and *Starting Point* by C. Day Lewis. Reed also checked out two short story collections, *Stories of Three Decades* by Thomas Mann and *The Gay and Melancholy Flux* by William Saroyan, and the poetry collection *The Still Centre* by Stephen Spender, whom Reed met in England. Besides the three volumes of Strindberg plays, Reed borrowed one other play, *On the Frontier: A Melodrama in Three Acts*, by two of his favorite authors: Auden and Isherwood. Charles Morgan was another author that Reed checked out more than once, borrowing *The Fountain* in March 1939 and *Sparkenbroke* in May 1939.

Many of the authors Reed took an interest in are now known to have been queer. What drew Reed to these books? Was there some coded language or signal? None of the publications had overtly queer storylines, but perhaps they contained subtexts that attracted Reed. Or perhaps the titles of interesting novels were shared among his circle of friends. According to the author Edmund White, "In the twentieth century gay content became widespread—especially in France." He cited many authors that interested Reed, like Marcel Proust, the author he studied for his bachelor's thesis at Harvard; André Gide, the subject of his essay for *Twice a Year*; and Christopher Isherwood, who according to White was "the best and most open of the twentieth-century English gay writers."

Reed was primarily interested in reading the latest books. Most of the items he borrowed were published in the 1930s. While he could have borrowed books by Black American authors, he did not. The lending library held a range of books by such authors, including W. E. B. Du Bois's *Darkwater: Voices from Within the Veil*, Jean Toomer's *Cane*, Jessie Fauset's *Comedy, American Style*, and Zora Neale Hurston's *Jonah's Gourd Vine* and *Mules and Men*, among others. Reed was clearly familiar with Langston Hughes but did not take out any of his works from the library.

Reed reached out to the Rosenwald Fund at the end of October 1938 to give them an update on his progress in France. He informed them that he had found nineteenth-century periodicals and works by Frenchmen at the Bibliothèque Nationale de France and planned to enroll in the Sorbonne the following month, which would provide him access to experts in his field. He outlined his research in a Statement of Work and Plans for the Coming Year. He intended to organize his dissertation by describing the meaning of decadence by various people and the significance of the nineteenth-century decadents by examining their social, economic, and literary backgrounds, their use of the term "decadence," the importance of the decadent writers in France, and their contribution to modern literature.

Next, he asked about the possibility of extending the fellowship for another year. What was their policy? The Rosenwald Fund's director of fellowship, George M. Reynolds, promptly responded that they were glad he was getting settled in Paris and

the fellowships were for one year and that they were only renewed for "very exceptional cases and there must be a very significant reason." He told Reed that he could ask for a renewal
and his request would be considered along with applications
from new candidates. The Rosenwald Fund sent him a renewal
application and requested the reference letters and bibliography
he said he had about Haitian literature. Reed submitted reference letters from his Harvard adviser Professor Baldensperger
and from Jean-Marie Carré, professor of comparative literature
at the Sorbonne, in French and translated into English, along
with his bibliography. Reed sent follow-up letters stating that he
expected an article about Stephen Spender to be published in the
journal *Les Cahiers du Sud* and an article on André Gide in *Twice
a Year*. He also hoped that the "international situation"—the impending war—would not influence their decision.

As a backup, in case his request for an additional fellowship
year was denied by the Rosenwald Fund, Reed decided to apply
for teaching jobs. He contacted Harvard University's Appointment Office and completed a registration form. Next to "Part of
the country preferred," Reed wrote, "I should refuse any state
south of Virginia." Perhaps Virginia was deemed okay because
both of his parents were born there. Ignoring his request, the
Appointment Office only submitted his application to historically Black institutions, and most of them were located in the
South—south of Virginia.

In November 1938, Reed checked out *Of Time and the River*
from the Shakespeare and Company lending library, about a
Harvard graduate from a small town in North Carolina who

moves to New York City and ends up traveling overseas—elements of Reed's own life story. It's a mammoth novel; the edition that Reed borrowed was 912 pages long. Not surprisingly, he didn't check out another book for almost an entire month. Once his classes began, he spent a lot of time researching and studying in the library. His next selection was a collection of short stories—*The Gay and Melancholy Flux*. He no longer had time to read another massive novel.

But before his studies at the Sorbonne started around mid-November 1938, he spent his free time getting to know Paris. Reed was "determined to do all that is in my power to enjoy Paris properly, make the right contacts, and make myself a big success." He declared, "I am becoming a real scholar in a big way," once he began studying at the magnificent Sorbonne and conducting research at the majestic Bibliothèque Nationale de France on the rue de Richelieu. He was loving Paris and the only reason he would return to the United States was because he missed his relatives and friends. In one letter to Laura he noted that the *Queen Mary* ship was on its way back to America. He jokingly suggested that she catch it on the return voyage across the Atlantic Ocean. He was missing her. He said, "I am wild about it here. I feel as if I had been here for three years instead of three months, and I know Paris will always be a second home to me if it is not blown up in a war."

Reed checked out the hybrid literary monthly book/magazine *New Writing* from Shakespeare and Company. Despite his earlier rejections from *New Writing*, he submitted several poems to the publication. He received the following response:

The Editor of NEW WRITING has read with interest the poems you so kindly submitted to him. Although he appreciates their quality, he regrets that he will be unable to find room for them in the limited space at his disposal. He now returns the mss to you with many thanks.

The copies of the poems are now lost to history. Was Reed aware he was following in his father's footsteps as a poet?

Reed looked at the other literary journals available and suggested to Beach that she order *Twice a Year*. Of course he was self-interested and longed to see his name in the table of contents of a journal for sale in the famous bookstore. He renewed his correspondence, begun while he was at Harvard, with the editor Dorothy Norman about publishing his André Gide essay. He told Norman, "Incidentally, I have spoken to the ladies of Shakespeare and Company (12, rue de l'Odeon, Paris Vie), and it has been suggested by them that they would be glad to receive a sample copy of TWICE A YEAR" to examine and consider selling in the bookstore. Later, he reported to Norman that he saw issues of *Twice a Year* at Shakespeare and Company. Reed longed to be part of a literary group like Auden and Isherwood.

Reed fretted about the pieces he sent to various publications—always waiting for his big break. Ultimately, he was more successful as a scholar. He published an academic article, "A Neglected Dutch 'Amphitryon' of 1679," while in Paris, in *Modern Language Review*, a journal founded in 1905. His piece began:

Undoubtedly Monsieur Jean Giraudoux did not count this seventeenth-century version of *Amphit-*

ryon among his "thirty-seven" predecessors, for it has been so consistently neglected since its period that most scholars of to-day regard it as one of the many translations of the play of Molière.

He published a second article in *Modern Language Review* entitled "The First French and English Translations of Sir Thomas More's 'Utopia.'" It opened with:

> An investigation of the editions of the *Utopia* of Sir Thomas More is an exciting subject in itself, but a comparison of the first French and English translations throws remarkable light upon the parallel developments of the two countries in Renaissance literary history.

He acknowledged that few people except for professors would be interested in the other article that he wrote for an academic journal, about translations in the sixteenth century. He still hoped to publish an article about the literature of Haiti. He knew a lot about the history of the island and thought more people should know about it.

MEANWHILE, REED ENTERTAINED THOMAS Handforth, a forty-one-year-old queer American artist and children's book illustrator from Tacoma, Washington, who was awarded a Guggenheim Fellowship in 1931. Handforth later received the very prestigious Caldecott Medal in 1939 for his illustrations of a children's book he also wrote, *Mei Li*, about a little girl in China, informed by his travels to that country. He and Reed had several friends in common, including Jan Gay. But they met via the Count, who had just passed through Paris a week or so before. Handforth stopped in Paris, where he had previously studied art, on his way back from China, heading to New York City. He asked to draw a portrait of Reed.

Using brown and black Conté crayons, Handforth concentrated on including Reed's hands resting under his cheek, with a ring adorning a finger on his right hand. Reed would've normally posed with a suit and tie but wore a sweater because Handforth preferred capturing his neck. The artist signed the portrait "HANDFORTH Paris 1938." Reed crowed that "he produced something that several critics here have already praised as quite remarkable." The portrait was scheduled for an exhibition in a New York City gallery on 57th Street. He asked Mary to watch for the exhibition. He also said, "I have been most interested to know how much it will sell for." He sent her a reproduction and planned to use the portrait as a Christmas card to send to all of his friends.

Reed hoped that the portrait would be a success and that others would ask him to pose as a model. He thought, "It seems a shame, after all that it is the artist and not the model who is payed [*sic*] for the portrait, but I could point out that I am a very interesting subject, but God is responsible for that, and not I." He also told Monty about the exhibition and suggested that he buy the portrait but doubted that his mother would allow him to purchase it. They remained in contact despite the fact that Monty hated writing letters. Monty wondered when they would meet again.

Always on the make, looking for a benefactor, Reed met another interesting, nameless person—an American millionaire—introduced to him by the artist Handforth. "He likes colored people," Reed said without complaint. He didn't mind being exoticized and liked that being an African American made him rather unique among his ever-increasing circle in Paris. He hadn't mentioned this same feeling back in the United States if or when he was the lone African American in a social group. He said:

> He is like me: he is so wild about Paris that not even a war can drive him out. He is an awfully kind soul . . . and apparently does nothing but travel, since he has so much money he doesn't need to work. He lives in a very beautiful house, all by himself, as far as I can see, except for his servants.

They talked about art and literature and smoked cigarettes and drank cocktails. Reed hoped he could somehow help him to learn how to get a book published—although he was not in that industry. Reed's charm was a source of real value—and a crutch, he marveled. "It is funny, really—I can get almost anywhere I want to socially, and if only I had a way of living, without being 'kept' by other people, I probably would have become something already." The one person who truly took care of him was Laura, whom he thanked for his recently purchased shoes. He expressed concern about her retirement—"I don't know what you are going to live on"—but perhaps he was more worried about how she was going to be able to help finance his lifestyle.

Reed wanted to move to the Hôtel Saint-André des Arts at 66 rue Saint-André des Arts, an avant-garde hotel populated with artists, singers, and actors. It would cost a little less than his current one and, like most hotels, changed the towels once a week and the linen once a month. Importantly, the hotel did not have a 10 p.m. curfew for visitors—something that vexed Reed about his last hotel. He had befriended a Frenchman named Marcel who invited him to listen to records at his place and played the piano for Reed too. Reed couldn't reciprocate the hospitality at the Hôtel de Seine. Instead they met at a café after Marcel finished his class at the Louvre after 10 p.m. on Thursdays. They shared an interest in "music, art, and literature." Marcel did not speak English, so conversing with him helped Reed with his French, and he also planned to elicit Marcel's help with picking out new clothes in Paris.

He seemed quite close to Marcel; was it a platonic friendship? They met several times a week and Reed would sometimes spend the night with Marcel. When Marian Anderson performed in Paris, Reed couldn't get tickets or couldn't afford to get one before her concert was sold out. Marcel attended the concert and met Reed at a café afterward to discuss the performance, and Reed no doubt shared his experience seeing Anderson perform at Carnegie Hall in New York City. Marcel was thrilled and reported that Anderson's singing was exceptional.

Reed's current landlady discouraged him from changing hotels by telling him she was sure that his new place had bedbugs. The point was moot when his plan collapsed: the occupants of his desired room delayed their move. Instead, he relocated to the nearby Hôtel des Deux Continents at 25 rue Jacob, where he remained for the rest of the academic year and the summer. Marcel helped him move his things in the rain. He paid 330 francs, or ten dollars, a month for his room, which was on the fourth floor overlooking the street with two large windows as big as doors that opened in two halves across the middle. It was ideal for reading. Perhaps he created a little reading nook. The room contained three chairs, including a large armchair. At first he piled his books on the mantelpiece above a beautiful fake fireplace. But one day when he returned to his room, he discovered, to his delight, that the two female proprietors had given him bookcases. He was glad that he had packed cocktail glasses, because tea or wine was served in the afternoon at the hotel. He told Laura, "I do think I shall be very happy here. . . . I do hope I can stay here a long time now, for this is just the sort of private room I have always dreamed about." He wished he had moved there earlier despite the squeaking bed. He assured Laura that he would not be moving again, "But you know I have never liked staying in one spot long. Just like my father, I hear you saying."

Reed remained in Paris for Christmas and Newton came for a three-week visit, renting a room in Reed's hotel at a reduced rate. They hadn't seen each other since their trip to Warsaw in September. Newton wanted Reed to visit him in Switzerland, but he didn't have the funds. He resented Newton not realizing that the ten dollars his father sent to him every week really helped his budget. Newton planned to return to Paris in March to stay for two months to do work in the libraries. Newton found that the hotel was too cold for his liking and often wore his coat and gloves while typing in his room. Only after leaving Paris did Reed reveal to his family how cold his hotel room was in Paris, even with radiators. It felt like an "ice box." Toni also planned to be in Paris during the holidays.

At the start of the new year, Reed resumed his normal activities with schoolwork and his extracurricular reading. In January, he borrowed *Phoenix: The Posthumous Papers of D. H. Lawrence*. The *New York Times* reviewer described it as an 852-page book divided into seven sections, including reviews, short essays, and long essays on a variety of topics and places including flowers, women's suffrage, Thomas Hardy, and Florence. The reviewer called *Phoenix* "an appealing and provocative book, disappointing and disturbing, exciting and exhausting." Later in January, Reed borrowed *The Guermantes Way* by Proust.

Besides making American friends in Paris, Reed also made some French friends, including Claude, a fellow student at the Sorbonne. They agreed to exchange language lessons, with Reed teaching Claude English and Claude supposedly helping Reed with his French, although all indications were that Reed was already fluent in the language. Perhaps Reed was playing along. They planned to write an article about Stephen Spender for *Les Cahiers du Sud*, and another friend would translate his poetry. Reed hoped the article published for the general public would bring fame or money or both.

Spender visited Reed several times while in Paris with his wife, Inez Pearn, in January 1939. Their short-lived marriage ended after the trip, probably because of Spender's numerous affairs with men. Reed was excited to introduce the French public to Spender, who was already well-known in England and somewhat in the United States. Reed wrote, "I am quite flattered with the honour, for if he becomes a very famous writer some day, I will go down in history as the first person who introduced his work to another country."

Claude invited Reed to dinner, and he was happy to go. Reed recalled, "When I found the house, I was surprised to find myself before a door almost as large as a cathedral door." When he rang the bell, a butler opened the door and took his coat before leading him into a large room. Reed said he nearly fainted when he realized that he was going to be attending a formal dinner. He had not expected that. There was a large group of people that included Claude's parents, his brothers, and his sister-in-law. Reed found Claude's mother to be quite charming but initially didn't know why she was wrapped up in a blanket. He thought she was perhaps paralyzed, but later discovered that she was just cold. He was surprised that this majestic home was no warmer than his hotel. The butler returned and announced, "Madame the Baroness is served." Reed had no idea that Claude's parents were French nobility—a baron and baroness. She entered the dining room first, followed by Reed since he was the invited guest, then the rest of the family. He had a wonderful time and they invited him to return. He was sure that the invite was sincere.

Later, Claude's brother, a journalist, hired Reed to help him translate an article he was writing into English. Reed was doing it as a favor but was happy to find out that the brother planned to pay him a hundred francs, or three dollars, according to Reed. It was the first money he had made in over a year and he considered framing it. This unnamed brother was married and lived in a different part of Paris from his parents. Reed went to the movies with him, his wife, and his grandmother. The brother invited

Reed for lunch one Friday and he ate every serving that was offered to him. There was so much work to do that he was invited to stay for dinner and enjoyed cognac and hard-to-find American cigarettes afterward. The brother drove him back to his hotel at eleven and invited him to return on Sunday, where he enjoyed dinner, more cognac and cigarettes, and an invitation to go to lunch on Monday to continue working. Since the brother was getting paid for the article, he thought it was only fair to pay Reed. The baroness invited Reed for dinner the next night. Besides being paid for translations, Reed figured he saved a lot of money by eating so many meals with this family.

Reed returned his copy of *The Fountain* by Charles Morgan to the Shakespeare and Company lending library and renewed his subscription on March 27, 1939.

Although he missed Laura, he couldn't leave Paris now. Reed thought:

> This is a point in my life in which I must be very careful what moves I make next. I am a man, after all: no longer a boy, and not only a man, but a man with extraordinary gifts in different lines. I must act so that these gifts may be most appreciated.

He feared that "I may be forgotten, and this brilliance of mine may not be properly appreciated."

While he was enjoying the life that he was building in Paris, one thing was still missing. Romance.

SEVEN

Arne

After his initial whirlwind of travel to various European countries upon his arrival in Paris, Reed had not left the capital city since the fall. In April 1939, he took a trip to Fontainebleau, about thirty-four miles southeast of Paris, with Paul, a Danish actor he'd befriended. They toured the Château de Fontainebleau, an Italianate palace with décor from the French Renaissance for the monarchs of France from the Middle Ages into the nineteenth century, including Napoleon Bonaparte. Afterward, they headed to their hotel a few miles away and had dinner. The next morning, they were served breakfast in bed, and spent an afternoon hiking in the forest that surrounded the chateau. Reed declared, "It was such fun, really, for I haven't been in any such spot for God knows when." They returned to Paris on Sunday night and Reed was very sore—but he did not regret it since he was delighted by the excursion.

It was Paul who introduced Reed to his Danish friend Arne, an artist. In a letter written on May 19, 1939, on the second page, in the penultimate paragraph, Reed casually told Laura about meeting the man who would become so pivotal in his life. He described Arne as "a very charming fellow."

They spent a lot of time in Arne's Parisian apartment cooking meals together over his electric stove. Reed spent so much time there that it was almost like he had moved in. Arne was returning to Denmark in June and invited Reed to visit; Arne was sure that he could find someone to provide housing for Reed, and indeed he was also sure that Reed would get plenty of invitations for meals. Reed didn't know Danish, but no matter—he had been able to successfully navigate Poland without knowing Polish.

Reed's new companion was Arne Gerdahn Hauptmann, a tall, thin, blond twenty-two-year-old University of Copenhagen student, studying fine arts and painting at the Sorbonne. They had lived parallel lives with an interest in studying abroad and living a creative life filled with poetry, art, music, and writing.

Arne was born on March 11, 1916, in Copenhagen, in the Østerbro section of town, to a father, Birger Jens Johan Hauptmann, who'd had a rough start in life and came from a similarly humble background as Reed's own. In 1870, when Birger was just seven years old, he lived in a poorhouse in Odense with his brother and widowed father. Arne's mother, Ane Margrethe Cathrine Mathiesen, was born in 1874 in Esbjerg. Arne was the youngest of nine children, and Birger died in August 1920, possibly of tuberculosis, when Arne was just four years old—around the same age that Reed lost his father to mental illness.

After a brief but intense relationship, Arne returned to Copenhagen and Reed remained in Paris, but they made plans to meet again in Denmark in the near future. Reed was aware that war could begin while he visited Copenhagen, but he thought, with the optimism of the newly smitten, "since Denmark was not in the last one [World War], she probably would not be in this one either."

Reed was buoyed by this new relationship, but his joy was tempered by earlier bad news. He found out on May 2, 1939, that the Rosenwald Fund would not extend his fellowship. He must've been crushed and immediately dashed off another letter on the same day hoping to find another option. He asked, "would the Committee consider prolonging my present fellowship, to the extent of, let us say, $500.00?" Instead of contacting Reed, George M. Reynolds wrote to his adviser, Professor Baldensperger, asking, based upon his progress, if an extension of his fellowship was justified. If Baldensperger responded, the correspondence is not included in the records, but Reed's request was turned down.

Reed was angry at the Rosenwald Fund and admired a man who got his fellowship renewed three times and another who asked for more money so he could support his wife. Reed observed, "In short, it takes nerve, as well as brains, to get what you want in life. Although up until now, I thought I had as much nerve (if not more) than any one else." He also hoped to make money from a novel on an unnamed subject. He felt confident that he had enough money to make it through the summer.

His prospects back home weren't looking much better. He had been rejected for employment opportunities from Wilberforce University, Shaw University, the North Carolina College for Negroes, Dillard University, Atlanta University, Lincoln

University, Fisk University, and the Hampton Institute. These historically Black institutions did not have a need for a comparative literature professor coming out of the Great Depression and given the fear of an impending world war that would probably negatively effect the economy.

Reed eventually accepted a job at West Virginia State College teaching German, French, and Spanish. At least, he argued with himself, he could easily travel to Boston and New York City from this location. The college was formerly the West Virginia Colored Institute, a historically Black institution founded in 1891 in Institute, West Virginia. Reed made plans to remain in Europe through the summer and reluctantly return to the United States, taking the job offered by William Bradford Pratt at West Virginia State for a salary of $1,800. He said, "I feel that I am worth that much."

The administrators at West Virginia State College wanted Reed to study for one more year—perhaps to strengthen his knowledge. Because it was difficult for African Americans to be accepted into doctoral programs, historically Black colleges often hired people with master's degrees—which bolstered the argument from white institutions that African American prospective students did not need to enroll in a Ph.D. program in order to obtain a job since it was unlikely that a white institution would hire them. West Virginia State College would pay Reed a higher salary with this additional training. Reed promptly wrote the Rosenwald Fund to reconsider his application and to extend his fellowship in light of the suggestion by West Virginia State College. He felt that the Rosenwald Fund should want to help him in service of the "culture"—the Black community. He was rejected again, and they wished him luck finding a way to remain in Paris. Not giving up, Reed asked if the Rosenwald Fund could provide a recommendation because he planned to apply for funds from other foundations. They agreed and returned the material he used to apply for the renewal: a short bibliography of Haitian literature and letters of recommendation. Reed now turned to the John Simon Guggenheim Memorial Foundation for a fellowship.

Laura celebrated her seventieth birthday on July 1 and Reed sent her a letter, followed by pearls. He fretted and regretted how much she had to pay to customs, but at least she could say that the pearls came from France. How did he afford them? He said he hadn't worked in a year. Perhaps he saved the money that she sent him or from his Harvard fellowship funds. He asked for a picture of her wearing the pearls. She sent him a picture of her with a bouquet of money, $45, that she received for her birthday. He said that no one would believe she was seventy or that he'd be twenty-five, "which only goes to show how good-looking we all are in our family."

Although Laura was missing Reed, she was not alone. Her sister Nona lived with her, and when school was out for the summer, Mary traveled to Boston with her sons Phillip and Vincent to spend the summer with her mother. Phillip Sr., her husband, presumably remained in New Jersey.

Reed celebrated his own birthday, his twenty-fifth, at the end of July. His first birthday in Europe. Laura sent him a gift of cash, which he planned to use during his travels in August. The next letter from Laura included a note from Harvard's bursar. Reed had to hand over his $10 gift and inform the bursar that he would "cooperate" in paying the rest before the bursar began to think that he had died. He considered dipping into a bank account that he had in Bayonne, New Jersey, as a child, although he could not recall how much was in the account. Or, Reed thought, toying with an idea that was clearly beginning to take form:

> I suppose I might as well wait until the Bursar starts to send a policeman after me. Of course it may be that the policeman will be waiting for me at the gangplank when I get off the boat. . . . That makes as good a reason as any for staying over here, doesn't it?

He knew Harvard wasn't exactly hurting for money. He thought they should give him a break, stating, "(but it might very well be a break in the head.)"

July 1939 was full of friends and celebration. Newton returned to Paris to see Reed after finishing his studies in Switzerland. He was heading to England to catch a ship back to the United States. Although they had traveled to Europe together, Newton returned to the United States alone. Reed enjoyed celebrating France's Bastille Day on July 14 with fireworks and dancing in the streets. Clarence stopped by to see Reed in Paris and invited him to dinner before leaving at the end of July to travel to England, Poland, and Russia.

Things were winding down in Paris. Reed checked out several more items from the Shakespeare and Company lending library before ending his membership; he returned the last item he borrowed from the lending library—a volume of Strindberg plays—on July 29. He also made plans to visit a few more countries before he had to reluctantly return to the United States.

Back in Dorchester, Laura finally retired at age seventy on Monday, July 31, 1939. No more cleaning schools or private homes. After decades of backbreaking work, she could now retire knowing that her grandson had attained opportunities beyond her wildest dreams.

When Clarence returned to Paris after his trips, he unexpectedly gave Reed $20—no strings attached—for showing him around Paris during his earlier visit. Reed was ecstatic to finally have enough money to travel to Copenhagen in late August 1939 and to leave the heavy atmosphere of anticipatory doom in Paris.

Two unnamed friends with an apartment in Bern, Switzerland, invited Reed to spend early August with them. While there, he missed Paris and found that Bern was too small and quiet for his liking. He planned to rest and to do a lot of writing because he didn't know anyone besides his hosts.

When he returned to Paris, Reed made arrangements to go to Denmark, where a friend said an acquaintance had an apartment in Copenhagen where he could stay. When Paul went back to Paris after a trip to the African continent, he gave Reed a gift of a large silver ring and said he was looking forward to seeing him in Copenhagen at the end of the summer before he returned to the United States. Reed had several letters of introduction from Danish friends he met in Paris. A Danish lady said she had a friend in Copenhagen who was a millionaire who could possibly find work for him as a private secretary. This friend was "interested in literature and colored people (he often takes trips to Africa so that he can be with them), and since I represent both things, it may be that I could suit him," Reed said. He didn't mind being fetishized if it could bring him money, which would mean not just more travel but a possible extension of his time in Europe.

He eagerly anticipated going to Denmark and reuniting with Arne. He mused, "If things turn out in Denmark the way I want them to, I shall perhaps be here much longer yet. But we shall see. Life is a big adventure after all and we can't make predictions." More than anything, he was desperate not to leave Europe just yet. He thought that being an African American would help him to stand out in Copenhagen:

Particularly because they very rarely have colored people there, and since they have heard so much about the ill-treatment of Negroes in the U.S., they will be very glad to have something about some one who has been able to do things (or, at least, shows promise of being able to do things as he grows older).

On August 10, 1939, Reed uncharacteristically wrote a letter to his mother, Mary, instead of to Laura. Possibly, he wasn't brave enough to write to Laura directly.

Dear Mother, I know that it may sound quite mad, possibly even as if I have lost all my senses, but I really am _not_ returning to America at once. I have known all along that I would not, although I had hoped that I would have some definite plans in mind before I finally said that I intended to stay here longer. But as the summer draws to a close, and September almost rears its head, I know more and more that I don't intend to return next month.

He reminded her how much he always wanted to go to Europe and liked being there, because "I have made friends of practically all nationalities, I have been wined and dined by all classes of people, from the nobility on down." Even a possible impending war wouldn't tear him away. Even if the war started, he said, he would stay—after all, others would have had to live through it. Of course, there was the issue of money—he had no means yet to support himself beyond the three months of savings he currently had. He said, "In fact, dear, I shall <u>even work</u> if necessary."

He admitted:

I could have told you before I left that I wouldn't be back in a year, but you wouldn't have believed me then. But now you know, and I have a greater determination to make good than I have ever had in my life. Don't worry about me. Please, you and Aunt Nona and every one, take good care of Nana, for you all know how much she means to me, and she knows that I am with her, and love her deeply no matter where I am and no matter how long I stay away.

Reed said the last sentence nearly made him weep as he wrote it.

He added a handwritten note to Laura:

Dear Nana, Courage, darling. I know you expected to see me soon again—but I know also that you have always understood that whenever there is an important choice to be made, I alone can make it. . . . Your work is now finished, and you can rest and live like a lady. My work is just beginning. . . . You have given me so much to start with darling, that I feel full of optimism.

Meanwhile, tensions in Paris were becoming more serious by the day. The *New Yorker* columnist Janet Flanner noted that everyone from government officials to housewives were preparing for an inevitable war. There were official announcements instructing people what to do in case of a gas attack and how to black out headlights and lamps. During the nights, "Paris was only partially illuminated." The French government urged people who could to leave Paris and discouraged those who remained from hoarding essentials like sugar, rice, and flour. Citizens could only buy one candle instead of a box of them. Government officials tested the air raid sirens at noon every Thursday to make sure they were in working order, but for a very short time so as not to alarm citizens that it was the real thing. Information on the radio and in newspapers was scarce.

Despite the ominous signs, Reed left most of his belongings behind in his Paris hotel, expecting to return after a short stay with Arne in Copenhagen.

EIGHT

"Life Is Very Peaceful Here in Denmark (So Far)"

A nyway, you see I was right in not buying another ticket and leaving for the U.S. at once when I found that I could not get back to Paris," Reed wrote to his mother, Mary, back in Bayonne, New Jersey. "I might very easily have been one of the victims in that frightful torpedoing which happened this morning."

On Sunday, September 3, 1939, Britain declared war on Germany. That night, SS *Athenia*, sailing from Glasgow to Montreal, carrying over a thousand people, was hit by a torpedo from a German submarine. One hundred seventeen people, both passengers and crew, were killed, including many Americans. Reed had left Paris to vacation in Arne's country, arriving on August 23, 1939. His planned short visit turned into an odyssey. Back in Poland, Reed's friend the Count, Antoni Sobański, fled from Warsaw to London when the Nazis invaded his country.

In Reed's letter to Laura, dated August 31, he said, "I must say things couldn't be better with me than here in Copenhagen, and people are treating me beautifully." He spent a lot of time reassuring her that he was okay and to not worry about him, because "I am a man, and can take care of myself."

While he was upbeat in his letters to his relatives, Reed's letter to his friend and editor Dorothy Norman was less optimistic. He told her that "recent European events have caused me to leave France for Denmark." He said, "I hope you will also join your prayers to mine for humanity, civilization, and culture."

The day after the sinking of the *Athenia*, Reed may have had second thoughts about being in Denmark. A little before 4 p.m., a plane dropped bombs in a harbor, a courtyard, in a field near the airport, and on a three-story apartment building in Esbjerg, a Danish seaport town about a three-hour train ride from Copenhagen, costing two people their lives.

A group of African American entertainers scheduled to perform in Esbjerg that day were so frightened that one performer, Rollin Smith, lost his voice and had to leave the stage. Fellow African Americans, husband-and-wife singers and dance duo Ola Mae and Eddie Alston, known professionally as Ola and Eddie, were able to complete their performance.

Ola, born in 1910 in St. Louis, had a style reminiscent of Ethel Waters, dazzling audiences with her singing. Eddie, born in 1905 in Savannah, Georgia, performed in America before going to Europe in the mid- to late 1930s with his wife, touring France, England, Romania, Hungary, Greece, the Netherlands, Egypt, and Turkey before arriving in Denmark in February 1939. They had a contract to perform until September 30, 1939, and had secured tickets to return to the United States before the outbreak of the war.

After leaving Esbjerg, the Alstons returned to their hotel in Copenhagen. Because of the sinking of the *Athenia*, there was a temporary ban on ships sailing across the Atlantic. The hotels in Copenhagen filled with American families wanting to leave. The atmosphere in Denmark was tense and the American embassy said every effort was being made to get stranded citizens safely back to the United States. But while Ola and Eddie were trying to leave Denmark, Reed was trying to stay.

Back in Paris, many Americans were fleeing. Tyler Stovall noted in *Paris Noir: African Americans in the City of Light*, "Virtually all of the exiles finally did leave Paris at the beginning of World War II, as the possibility of a German invasion became daily more menacing." He continued, "Yet a very few, most notably Josephine Baker, chose to stay with the people of France."

On the day of the bombing in Esbjerg, Reed went to the American consulate in Copenhagen. They told him he could remain in Denmark or Sweden for as long as he liked—or so he told Mary and Laura. For more than a year, the US embassies in Europe had posted signs outside their buildings urging Americans to leave. Because of his fluency in several foreign languages, Reed hoped to get a diplomatic position and dropped vague hints about this desire. He wrote, "I still think it's funny that I should know how to speak German, French and Danish! Many people have learned German and French, and I have dabbled about with Latin, Greek, Spanish, and Italian, but who in hell knows <u>Danish</u> except Danish people?" He said, "I wish I knew Danish better, but I am learning it fast and carrying on little conversations with people even by phone." He concluded that he would soon be able to speak Norwegian and Swedish.

Since Reed was unable to return to Paris, his Danish actor friend Paul rented a hotel room for him. On the day he was supposed to move out, he received an invitation to stay in a room in the fourth-floor apartment of Albert Budtz-Christensen, called "Bertie"—a friend of the Count's, located at Nyhavn 31B. Bertie allowed Reed to live in his attic room on the fifth floor without paying rent while apologizing that he could not offer better accommodations, but Reed was quite satisfied. He was just happy to have a room with a desk to write on and a bed to sleep in. The entrance had a separate key, so it was almost like he had his own apartment with views of the neighboring rooftops, which he found to be quite romantic while he spent his days writing. Nyhavn was once described by a Jamaican man, writer Roy De Coverley, who lived in Copenhagen in the 1930s, as "a lovely street, threaded with a canal down its middle, lined with naughty cafes and peopled with sailors from every port in the world." In other words, a sort of red-light district where sailors could drink and find companionship for the evening—for a price.

Fortunately, Reed had his manuscripts and typewriter with him. He saw himself as a writer and could not be detached from his instrument, seeing it as his "meal-ticket." But a subsequent letter to Mary was handwritten. He explained, "My typewriter is being repaired at the moment (it's not in hock, really), so you'll have to put up with my handwriting. I must have used it so much that it cried 'ouch' and stopped running."

Reed compared Copenhagen to Boston because living near the canal in Copenhagen reminded him of the Charles River

near Beacon Hill. He could also see the king's castle, Amalien-
borg, from his window and told the apocryphal story of the king
riding his horse around town early in the morning. But he said,
"Of course, I don't see him, because I'm never up at 8:00 a.m."
The only downside was there was no hot water or bathtub. He
fantasized about getting a hotel room. But Bertie was very generous. He had once invited a friend to stay with him for two
weeks and the friend remained for two years.

Bertie was quite the host. He planned a party for Reed and
took a day off from work to go sightseeing with him outside Copenhagen in Helsingør where he had once lived in 1925 as an
apprentice in the clothing business. They saw Kronborg Castle,
the setting for Shakespeare's *Hamlet*, explored old churches, and
climbed walls.

Besides not charging Reed rent, Bertie gave him bread, pastries, and tea for breakfast every morning, although Reed lamented, "I haven't the heart to tell him how goddamed [*sic*] tired
I am of tea." Later, he reported, "I still have plenty of tea to drink
every day! I think I shall be pissing tea very soon."

Although Bertie took his lunch and dinner with his own family, he did not invite Reed for some reason. But Reed was not
bothered by this and bought his own lunch and dinner for thirty
to forty cents per meal.

Reed never imagined that he would live in Denmark but
looked upon his circumstances as an opportunity: "After all, I
have always wanted to go places," and "I shall certainly have lots
to talk about when I get back." Later, he claimed, after receiving
letters from friends in the United States, that they were quite en-
vious of his adventures, stating, "I don't feel in any danger, and

the experiences I am having are something that I shall be able to talk about my whole life." He was also glad to hear from Laura that people had inquired about him—he didn't want to be forgotten.

Reed assumed Copenhagen would be a safe place to stay because Denmark had been neutral during World War I. But the Danish government feared that they would be dragged reluctantly into war. The Danish prime minister, Thorvald Stauning, and the Danish foreign minister, Peter Munch, known as P. Munch, reached out to possible allies but did not receive reassurances that Britain, Norway, or Sweden would help if Germany invaded Denmark. If the Germans attacked, a defeat for Denmark was almost inevitable, and the other countries were worried about their own fates. Denmark did not have the military strength to defend itself against the Nazi war machine, so the Danish government tried not to provoke Germany through their policies, statements, antagonistic newspaper reports, or a conspicuous marshaling of military forces. But Reed probably did not know enough about Danish politics to understand this. For him, possible conflict was more of an inconvenience, a wrench thrown into his plans for European adventures. He called it "a silly old war."

Reed hoped that the United States would not enter the war. But most interestingly, he compared his plight to his father's, stating, "But you needn't think, dear, just because I am the same age my father was when the last war broke out that I am going to go mad too." Instead, he compared himself to Laura. "I am like you: I have determined to live through it all, and see if the new society, after this war is over, will have any more sense than the old one."

Because Reed was a foreigner, he was required to register with the Danish police and to show proof of financial support. He explained that he was in Europe to study at the Sorbonne and received a stipend of 250 to 300 Danish kroner a month, equivalent to thirty-six to forty-five US dollars, from his Harvard travel fellowship. He could only receive these funds if he was in a neutral or non-belligerent country like Denmark. He also had a return ticket to the United States on the Holland America Line and discussed exchanging it for a ticket on a Scandinavian line.

Despite a limited wardrobe consisting of two suits, five shirts, shoes, and socks with holes, Reed dressed as well as he could while wandering around Copenhagen in his raincoat and a blue scarf borrowed from Bertie. He eventually purchased another shirt and hoped that he would not need a winter coat in Denmark—he only had to use a raincoat in France during the winter. He was glad that he had Aunt Nona's ring and his own towels and washcloth, since he said, "I always carry my own toilet things when I am travelling." He regretted all of the things he had left behind in Paris, particularly his clothes, his books, and a portrait. He was resigned to the fact that he might not ever see his belongings again after contacting the Hôtel des Deux Continents and asking the proprietors to send him his belongings but getting no response. He was also sad about the loss of his two Harvard diplomas, because they didn't reissue replacements, but was glad he had his Phi Beta Kappa key, which proved he had gone to Harvard. Later, the hotel proprietor assured him that she would not charge him for his room and would safely store his belongings—saying nothing of the possibilities if Paris was invaded or bombed. Embracing the dramatic flair it provided, Reed liked that he could say, "Oh, I lost that in Paris because of the war."

Life continued in a fairly normal manner in Copenhagen despite the war in other European countries. Unlike his friends in
France, who now carried gas masks with them as he'd seen in
England last year, Reed attended concerts and operas and went
to restaurants where he found himself "hobnobbing" with interesting Danish people. He sometimes took the streetcar down-
town for lunch, eating quickly, in less than an hour, which meant
he did not have to pay for a return fare. Despite everything he
was going through, he felt he was still "elegant and charming."
According to him, the Danes liked listening to him read his
writing and often invited him to join them at various events. He
attended a concert one night where King Christian X and Queen
Alexandrine were in the audience. Through the force of his personality and no doubt because of his perceived exoticism as an
African American, he received invitations to the homes of the
Danes for tea and cakes. Reed told Laura, "People here love pastry. In fact, Danish pastry is famous throughout the world." He
seemed to enjoy the pastries but not the tea since he had had his
fill at Bertie's. He tried to ask for coffee if he was quick enough
to do so before his hosts could serve him more tea. He felt that
the Danes were much friendlier in this respect than the people
he encountered in Paris. Another couple invited him to their
home in "a very charming apartment with all modern decora-
tions and a very excellent radio and phonograph." They listened
to music and to news from Paris and could occasionally get news
from the United States too. Reed claimed to be quite popular
in Copenhagen, speaking to people in English, German, and
French, with Danish as a last resort. He thought, "I've never
been in any city before where people are so kind and so friendly

as they are here." He speculated it might be because of the war and their lack of visitors.

He continued observing Black people much like he did in New York City:

> There are quite a few colored people here in Denmark: that is to say, more than I expected to meet. I have seen about a dozen or so, and they are mostly visiting here from Harlem in shows. Some of them are dancing, some of them singing, and some playing instruments.

Some of the performers he mentioned could have been Ola and Eddie Alston, who lived in Harlem when not touring around the world.

He was excited to tell Laura about encountering an African American celebrity in Copenhagen:

> I just met "Valaida" (ever hear of her? I'm sure Aunt Nona has), a very famous colored singer from America, who is often called "the queen of the trumpet." She is singing at a night club in Copenhagen, and is very popular. People here are very fond of American jazz, especially colored jazz, and they are all disappointed that I don't sing.

Valaida Snow was known in the United States for playing the trumpet and leading the band in the hit musical *Rhapsody in Black*. She was often compared favorably to another jazz trumpeter, Louis Armstrong, and was described as "dashing and charismatic." Born in Chattanooga, Tennessee, sometime between 1901 and

1904, Snow was quite a storyteller, and many questioned the veracity of some of her tales, including about her real age. She performed in vaudeville in the United States before entertaining around the world. She was often accused of theft and drug addiction. A young Danish woman was found dead in her hotel room in Copenhagen after an overdose. Her chaotic personal life overshadowed her talent and success as a woman in a man's world of jazz where she played an instrument that women did not often play, and she was also a bandleader who sang and danced.

Reed was enthralled. Snow had spent the last eight years traveling in Russia, China, France, and Hungary, among many other places. In keeping with her creative storytelling, she told Reed that they were the same age, but she was really a decade older. Reed invited her to visit with his Danish friend who owned over four hundred jazz albums, including some by Ethel Waters and Duke Ellington. Reed recalled, "We filled her up with gin until she got quite high and began to shout 'Hi-de-ho' with the records." They had a great time, and she gave both of them a photograph of her playing the trumpet as a gift.

Although he loved and preferred classical music, Reed wrote a piece, "Jazz in Copenhagen," that he submitted to an unspecified American publication about an evening he spent with Valaida Snow. He continued hoping to earn money from his writing, feeling that he was "born to be a writer if I ever get the proper breaks."

In the meantime, Laura continued sending Reed checks even after her retirement. He used the money to buy socks, handkerchiefs, cold cream, and soap.

He was often reflective, telling Laura, "I wrote Mother just the other day that I am leading a very funny life: it almost reminds me of my father and the frayed suits that you used to tell me about. Today, for instance, I was patching my trousers for an hour so that my arse wouldn't be out."

He concluded, "Well, that's life. It gives me plenty to think about, and write about."

Reed asked Dr. Beryl Orris, the American psychologist he had befriended in Paris, to take his ticket and bank book from his hotel in France and give it to Laura. She could cash the ticket and send the money or the ticket to him in Copenhagen. With this additional money from the ticket—about $80—Reed could rent a hotel room with heat. He cautioned Laura, "But you needn't tell those two Browne bitches anything about it." He didn't want sisters Margaret and Hattie to know that he was struggling.

Copenhagen residents were required to use less light and faced restrictions on driving automobiles to save gasoline. If things took a turn for the worse, Reed said he planned to catch a ship back to the United States. But now he was living quite comfortably and had many friends and was getting a lot of writing done.

Reed wondered if the Danish police suspected him of being a spy because he spoke so many languages, but they must not have been too concerned: he received permission from the Danish government to stay until January 15, 1940—if they were not at war. His letters home were full of gentle reassurances, as well as logical reasons he was reluctant to come home to the United States: He didn't want to leave his belongings behind in Paris.

He didn't feel safe crossing the Atlantic Ocean at this time, and he was still thrilled to live cheaper, "like a king," in Denmark with his American money. But it's hard not to suspect that a budding romance with Arne—who he leaves out of most of his letters during this early part of his stay in Copenhagen—might have been his biggest draw to staying in this otherwise foreign place.

He said, "This has been one of the most charming months I have spent, and sometimes it is very hard to believe that there is a war raging on all sides of this country." As the war continued in other parts of Europe, Reed advised his friends, family, and potential publishers to contact him by cable instead of through letters because ships were often torpedoed. Communicating with people in the United States and friends in Europe was a lifeline for him.

While grateful for the free housing, Reed loved visiting other friends because he could toast his "tootsies at their fire." Bertie's apartment was heated by a stove that only warmed one room, and sometimes his room was so cold that he could not type. Reed was ready to find alternative housing even though he was reluctant to spend money. He said, "Bertie is quite willing to let me stay here as long as I like, but I just don't like." Bertie once had a Polish friend stay all winter in the room where Reed resided, but Reed could not fathom how he was able to do that. He pined instead for a small room like what he had at Columbia, with a bed, desk, chair, and a radiator.

He had been in Europe for over a year and a half and his longed-for reinvention was finally clicking: he had a network of friends—quite possibly some romances, including one major one—and the kinds of connections that would keep expanding his life. He attended events with nobility, partied with an American celebrity, studied poetry and literature, and listened to music late into the night. The world outside might be threatening to turn violent, but in Reed's little corner, the future started to spread before him.

NINE

The Central Hotel

Strangely absent from Reed's early letters from Copenhagen was any mention of the real reason why he was in Denmark—Arne. In November 1939, Reed and Arne rented a room at the Central Hotel located at Reventlowsgade 16 by the main train station in the Vesterbro section of Copenhagen. The Central Hotel was a five-story building with a parapet located on the corner of Istedgade—the notorious street at the heart of a red-light district. Performers Ola and Eddie Alston resided nearby at Hotel Welander at Helgolandsgade 14. They must have noticed each other as the few African Americans in the streets of Copenhagen in 1939.

Reed's and Arne's room cost eleven dollars a month for heat, hot water, and food service. For fifteen cents they could get breakfast in bed—later reduced to ten cents after they became long-term residents. They could also get a bottle of beer for ten

cents. Reed felt well suited to living in hotels after his experiences in Paris. He liked the idea of being able to "pick up and
leave at the slightest notice." He said, "My hotel room is so warm
and comfortable that I almost forget how cold I used to be in my
other room, where I was warm only in bed." Despite the shortage
of items like coal and coffee, Reed was able to get sugar for his
tea. He was annoyed that the streetcars were so cold that you
could not see out of the windows due to the frost. But while he
described life as being very pleasant, he wished he could know
what would happen in the future. The uncertainty was clearly
causing him stress.

With his typewriter repaired and Arne by his side, Reed hit a
new stride, working simultaneously on several writing projects,
including composing poems. He was "writing more now than I
ever have before, and feel sure that this particular time has really
been good for me in making use of all the talent I've got to pro-
duce something." He planned to collaborate with a Danish artist
named Bent to provide illustrations to accompany his poems.
The artist was also going to help Reed translate his stories into
Danish in order to get published in Danish magazines and newspapers. Reed said:

> I like Bent better than any one I have met since I met Ber-
> tie. We speak French together most of the time, because he
> lived in France for a while too. He has done several sketches
> of me, and may have some of them exhibited this January.

Bent used a larger-than-expected payout for one of his submissions to take Reed to a fancy restaurant where they dined on

roast duck and so many sides that Reed couldn't finish his meal. He liked his dessert and the Danish custom of topping ice cream with whipped cream and strawberry preserves and the delightful pastries that Denmark was known for.

Reed was also expecting information from the United States with names and addresses of publishers so that he could submit his work, including a novel that he did not describe. He also wrote a children's book manuscript, "The Adventures of Pusé, the Little French Cat," that he hoped to sell in America and in Denmark, believing that the Danes were interested in publishing it. It was about a cat on an ocean voyage. The ship sinks but Pusé is rescued by fish. She is later arrested as a spy, but eventually makes her way back to the United States. He planned to dedicate it to Laura and use a pseudonym, Bernhard Reed, claiming that no one could pronounce Peggram, keeping Reed as a surname to honor Nana, and Bernhard after his patron saint—actually spelled Saint Bernard.

Arne and Reed continued writing and Reed thought they made an excellent team. In Paris, they developed pseudonyms. Reed would go by Edwin Reed instead of what he called the "cumbersome" Reed Edwin Peggram, and Arne Hauptmann selected Arne Weitløv as his pseudonym—an ill-conceived one because the Danish letter ø was not easily replicated in other languages or on typewriters. They worked on a 120-page manuscript, "Poems and Sketches," a translation of the work of the nineteenth-century Danish author Jens Peter Jacobsen (1847–1885). Despite living a short life, dying of tuberculosis at age thirty-eight, Jacobsen published short stories, poems, and two novels: *Marie Grubbe* in 1876 and *Niels Lyhne* in 1880. He was a contemporary of other Scandinavian writers including Henrik

Ibsen, Knut Hamsun, and August Strindberg. One of the found-ers of the naturalist movement in fiction, he presented his char-acters without moral judgment and was considered influential in Europe and also for Harlem Renaissance writers Nella Larsen and Zora Neale Hurston, who read an English translation of *Marie Grubbe*, an account of a woman criticized for her various romantic liaisons.

Although Reed received a rejection for an article, he was heartened by the news that the editorial staff was divided, and that the editor asked to see his novel. He planned to finish two more chapters. He also contacted editor Dorothy Norman re-garding an essay about Haiti that he wanted her to consider for *Twice a Year*. He was disappointed when some poems he submit-ted were rejected, but not entirely discouraged—a momentum seemed to be building.

Reed had met a network of artists in Copenhagen and was invited to join a group of them renting a large house in the coun-tryside as a retreat where they would do their own cooking. Reed brought his typewriter and wrote. Arne was possibly a part of this group. Reed was living the life that he imagined, in pursuit of creative projects, surrounded by like-minded individuals.

In December 1939, Reed assured his mother, Mary, that "life is very peaceful here in Denmark (so far)." He continued, "how friendly people seem to be here. I am more impressed by Den-mark. I think it is the most civilized country I have ever lived in. The rich are not extremely rich, and the poor are not ex-tremely poor."

Reed continued asking the Rosenwald Fund to extend his fel-lowship for another year. He felt that they were making a mistake in not giving him more money since the fund was designed to help people like him.

The Rosenwald Fund sent a form to Reed while he was in Copenhagen asking for "up-to-date information" that included the "bare facts," and wanted to know "anything interesting that has happened to you, or that you have accomplished either during your tenure of fellowship or since you finished your work." Reed replied:

> At the present moment, [I] am attempting to support myself by publishing articles of a literary and journalistic nature for American publications, and compose chapters of my dissertational work in whatever time is left. While my financial status is nothing to boast about, I am receiving spiritual stimulation from daily association with Danish intellectuals and an unexpected insight into Scandinavian culture. Have completed a book of children's stories, which I am trying to sell to Macmillan's, with illustrations by a Danish artist.

Under "Publications since you were awarded the fellowship," he listed the two articles in *Modern Language Review* and the forthcoming article on André Gide in *Twice a Year.*

Reed continued making friends, including a Danish actor with the surname Andersen, who invited him to dinner with his mother and grandmother—former actors who had performed on the stage in the United States. They drank beer with their meal, which began with little shrimp croquettes, then a meat course with pickles, cranberries, and two types of potatoes with gravy.

He was unsure if the meat was veal, lamb, or pork. The grandmother made apple pie in honor of Reed, and he ate three slices. He shared his poems with them. They served tea, cookies, and cakes with jam around 11 p.m. The meal reminded him of Thanksgiving. He was missing home. Back in the United States, Laura planned to go to New Jersey to spend the real Thanksgiving with Mary's family.

On another night, Reed went out with a group of Danes. They asked him many questions about jazz and raved over the singer Bessie Smith, whom they adored. They fantasized about going to Harlem and listening to swing bands at the Savoy Ballroom. Reed told them about his wild night out there with friends before he sailed for Europe in August 1938. During his nights out, Reed encountered other African Americans in Copenhagen, including some he jokingly called "coons." Performers from Harlem who sang and danced in Europe were increasingly concerned about returning to the United States because of torpedoes possibly downing passenger ships. He liked them and noted that these were the types of people that his nana, grandmother Laura, disapproved of and discouraged him from associating with. Perhaps they were Ola and Eddie.

Meanwhile, the city of Copenhagen was getting ready for the Christmas season. Reed was surprised to see a lighted tree in the plaza in front of the city hall, Rådhuspladsen, because of the edict to save electricity. He had little of what he called the "hi-de-ho spirit" in him. Perhaps he was a little down because this was the second Christmas and New Year's spent without his family.

But still Reed did not seem keen to return home, and had no intention of looking for a job. He hoped to spend at least a year working on his book and informed Laura that he was concerned he would annoy her with his incessant typing if he lived with her back in Boston. He was able to live in Copenhagen for fifty dollars a month and couldn't do that in the United States. He was content in Copenhagen, he said—he just wished he had a second set of shoes; when he had his only pair resoled, he considered remaining in the shop and reading a book while they fixed them. None of his friends had a pair his size to loan him. He finally borrowed a pair that was one size too small and was relieved to get his own shoes back. He eventually purchased an expensive pair of shoes right before Christmas.

Reed did not have enough money to send presents home, but he sent Danish Christmas cards to his mother and to the boys—as he often referred to his two younger brothers—Vincent and Phillip. He also described the rituals of Christmas in Denmark:

Christmas is a big festival in Denmark. They close up everything for three days, Christmas Eve, Christmas Day, and the day after, which they call "Second Christmas." When I say everything, my dear, I mean everything. Stores, restaurants, theatres, movies, cigar stores, EVERYTHING. I still think it is very silly of them, because there must be some people who don't have any families to go to, and would like to be doing something those three days, but they don't think of that. The railroad station stays open, after all, and people who don't have homes to go to can always eat there.

Reed remained in touch with Bertie after moving out of his apartment. They spoke by phone every day and Reed visited him at his store located at Vennemindevej 5 in the Østerbro section of Copenhagen. Bertie dropped in on Reed on Christmas Eve and gave him a picture of himself as a present. Someone else gave him a pair of socks—a practical and much-needed gift.

Despite making so many friends in Copenhagen, Reed dined alone on Christmas Eve at a restaurant in the railroad station and then attended midnight mass. Afterward, he went to a party at 2 a.m. that lasted until 5 a.m. Reed didn't consider it to be a true Christmas party since people just sat around drinking scotch and soda, listening to the radio, and dancing. He slept in the following morning and wrote a little in the afternoon before joining the Andersens for dinner. They consumed a feast of meats, vegetables, fruits, nuts, and drink. Reed ate "until the food didn't taste good any more." Afterward he partook in the Danish Christmas tradition of dancing around the Christmas trees and singing Danish songs. He thought, "lots of fun if you don't have to do it every day."

Reed seemed down during the holiday season. Perhaps he was missing his friends and family in the United States. Monty sent pictures of himself from the United States and promised to replace a large photo that Reed had left behind in Paris. Monty seemed well and was enthusiastic about his music. Newton, living back in New York City, said he was very bored after all of his European adventures. Clarence shared a letter he received from Reed with Newton.

Back in Copenhagen, the Andersens invited him to spend New Year's Day with them, but he didn't want to, feeling bad about going without having any presents to give them. He also didn't think he would like to spend the time drinking coffee instead of out with the crowd of people gathered at city hall for the New Year festivities.

Reed and Ola and Eddie were summoned to the police station on January 12, 1940, to report on their current status and plans to return to the United States. Maybe, because Reed had a steady source of income from his Harvard fellowship, the Danish authorities did not meet with him as often as they did with Ola and Eddie, who were in an even more precarious financial situation. They had difficulties getting work permits to perform since the Danish government favored their own citizens. During these tough times, the Alstons lived on very little money, cooking their meals in their hotel room.

Ola and Eddie explained to the readers of *The Chicago Defender* that in Copenhagen, "night life and the social whirl is still at top place." But "there is, however, a bit of nervous strain as everyone seems to think that the Germans may invade Denmark most any day . . . but these busy folks of Copenhagen go about their daily tasks with a smile." Fearing the invasion by the Nazis, Ola and Eddie were ready to leave Denmark as soon as possible. Since they could not get work, they told the readers of the *Defender*, "We've stayed as long as possible, but now conditions are such that we have been forced to take a liner and start back to American shores." Eddie signed a promissory note agreeing to repay the Danish authorities for a loan to cover their expenses, including for tickets on the Swedish American Line. They sailed on SS *Drottningholm* from Gothenburg, Sweden, arriving in New York City on January 29, 1940.

Reed, on the other hand, asked for an extension of his residence permit until April 15, 1940. The US government urged all

American citizens to leave Europe, but Reed pondered staying "until the last horn blows . . . until the last gun is fired." Possibly realizing that the war might go on much longer than he anticipated, he now said he planned to return to the United States instead of to France. He claimed that the US government had issued a statement ordering Americans to return home during the next three months or risk losing their citizenship. Reed thought, "I know it would be exciting to lose one's citizenship, especially in these days, but I am not sure I would like to go through with that." But this equivocation might have been due to a new plan that seemed to be brewing: he might go back, if Arne could go with him.

Reed mentioned Arne in letters to his family, describing him as "a very good friend of mine, named Arne Hauptmann, who is a writer," and as the person who took care of Reed when he became really ill. Reed was not explicit about the nature of this relationship, but perhaps Laura and Mary suspected that it was romantic.

He had finally found a soul mate in Arne. He was in love, and despite the danger of the war, he did not want to lose this opportunity to have a relationship in a place where secret tribunals weren't seeking him out in order to destroy him. In Copenhagen, he could live with the man he loved, and they could enjoy some degree of openness, however small.

Reed wrote:

Arne Hauptmann and I are doing lots of writing together, and I personally think we could make a good writing team. We have a double room in the hotel together, and do lots of work every day. I am hoping he can get permission to come to the U.S.A. with me when I leave, for I think it would be a shame for us to stop writing because of a silly old war and lots of stupid passport regulations.

Reed and Arne were most likely sharing one hotel room, but they continued to obscure the true romantic nature of their relationship. While little is known about the interwar period in Denmark for homosexuals, Copenhagen did have a reputation for more tolerance of homosexuality and a homosexual subculture. While in the nineteenth century sodomy was punishable by death, gay men no longer faced execution in the early twentieth century, even though they could be imprisoned. By the 1930s arrests were often limited to homosexual prostitution or same-sex liaisons with a person under the age of consent—eighteen. The age of consent was higher for same-sex partners than for heterosexual ones until 1976, when an equal age of consent was established. In 1989, Denmark became the first country to recognize domestic partnerships.

Nevertheless, gay men living in Copenhagen in 1939 and 1940 still had to be discreet. Although homosexual sex was decriminalized, police sometimes surveilled and harassed gay bars and street hustlers. Intellectual men like Arne and Reed often met in the private homes of men in a secret network. Reed did not discuss his movement within gay circles in Copenhagen with Laura or Mary, but perhaps he did occasionally patronize Café Intime. Established in 1922, it was a piano bar—an instrument that Reed adored. He would've loved the smoke-filled ambiance behind stained-glass windows off a tree-lined boulevard in

Frederiksberg, a municipality surrounded by Copenhagen. The red walls were decorated with paintings in gilded frames and the floor was covered with plush carpet. The bar had stalls for discreet assignations, and its proximity to public bathrooms was another draw to the clientele.

Arne and Reed began making plans to return together to the United States, and Arne sought permission to get a visa for his passport. Reed hoped that they could live together in Boston or preferably in New York—the only other city he deemed suitable. Reed noted, "And even that is no Paradise. Europe, even in war, is much more interesting than you think." Although he did not explicitly state this, he must have considered that larger cities might be more tolerant of a gay couple.

Reed considered asking Laura to send him money, explaining that he would pay her back once his writing career took off. Although he had two Harvard degrees and was studying for a third, he had no qualms about relying on financial assistance from Laura, now a retired cleaning woman with very little formal education. He often thought he was on a verge of getting something published. He wrote to Mary, "These have been a two year period I shall never forget. I'm sure you'll hardly know me when I get back. Personally, I think I ought to write a book about my adventures instead of trying to write novels. They are more exciting."

Meanwhile, Harvard hounded Reed to pay his student loan. Irritated, he said:

Of all things! That damn loan coming up at this point! They write me that I owe them $149, so I sent them $5.00

to show that I was trying, and wrote them that I shall pay them in full when I publish a book.

Always looking on the bright side of things, Reed wrote, "As long as I have a debt as large as that, I won't have any worries about income tax." His money troubles continued after he learned that the cost of a ticket on a ship had increased to $200 because of the war. Reed only had a ticket worth $83 and had no idea where the rest would come from. He was optimistic that the money would somehow arrive. After all, he had wanted to go to Europe and had found a way to do it and a way to stay for two years—although he was partially supported by Laura.

Just as Reed was about to contact his bank in Boston to send him the last of his savings, he received an unexpected telegram informing him that he had received a wire transfer for $100—equivalent to approximately $2,000 today. He rushed to the wrong bank and spent "a flustered morning" calling around and speaking in both English and Danish. He didn't know who had sent the funds, but suspected Laura had, although he wasn't sure how she was able to manage it. He improbably hoped that the money came from one of his writing projects. He told Laura:

Needless to say, I shall be much happier if I find out it was something I earned. If you were a rich lady, I would let you send me any amount you like. But since you aren't, I always feel badly when I take a large sum from you.

Reed and Arne made plans to leave Copenhagen with these unexpected funds. They thought the safest and cheapest route across the Atlantic Ocean was through Italy. Reed had a return ticket for a Dutch ship on the Holland America Line, but he would have to take an expensive airplane journey to get to the embarkation port. Going to Italy was cheaper even if it was farther away from Denmark because they could take a train. The catch was that they would have to go through Germany. Most people were reluctant to take this route during the war, so the tickets were cheap. Reed figured that people went through Germany every day and were not harmed. He also thought an added bonus would be the ability to have something to talk about when he returned, imagining starting conversations at a dinner party with, "When I was in Germany during the war . . ." Although he must've been concerned, to Reed, this was also a big adventure, something that made his life more interesting and exciting. He hoped to do a little sightseeing in Italy before catching a ship back to America. As with the "silly old war," Reed considered Mussolini's dictatorship a minor flaw in what he had heard was a beautiful country. Arne finally received his passport and they both planned to get their visas for Germany and Italy.

But their plans quickly collapsed when they were unable to secure permission to travel through Germany by train. They were now passing through Paris instead. This route was quicker and safer, but it was three times as expensive; they would have to catch an airplane for part of the way because some train lines had been discontinued. It did mean, however, an opportunity to stop at the Hôtel des Deux Continents to pick up the belongings Reed had left behind in August.

Reed finalized his plans to go to Italy and found the people at

Reed's mother, Mary. They had
a complicated relationship.

Reed Peggram, Edward Everett
Elementary School in Boston,
Massachusetts, 1927

Reed (front row, second from right) was the business manager for the Dramatic Club at Boston Latin School. *Latin School Register*, 1931.

Reed (middle row, far left) was a member of the Literary Club at Boston Latin School. *Latin School Register*, 1931.

CYRIL LEO TOUMANOFF

Born on October 10, 1913, at St. Petersburg, Russia. Prepared at Lenox School. Home address: 57 Gorham Street, Cambridge, Massachusetts. In college one year as undergraduate. Price Greenleaf Scholarship.

Cyril Toumanoff, Harvard University
Class of 1935 classmate and one half of a
queer couple who Reed called "the kittens"

Reed Peggram (back row, far right) and the
Harvard University Phi Beta Kappa Class of 1935

Montfort "Monty" Schley Variell, Reed's Harvard classmate, Class of 1936. He was a close friend during his short life. His death provided Reed with a lifeline.

Reed Peggram graduation photo. Location and date unknown.

Portrait by Guggenheim fellow Thomas Handforth, created in Paris in 1938. Later included in a 2019–20 exhibition at the Cascadia Art Museum in Edmonds, Washington, and related book, *The Lavender Palette: Gay Culture and the Art of Washington State* by David F. Martin.

Reed Peggram and Arne Hauptmann in Italy, 1944

Arne Hauptmann and Reed Peggram talking with reporter Max Johnson from the Baltimore *Afro-American* newspaper, who wrote, "If Peggram's story proves to be correct, it will undoubtedly become one of the greatest human-interest stories yet revealed in this war"

Reed's maternal grandmother,
Laura Reed. She was his
champion, legal guardian,
and most ardent supporter.

the Italian consulate treated him well. He expected Italy to be warm, or at least warmer than Denmark. He hadn't been prepared for the weather and now wore two sweaters to fight off the low temperatures. Arne gave Reed two of his own sweaters and a pair of gloves, which helped, along with Bertie's scarf. The suits he brought with him from Paris had turned to rags, but he had the new suit he purchased in Copenhagen.

He assured Laura that "Italy is sure to be neutral for some time to come. They are very glad to have visitors, and I have even heard that Mussolini and the Pope are trying to get together and make peace. Just how far they will get is another matter, but it's certainly an idea worth trying." Before signing off, he added, "Arne sends you his greetings, and still looks forward to meeting you in a few months." Reed was filled with optimism. He said that Arne's "parents are quite willing to let him leave, and we really find it quite adventurous trying to make our plans about how we shall finally get to America." But this couldn't be true, since Arne's father was long dead. Perhaps he meant a stepfather?

Reed told Mary, "Now don't worry about me. . . . I think I'm going to like Italy," and insisted, "But it's fine really. I only hope you both won't turn grey worrying about me." He assured her, "I'm really not depressed at all, although anyone should think I would be. Personally, I think God takes care of the bright and the lazy, and I'm sure I'm both." He recalled how his friend Jan Gay ran out of money while traveling in Buenos Aires but was able to earn money by writing a book. Reed yearned to do the same.

In late March 1940, Reed and Arne made plans to go to Venice for what they hoped would be a short stay. Because of the cost, Reed might not have been able to contact his family right away with a telegram but wanted them to be assured that he would be safe.

But a few days later he playfully wrote the following:

STOP! As one says in a telegram. LOOK! As one says on a radio program. LISTEN! As one says at a railroad station. (I got the last two twisted around, but you know what I mean). CHANGE OF PLANS: GOING TO MILAN, NOT VENICE.

They decided to go to Milan instead of Venice because the train from France arrived in Milan first.

A friend in Boston was going to try to get two of Reed's poems published. Reed also completed another story that he sent to the United States for possible publication. Arne translated the story into Danish and they hoped a radio producer they met would use it. They would earn four dollars per minute. They hoped the show would last an hour and that the money would be forwarded to them in Italy. Reed told Mary he was her "wandering boy."

Once again, on March 2, 1940, Reed contacted the Rosenwald Fund to inform them that he was heading to Italy and that he would have a change of address. He ended with, "I would be very happy if the cooperation of the Foundation would make it possible for me to buy a return ticket to the United States, the price of which has been doubled since I sailed from New York in 1938." Edwin R. Embree, the president of the foundation, wrote on the letter, "I don't see any obligation on us, do you? Should we tell [unclear] about this case, for his information and possible suggestions?"

Leaving Copenhagen was taking longer than expected as Reed waited for his visa to travel through France. During this time, he fell ill again, and Arne took care of him, feeding him tea with lemon and making sure he was wrapped up warm in bed. Reed hoped that the Rosenwald Fund would give him money. The cost of the plane ticket was so high that he wouldn't even mention the figure in letters home lest "you think I am completely mad." In order to save money for the expensive trip, Reed and Arne tried to cut down their expenses as much as possible. They ate very little besides tea and bread, but both became ill and had to resume a normal diet. Reed tried to sell his return ticket to the United States, but it was now only worth fifty dollars. He also tried to sell the ring that Aunt Nona had given him, only to discover that the diamonds were fake. Finally, Arne was able to borrow another hundred dollars from an uncle and they had the funds they needed to leave.

Despite his cheery front with his grandmother and mother, no doubt he couldn't allay their fears. Surely the news in the United States indicated that war in Europe was going to spread to other countries. Reed could feel war was coming and had to admit that this was a threat he couldn't dodge with his charm and usually unshakable optimism. He now wrote in his last letter to his grandmother from Copenhagen dated March 11, 1940:

Between you and me, we know that it's good to get out of this part of Europe as soon as we can. The Northern countries are going to be in the war very soon, and then we would be in a hell of a mess. One shouldn't say so now, because they are still at peace, but we've heard enough to know that it's a good idea to get out now.

They prepared to leave Denmark.

Reed and Arne flew from Copenhagen to Brussels—Reed's first ever plane ride. From Brussels they took a train to Paris and arrived around midnight. Paris looked the same to Reed except for ominous signs indicating where to go during an air raid and the number of soldiers walking the streets. At night, there were no streetlights, and stores and restaurants had heavy curtains draping their windows and doors.

Their train to Italy was leaving the following day, so they stayed in a hotel after Reed was unable to contact his old hotel; their phone had been disconnected. The next day Reed returned to the Hôtel des Deux Continents to retrieve his trunks. The proprietors were so happy to see him alive; they had been so worried about him. They had packed his bag and Reed went through it, removing anything he didn't need. He was dismayed to find that his old gray coat was gone—the proprietors had given it to a poor unfortunate man. So they gave Reed a raincoat that he thought was better than his previous one. He was happy to be once again surrounded by his books, pictures, old letters, and clothes—especially because the clothes he had in Denmark were so worn.

Reed and Arne returned to the station that evening to catch the train to Italy. When they got there they had only five minutes to spare and ran around with their suitcases like "chickens with our heads cut off" and promptly got on a train headed in the wrong direction. By the time they returned to the station, their train had left. They returned to the Hôtel des Deux Continents, to the amusement of the proprietors, who gave them a discount for the night and served them breakfast for free after noting how thin Reed looked.

They returned to the train station the next day a half hour before their departure and ran into the composer and pianist Howard Swanson, Reed's fellow Rosenwald Fellowship student. Swanson remained in Paris and suggested that they go to Florence because he knew some people there. Reed hoped to persuade Howard to join them in Florence because, first, "He is a really good friend of mine" and, more likely, because "he also has money."

This time they boarded the correct train and were headed to Italy. Reed was determined to "do everything in my power" to bring Arne with him to the United States.

TEN

"Italy as a Whole Is Very Peaceful"

Their train finally arrived in Italy, and they got off in the city of Genoa, where they had to spend the night in order to complete the customs inspection the following morning. Reed found the city to be both dirty and depressing and couldn't wait to leave for their ultimate destination of Florence. They hoped that this would be their chance to leave Europe and to be together in the United States. Reed could finish his Ph.D. while teaching as a university professor.

Iris Origo, a British woman married to an Italian man, kept diaries before and during World War II capturing the atmosphere in the Tuscany region. She later published *A Chill in the Air: An Italian War Diary, 1939–1940* and *War in Val d'Orcia: An Italian War Diary, 1943–1944*. Before Reed and Arne's arrival in Florence, the city was already filled with anxiety. Origo documented "the increasingly oppressive atmosphere of a country on the brink of a war for which it is entirely unprepared." Residents received news from the Italian papers and *L'Osservatore Romano*, *The Times*, *Le Temps*, and the *Journal de Genève* and listened to news on the radio from the BBC and Paris PTT. There were some restrictions on the use of private motorcars, and restaurants were limited to serving a single dish of either meat or fish. The sale of coffee was forbidden and residents could not procure tea. Hospitals, factories, and charitable institutions were purchasing gas masks but were only able to provide them for about 20 percent of their employees. Other citizens were encouraged to get masks, and the elderly and children were urged to leave the major cities, although there were no concrete evacuation plans. Now that war had begun, pitting Britain and France against Germany, and after the sinking of SS *Athenia* back in September at the start of the war, people wondered if Italy would remain neutral.

After clearing customs, Reed and Arne took a train 124 miles to Florence. They walked around for hours looking for an affordable room to rent. Two little boys offered to help them by introducing them to two men who, for a fee, helped them to find a suitable place that they could afford. They settled on the Pensione Marchetti, for thirty dollars a month, which included meals with their lodging. They only had enough money to pay for the first two weeks. Arne was expecting some money from Copenhagen from an unnamed person, and Reed was hoping that he would hear something positive from one of the editors about his writing submissions. They later discovered that Howard Swanson's friends had gone to Greece and Howard would not be coming to Florence after all.

Despite the circumstances, Reed loved Florence. He declared,

"Florence is the most beautiful city I have ever seen," sending images of the city back home. He was "wild about its beauty." He liked that it was near mountains with fresh air and had a wonderful climate and great food that was not expensive. They ate a lot of spaghetti and macaroni, fruit, and vegetables, drank wine, and in the mornings and they somehow procured coffee and had prune jam with their toast because they couldn't get butter. As they waited for Arne to get a visa to travel to the United States, Reed gained back some of the weight he lost in Copenhagen, where neither the climate nor the food agreed with him. They considered going to Central or South America to wait for a visa to the United States because it would be safer than being in Europe—holding out hope that Italy would remain out of the war, though that was seeming less and less likely.

It is unknown if Reed and Arne knew what stance Italy had on homosexuality, but no doubt they thought it would be prudent to obfuscate the true nature of their relationship. In fact, to be a male homosexual under Fascism in Italy was to be under police surveillance. Homosexuality was antithetical to the image of the virile Italian man. Italy did not have explicit penal codes against it because the existence of such codes would suggest a problem. If homosexual men were discreet, wealthy, or connected, the police would often just issue a warning or caution. Overt homosexual behavior was severely penalized. Poor men who engaged in the sex trade were often targeted and imprisoned, or sometimes sent to penal colonies on islands under extremely harsh conditions. Or they were confined to mental asylums. To be in Florence during this time was to live in a repressive society. The prefect of Florence, a high-ranking official, reported on homosexual activity in the city directly to the prime minister, Benito Mussolini.

Their goal was to get a visa for Arne so that he could enter the United States, which proved to be very difficult. There were quotas and complicated requirements to fulfill and multiple documents to collect. Because of anti-immigrant sentiment steeped with antisemitism the process was deliberately slow. The 1924 Immigration Act set quotas for visas for different countries. This system benefited people coming from countries in northern and western Europe, which Arne had in his favor. But the United States didn't feel compelled to reach the set quotas and many slots remained unfulfilled, and these slots did not carry over into the following year. First, Arne had to register with the US consulate and get placed on a waiting list. He also had to have identification papers, certificates from the police confirming that he was a good citizen, and the inclusion of a police dossier and a prison record, if applicable. Arne would need multiple copies of a visa application, copies of his birth certificate, and a quota number that listed his position on a waiting list. Additionally, he would need affidavits of good conduct from several disinterested parties, and a physical examination at the US consulate in order to get a medical clearance stating that he was in good health. In order to obtain many of these documents, he would have to pay fees.

Due to the fear that immigrants would take jobs from American citizens, applicants had to prove that they had the money to support their stay and to obtain a financial affidavit that they would not rely on the US government for funds. Arne had to have an American sponsor, preferably a close relative who had to be a US citizen or permanent resident, who could guarantee that they had the financial resources to support him so that he would not become a burden on the US government. The sponsor had to provide certified copies of federal tax returns, bank statements, and a statement from an employer. Getting this affidavit was one of the most difficult parts of the visa process. By September 1940, the United States began requiring visa applicants to have two sponsors.

Arne hoped to rely on his uncle Søren Matthesen, his mother's brother. Søren, who took the more American-sounding name of Samuel, had immigrated to the United States from Denmark in 1903 at the age of twenty-two. By 1910, he worked as a bartender in a saloon in California and rented a room in San Francisco. He eventually became a naturalized American citizen, married a woman named Agnes, and became a wine merchant. By the 1930s, he owned a home in San Leandro, California, and a business. The couple remained childless. Perhaps it was knowledge of his uncle's thriving in the United States that gave Arne and Reed hope that he could assist them.

Reed told his family:

> The uncle is very rich and will probably send a lot when he gets around to it. It is probably because he is so rich that it takes him so long to make up his mind. We have waited far too long for his answer already. We even spent our last money on a telegram to him telling him to hurry up.

Additionally, Arne had to have proof that he had a ticket for a ship to the United States, which was often hard to obtain after submarines targeted passenger ships and many ports closed. Fewer ships took these risky voyages, which made obtaining a berth both very difficult and extremely expensive. Finally, Arne had to obtain entrance and transit visas from all of the countries he had to travel through in order to reach the ship's point of departure. The transit visas had to be collected in specific order and each one had an associated fee.

The waiting lists became extremely long, with more competition for visas in 1938 and 1939 as Europe veered toward war, and only grew after the war began. Some applicants could end up waiting for several years. If Arne was able to reach the top of the waiting list, he would have to submit to an interview at the American consulate in order to acquire a visa and make the journey to the United States with Reed.

They continued waiting to hear from Arne's uncle and repeatedly sent him letters or telegrams. The stress took a toll on their mental health.

Reed told Laura:

You can also understand how important it is that the uncle, or somebody in the family, simply MUST do something. We can't go on like this because the worry itself is making nervous wrecks of us. I can't understand how people can be so heartless as that family of his, especially when they can really afford it.

Arne added a note to Reed's letter apologizing to Laura for asking for money. He said, "I hope now the letter to my uncle will give results, and I shall give you all back again." They kept promising to repay Laura, with no prospects for earning money in sight other than wishful thinking.

Out of desperation, Reed sent Laura the name and address of Arne's uncle so that she could forward a letter that he had written as if it came from her. Reed wondered:

> Why in the hell doesn't he, or someone else in the family do something for Arne who is suffering very much in Italy because he is out of money. I mention in the letter that you have helped us as much as you can, but that you can't afford it, and that you think it is a damned shame that a family as wealthy as that can't do something.

It does not appear that Uncle Søren ever responded to any of their requests.

None of the procedures and obstacles they faced in obtaining a visa for Arne were shared with Laura and Mary. His letters to them were optimistic.

Reed knew what awaited him in the United States. A dreary life of looking over his shoulder, sidestepping both racism and homophobia, comporting himself in just the right way to get taken seriously. He would have to do it all without Arne. Reed had studied Romance languages, was moved by music and art. He was, after all, a romantic. The loss of this dream life was pain enough—he would not leave the man he loved.

In the shadow of the stunning, iconic terra-cotta dome of the Duomo cathedral overlooking Florence, Reed and Arne huddled together in their pensione, with little in the way of funds. Since they were foreigners, they were not allowed to work in Italy. They lived on a Swiss Legation allowance of one thousand lire (fifty US dollars) a month for a while, and the Italian government gave them eight lire (forty cents) a day.

Reed briefly considered asking an unnamed friend for funds but decided against it. In the meantime, Laura sent Reed another hundred dollars. He felt ashamed about her dipping into her life savings and promised to repay it. He lamented:

> It pained me like hell to have to ask you. You are so good to me that I know you would deprive yourself just to see that I was not badly off. I don't know why, but I always seem to make such a terrible mess of things. All I seem to have given you is trouble my whole life, but I hope it won't always be that way.

Reed still hoped that he could support himself through his writing and continued submitting while in Florence. He was grateful to receive a twenty-five-dollar check from the editor Dorothy Norman, which he said "rescued me from embarrassing situations." She had heard about Reed's plight and sent the money before the publication of his essay in *Twice a Year*. Reed asked Dorothy, if the issue had not gone to press, to publish the article under the name Edwin Reed instead of using Reed Edwin Peggram, which he called "cumbersome." He also informed her that he planned to stay in Florence as he could not purchase a ticket to travel by ship because the rates had doubled. But, he said, "Firenze is very pleasant, however, and I do not in the least regret being marooned here. Its climate, its scenery, as well as its Renascimento contours inspire to creativity."

Reed's essay, "André Gide—Novelist," was eventually published in *Twice a Year*. He said receiving it "was a breath of life, of peace, and of Art." It appeared in a double issue in 1941 after an article by *Tropic of Cancer* author Henry Miller. Reed would've been thrilled to see this journal with his essay sold in Paris at the Shakespeare and Company bookstore. The essay began:

> André Gide is a man who has something to say. His manner of saying it is at best incidental. He dislikes creating something "beautiful" just for the sake of its beauty. With him everything has to mean. Gide is first and foremost a moralist.

Norman later sent Reed a rejection letter for his submission of ten poems but with some encouragement. She wrote, "By the way, we liked the first and tenth poem best, just in case this might be of any interest to you."

During his time in Italy, Reed continued reaching out to Dorothy about various writing projects and hoping for a sympathetic ear about his plight. On January 15, 1941 (Reed mistakenly wrote 1940 as is common at the start of a new year), he wrote to her:

> It is my eleventh month in Italy, where I have been stranded, moneyless, ever so long, while friends, relatives, acquaintances and cultural foundations, whenever they

have pretended to listen at all, have only responded with advice, reproofs, or some sentimental consolation, whereas in reality they knew that they ought to realize that I am struggling for my life and that if some one does not help me very soon, I shall just simply die.

He continued:

Our mutual experience with art and with life had assured us that our collaboration would bring fruitful results, richer and more profound than either of us had produced separately. Our unprinted MSS. have convinced us the truth of our belief, so much so that we are now more determined than we were a year ago. In the meantime, pedantic doubts, procrastinations and downright refusals from our American sources not only ruined his chances of entering the U.S.A. as quickly as we desired, but also permitted our entire economic basis of existence to disappear. . . . Our aim is to leave Europe the moment we have the financial possibility of doing so.

Reed contemplated possibly going to Latin America or the West Indies. He stated, "It is probably the best thing for both of our futures, everything considered, that we don't go to the U.S.A. at this moment." Anywhere was better than returning home, where he knew he would face limitations as an African American, and he was possibly alluding to their sexuality. He explained their plans and philosophy:

We wish only to live, to write, to create, to say what we have to say as only we know how to say it. It is because we know we must do this together that we are only annoyed, rather than grateful, when people offer me a ticket to NY as some have indeed attempted—without explaining, by the way, how my collaborator could ever be saved through this philanthropy.

He further explained:

When one has grappled with life closely enough to feel the whys and wherefores of existence, one does not give up, even after a year of physical and mental suffering. One knows one's goal, and one will fight for it to the last, come what may. When it happens that those who are materially able to help are spiritually too poor to know what it is to be a Man, then one can only seem ridiculous in the eyes of all except those few who have a mature concept of living.

He assured Dorothy that he was merely making

a statement of fact . . . that two young artists of more than ordinary ability need immediate financial help in order not to perish. In the name of art, of culture, of humanity in their deepest sense, this message must somehow be spread around where it will take effect at once, before it is too late. Even the length of time it takes for this letter to reach America prolongs our suffering.

Unable to declare his love for Arne, Reed could not explain why he would not leave Europe without him, instead hoping the urgency he placed on those scholarly projects would convince a would-be savior.

A few months later, in a letter dated April 9, 1941, Reed wrote to Dorothy again:

> Just how long it will take us to reach the U.S.A. still depends upon how soon acquaintances, consuls, attorneys, lawyers, etc. can experience sudden attacks of intelligence forceful enough to make them understand that we have been living here by necessity rather than by choice. But we know that even these will realize themselves in the end. However, it will make our struggle easier if we know that we have the moral cooperation of people who are capable of understanding what it means to live as one thinks, even though their approval does not express itself in any material way.

During this time, Reed sent Dorothy several manuscripts, wishing she would help them get a publishing contract, including a short manuscript consisting of an unknown topic, entitled "Echoes in a Stone Room." He sent her a sixty-page manuscript, "Twelve Novels," a work of literary criticism, as well as a 120-page manuscript, "Poems and Sketches," a translation of works by nineteenth-century Danish author Jens Peter Jacobsen. He worked on this manuscript with Arne. He told Dorothy, "You will also remember that I spent seven months living in Copenhagen, where I developed an intimate knowledge with the language."

Reed also contacted publishers seeking funds if they published some of his work. His friend Dr. Beryl Orris thought he could sell Reed's children's book manuscript about Pusé the cat to Walt Disney but was ultimately unsuccessful. Beryl also tried to raise money for Reed by giving a lecture in Chicago, but instead of earning money, he lost money because not enough people attended.

Origo wrote on April 7, 1940, that there were so many rumors circulating in Italy, often contradictory, and "extraordinarily little real information has leaked out."

On April 9, 1940, shortly after 4 a.m., Germany launched multiple attacks by air, sea, and land throughout Denmark and Norway. Clarence Lusane, author of *Hitler's Black Victims*, said, "While the Norwegians offered some resistance but would not be able to hold out, the Danes virtually surrendered on the spot." Reed and Arne felt lucky that they had narrowly escaped: "We got out by the skin of our teeth." They had originally planned to stay in Denmark until April 15 when Reed requested an extension of his visa. Reed's acquaintance, jazz musician Valaida Snow, would get stuck in Denmark. As the Danish government expected, allies like Britain and France did not come to their aid. Reed worried about Bertie and whether he could manage during the Nazi occupation. They heard that boats were no longer leaving from Denmark, and that the waters were filled with mines and telegraph communications had ceased.

Reed and Arne were depressed about what was happening in Denmark and no doubt Arne was worried about his family. Reed seemed more concerned about not getting paid for their radio play. They could no longer receive any money from Denmark, including from family or friends, and so it was more urgent than ever that Arne's uncle in the United States would send funds. However, now that Denmark was occupied, it was even more difficult for Arne to get a visa to enter the United States. The State Department was more cautious about issuing visas to applicants who had family, like Arne had, in Nazi territory, fearing that they could be potential spies in the United States.

They hoped that the Vatican and the pope would do something to stop the war from coming to Italy. Reed still wanted to believe that Italy would remain peaceful while celebrating a major holiday, Natale di Roma, or the birth of Rome, in Italy with parades and speeches on April 21.

The money that Laura sent helped them cover their room and board, and gave them a brief sense of relief. They took the opportunity to take a trip to the country and climbed rocks and lay in the grass "for an hour or so, appreciating the fine country air." Reed found respite in nature outside of major cities, just like the excursions he took in upstate New York with friends from Columbia, his trips outside of Copenhagen and Paris with Bertie and Paul, and the artists' retreat he went on in Denmark.

Back in France, the battle for their other former home, Paris, began in May 1940. But in Italy, on May 13, 1940, Origo wrote in her diary, "I go up to Florence, to see whether it would be advisable for my mother, who is English, to leave. But the advice of both the US and the British embassies is still 'No hurry.'" But eventually, the Swiss Legation helped Origo's mother and stepfather obtain a special visa to go to England by traveling through Switzerland.

Meanwhile, Origo noted, "In Florence the atmosphere is very

tense." The news said that Churchill was considering sinking SS *President Roosevelt* in order to draw America into the war. People thought that Germany was invincible.

As two foreigners living in Italy during World War II, Reed and Arne were being watched by the Italian government and treated with suspicion. In May 1940, letters that Reed sent to the United States to Laura and to his friend Monty were seized, translated into Italian, and assessed. The letters were most likely destroyed afterward, because it appears that Laura never received hers. Reed's letter to Laura described what he thought of Victor Emmanuel III, the king of Italy, Pope Pius XII, and Mussolini's positions on the war. He believed that Italy did not have funds to go to war, unless the pope agreed to finance it. But he felt that Italy had enough men and the weapons to fight. He discussed how people demonstrated in support of the pope and peace, and how other groups demonstrated in support of Mussolini. Reed said that Mussolini sent police to confiscate a newspaper that the pope published, in order to prevent citizens from reading the pontiff's messages. "Everything is like a game," he said. "I personally hope that the Pope will win because I don't like war." In Reed's letter to Monty, he blamed England for goading Italy into war by holding up their ships until their goods were spoiled or damaged. He stated that Italy was not rich and depended upon these goods and food for funds. He admitted, "I'm losing faith for the cause of the allies." And he feared the German war machine. But as of now, he thought that "Italy as a whole is very peaceful." He was still, as ever, optimistic.

A "strictly confidential" document labeled "correspondence review," dated June 16, 1940, evaluated the two letters and concluded that they contained "appreciations regarding the current state of mind in Italy, in relation to the conflict between Germany and the allied powers." After evaluating Reed's letters, they concluded that he did not say anything that was objectionable.

Expecting him to catch a ship home, Laura and Mary grew increasingly impatient with Reed. They told him to return home but he refused. He argued:

> I can't leave until Arne gets his papers in order. It would be very unfriendly of me to leave him here in a strange country, where he can't even speak the language. As you know I speak so many languages I can get along anywhere. At the moment, we are waiting for the money to arrive from his uncle in America, and then we shall see how long it takes before the American Government is willing to let him into the country.

They moved to a boardinghouse located at Via Nazionale 10, which provided them with a larger room. This boardinghouse had a piano in the dining room that only Reed played. He hoped that they could move it to his room, which was large enough to fit a grand piano.

Meanwhile, Reed assessed his possibilities back home in the United States, wondering about the health of his stepfather, Phillip Farrar Sr. He questioned if Mary would receive his pension and insurance payout if he died, no doubt self-interested, and if it would be enough to support her and his two brothers. He wondered if they would relocate to Boston to live with Laura after his death; if so, he and Arne would not try to live there because there would not be enough room.

Reed assured his family that even if Italy entered the war, he, a foreigner, would be safe. He estimated that there were twenty thousand Americans in Italy—though it is unclear where he got that figure. But now the United States was encouraging citizens to leave and even providing transportation. Iris Origo's May 28 and May 29, 1940, entries in her diary stated that an American told her "that they received a most definite order from Washington to pack off all Americans on the [ocean liner] Manhattan on Saturday." Here was Reed's opportunity to leave with the help of the US government, no expensive ticket needed. African American club owners Bricktop and Eugene Bullard, who had remained in Paris, eventually left for the United States on the *Manhattan*. Reed made no mention of the order.

Awaiting word from Arne's uncle, they turned to Laura to fund their life in Italy. Laura sent another $40 that arrived on May 25. They spent some of the money sending a telegram to Arne's uncle. Reed's friends Monty and Peter were looking into getting a $5,000 bond for Arne—perhaps this would help him get a visa to the United States if he could prove that he had funds to support himself. Eventually they told Reed that they couldn't sign a bond for Arne because they were being asked too many questions. They were probably reluctant to vouch for someone that neither had ever met, or perhaps the questions were about the nature of the relationship between Reed and Arne.

Reed and Arne had been in Italy for over two months. Laura and Mary must've been frustrated to have to continue sending money to Reed, who was no closer to returning to the United States.

On June 3, 1940, loudspeakers were installed in the squares of towns and villages—an ominous sign of an impending major announcement. People gathered in the nearest town or around a radio, anticipating a speech by Mussolini. There was still no news in Italy by June 7, but Origo observed bombers flying south and about fifty military lorries on the roads. The June 9 Italian newspapers reported that they were expecting France to fall but no confirmation was forthcoming. Origo said, "By now my chief emotion—and I expect that of most other people—is exasperation." Arne and Reed were likely reading the same newspapers and listening to the same news on the radio if the owners of their pensione had access.

On June 10, 1940, Mussolini announced that Italy was now allied with Germany and declared war on Great Britain and France.

ELEVEN

"We Are Worn and Weary and Weak"

Now that Italy had entered World War II, things were even more dismal for Reed and Arne. They were in dire straits, "worse than you can imagine." They hadn't paid their rent yet and it was the middle of the month. Their landlords continued feeding them, but they were also suffering due to their poverty and begged Reed and Arne to do something. Reed pawned his ring, fountain pen, and typewriter but received only $10. He considered pawning his watch and a tuxedo, but he would not get much for either item. He tried to sell his ticket, but since ships weren't sailing, he was told he had to sell it in New York.

Laura sent Reed $100 at the end of June 1940. He was able to get his typewriter out of the pawn shop. The money, along with another $40 she sent, allowed them to catch up on their debts but they said it did not give them enough money to leave Italy. He explained, "It only put us on a better footing so that we can face life with more courage." And "I sometimes wish my father would die so that I could get his money." It was not clear how his father's death would result in Reed obtaining money. Maybe a death benefit?

Over three months after Reed arrived in Italy, he was no closer to returning to the United States. Now he was living in a country that had entered World War II. In frustration, on July 8, 1940, Mary turned to the State Department and the secretary of state, asking them to make Reed return home. Laura co-signed the letter. Mary wrote, "Please let me know if you can get word and arrangements made for my son to come home from Florence, Italy." Interestingly, Mary wrote, "Arne Hauptman [*sic*] claims to have a wealthy uncle," suggesting they were skeptical, but they provided his name and address. They pled, "We can make restitution for my son coming home but simply cannot continue to try to support the two over there. The situation seems acute." Mary must've been desperate. She'd lost her first husband, mentally and physically, to the first war and didn't want to lose her firstborn child to the second. While waiting for a response from the State Department, Laura continued sending Reed money but expressed her frustration and perhaps anger in her letters to Reed, which deflated his spirits so much that he asked Arne to write to Laura on July 30, 1940, to try to explain their situation. Arne wrote:

> I am writing to you because Reed was depressed over the letter he got from you Saturday and over the letter his mother sent to the American Express that he asked me to try and explain things clearer than he has explained them so far. It is not because he wants to stay in Italy that he has not come home. If it were possible, he would have left long ago, but the war has made lots of difficulties. Please do not

think that it is my fault that Reed has not gone home. He has been very kind to me, and I know what I owe both of you. But dear Mrs. Reed, please understand how things happened this way.

He then reiterated much of what Reed said about their travels and difficulties and plans that fell through. He ended the letter with:

Dear Mrs. Reed, I am very grateful for what you have done for me, and I promise you, you will not regret it. Please do not be angry with me. Reed has never written to you how difficult we have had it together because neither of us have wanted you to have more worries than you already have.

Reed added a note: "Perhaps Arne's letter will explain better than I can why I did not come home as I planned."

The next day, July 31, 1940, Reed wrote to Mary, who was very angry that Reed was still in Italy. Both she and Laura had concluded that he only remained in Italy, consuming their funds, to be with Arne while waiting for his papers to the United States to be approved. Reed admitted that he must come across in his letters as "unclear and confused." He acknowledged, "I am hardly myself these days with all the worries I have, and I suppose it is because my letters have been so crazy to everybody that no one will help me."

The Department of State responded to Laura and Mary's letter on August 2, 1940. Geo. L. Brandt, administrative officer of the Special Division, said:

With the spread of hostilities in Italy and the resulting prohibition under the provisions of the Neutrality Act against the entry of American vessels into the Mediterranean, the Department is not able at this time to indicate what means of transportation to the United States may be obtained by your son. However, American consular officers abroad are generally in touch with the Americans in their districts and are under standing instructions to assist them in any way possible in obtaining transportation to the United States when desired.

Brandt told Mary that the American Export Lines offered "a weekly passenger service between Lisbon and New York and it is expected, therefore, that transportation facilities will continue to be available for American citizens who are able to reach Lisbon." Unfortunately, Brandt said:

There are no funds available from which transportation at Government expense may be furnished to your son. Upon the outbreak of hostilities in Europe and during the resulting emergency, loans for repatriation purposes were made from special Departmental funds to needy Americans in certain areas in Europe. Such loans are not at present being made to persons in Italy.

The Department of State contacted the American consul general based in Florence, asking them about Reed's "present whereabouts, welfare, and plans." The consul general was asked to inform Reed about his family's "desire that he return to the United States at once." When the Department of State received a response, they promised to contact Mary.

Reed told Mary and Laura that he went to the American consulate, and they said they did not have funds to support him but let him borrow enough money to send a cablegram. He said that the consulate did not help citizens. They advised people to get help and concluded that he should have left in 1939 when he had the chance. He told Mary and Laura that the American consulate did not understand his situation.

In fact, Reed had an earlier opportunity to return to the United States that included great prospects for his future. In the summer of 1939, he had been offered a teaching position at West Virginia State College. His friend William Bradford Pratt was a professor in the Department of Romance Languages. Pratt was also an African American graduate of Harvard in the Class of 1931. He graduated the spring before Reed enrolled in the fall term at Harvard, but remained in Boston to study for a master's degree at Boston University, and perhaps that's how the two men met.

Pratt told Dean Harrison H. Ferrell that Reed was their top candidate for a position in the department. Dean Ferrell received his Ph.D. in German from Northwestern University in 1928—the first Black person to obtain a degree in the German Department. Pratt most likely felt an affinity for Reed as an alum of Harvard, and Ferrell as a fellow linguist. In an unfortunate turn of events, West Virginia State College had to rescind their earlier 1939 offer due to financial circumstances. However, although

Dean Ferrell could not offer Reed a position, he was unusually interested in making sure that he obtained a position somewhere because of his academic achievements.

Now Reed wrote to Pratt telling him that he was living in "abject poverty" and did not know "what fate is in store for me." He also warned Pratt that when he responded to his letter, "please do not make any political comments, inasmuch as both sides censor letters and take the right of intercepting all those which displease them."

Reed explained why he was still in Italy:

> I have been obliged to remain heren [*sic*], not only unable to raise the necessary funds to depart, but forced to live in such abject poverty that I often have not the price of a postage stamp. . . . I don't know what fate is in store for me. The Italian officials have been most courteous in the tradition of Latin solicitude for tourists, and have assured me that I may remain here until the war is over if I like. This naturally presupposes that I shall continue to have sums of money telegraphed to me from American sources and at the moment I am rather perplexed as to what these sources may be. I have sold a few manuscripts, but not enough to keep me on a basis of comfortable security.

He assured Pratt that he would continue working on his thesis "whenever my nerves will allow it."

During this same time, Reed contacted Edwin Embree, the president of the Rosenwald Fund, but his tone was not very pleasant. He wanted funds, although they had already told him that they would not extend his fellowship or give him the additional $500 he requested. He wrote, "I can't understand why the Rosenwald Fund should insist upon leaving me flat a moment when its aid would be of such vital significance to me." Reed tried to explain why he hadn't returned, stating that there were many problems that he was not responsible for, including: World War II; the increased cost of passage back to the United States; his trip from Denmark through France to Italy to get his documents in Paris; the occupation of Denmark that prevented opportunities to get things published; problems with mail delivery; and Italy entering the war.

He ended with, "Your negative answer to Copenhagen, by registered mail, sometime in December, was supposed to be final. If so, I cannot see how your institution satisfies the ideals for which it was founded."

Despite Reed's rudeness, the Rosenwald Fund decided to supply the money to bring him home. On July 18, 1940, they sent a check to the American Export Lines with the following information:

Tickets and cash to be cabled to Mr. Reed Peggram:

Steamship ticket, Lisbon to New York	$250.00
Embarkation tax	12.00
Cable	5.00
Air ticket, Rome to Lisbon	102.00
Cash to passenger	50.00

For a total of $419 described as "(Extension of fellowship award of Reed Peggram)."

The next day the Rosenwald Fund sent Reed a telegram via Western Union informing him that "Transportation Italy to New York via Lisbon and fifty dollars will reach you through Lisbon office American Export Lines."

The American Export Lines sought accommodations for Reed on the steamer *Nea Hellas*, set to sail from Lisbon on July 30. Reed could return to the United States.

Somehow, Dean Ferrell at West Virginia State College became aware of the Rosenwald Fund's intervention and wrote to Embree thanking him. Embree replied, "Under normal conditions we are careful not to assume responsibility for men to whom we have awarded fellowships." Ferrell assured Embree, "Details of our conversation will be treated confidentially by me and not released to Mr. Peggram."

Ferrell contacted James B. Conant, the president of Harvard University, on July 13, 1940, informing him that Reed was able to secure funds to pay for his transportation back to the United States. Ferrell appealed to Harvard to assist Reed in finding a teaching position.

The following month, on August 16, 1940, Reed wrote to Mary instead of to Laura because he knew she was "disgusted" with him and very angry at Arne. He said, "But seriously, Mother, do you think I could have the heart to desert my friend here, even if I could leave at once?" It always came back to Arne, whom neither Mary nor Laura knew or probably cared about. Reed was frustratingly repetitive in his letters, with the same laments about his friends that would not help him and their hopes that Arne's uncle would send money. He warned that he might not be able to send letters for a long time because he could not afford stamps but assured his family that "I personally don't think we'll die here, although some times [*sic*] we come very close to it." He began using "we" and not "I" in his letters as if he and Arne were now inseparable.

The Harvard Appointment Office staff contacted Ferrell on August 22, 1940, and updated him about their attempts to find a position for Reed. They had contacted several historically Black institutions, but none were able to offer Reed a position. They intended to send inquiries to Virginia State College for Negroes, Sam Houston State Teachers College, Claflin College, and the Agricultural and Technical College of North Carolina. Dillard University declined because they had recently hired someone to teach French. Hampton Institute said they did not presently offer courses in the Romance languages. Lincoln University said they did not have any current openings in their Modern Language Department.

Meanwhile, Reed's friend from Paris, Dr. Beryl Orris, wrote to Laura on September 5, 1940, informing her that he regularly corresponded with Reed. He said, "In his last letter to me (written on July 31st), he wrote that you are much upset by the fact that he is unable (or does not seem willing) to come home." Beryl wrote:

> I believe that you are sufficiently a good judge of human nature to realize that I feel very close to Reed. Because of our intimate relationship, our conversations attempting to solve his problems, etc., I feel that I know him as well as anybody else in this world, except you. There is no one in

this world who is closer to him than his Nana, and he truly loves you as deeply as it is possible for anyone to love another person. Very often those we love do things which other people cannot understand, but because of our love, we are able to understand or at least to be patient until we are given an explanation.

Beryl continued, despite acknowledging that perhaps he was speaking in riddles, "somehow, I feel that you understand what I am trying to say." He said when Reed returned "(and I am sure that he will safely return)," Laura would understand why "he could not come back until he was able to come back as he wanted to." Beryl continued:

There are a number of reasons why he is not ready to return at present—some of these reasons are very practical (visa difficulties, financial difficulties, securing passage on a boat, leaving Italy for Portugal, etc.).

He cryptically added:

And other reasons are emotional and can only be explained in terms which sound foolish in a letter. I hope that in the not too distant future, I shall have a chance to discuss these things with you personally, and then I shall explain them to the best of my ability.

It appeared that Beryl knew the real reason that Reed would not return was because he was in love in Arne, and his letter indicated that he thought Laura might also know the reason why Reed remained in Italy.

In the interim, the Rosenwald Fund was informed on September 10, 1940, by the American Export Lines that their New York office received a cable from their Lisbon office: "PEGGRAM NOT READY SAIL UNTIL SEPTEMBER OR LATER HENCE NOT TRANSFERRING YET."

Finally, Harvard had some success. On September 16, 1940, the Harvard Appointment Office sent Reed a cable in Florence, "Position at Claflin University being held for your return cable." President J. B. Randolph of Claflin University, founded in 1869 in Orangeburg, South Carolina, offered Reed a position as a teacher in Romance languages for a monthly salary of $87.50 including room and board during the nine-month school session. Reed responded to the Harvard Appointment Office on September 21, 1940: "I regret that I was unable to answer your cable, as you requested, but my finances have in the past month fallen into such a disastrous state that I was even unable to secure postage for writing you before today." Further, "Under such unpredictable circumstances, I find it impossible to inform you of my plans. They depend entirely upon a change in my present economic circumstances, without which change I shall remain in Firenze indefinitely." In a tone-deaf addendum given the circumstances, Reed asked for assistance finding a publisher for his translations of poems by Jens Peter Jacobsen. To their credit, someone made a handwritten note on the letter, "Dean Mayo referred to Prof. Cawley," to ask for assistance concerning Reed's request.

Reed wrote to Mary on September 30, 1940, asking her about

the return of his unused ticket on the Holland America Line. He had requested a refund in July before the ticket expired in August. He expected to receive $83.50 and asked Mary to go to the New York City office to find out why his refund had not been sent to Laura. He hoped she could forward a portion of the refund to him.

Unfortunately, unbeknownst to Reed, two weeks earlier a ray of hope had come in the form of a tragedy. In Cambridge, Massachusetts, on Thursday, September 12, Reed's friend, twenty-five-year-old Monty, gave his usual weekly Thursday night concert in his apartment for five young men including two friends from Harvard, Theodore W. Sprague and Claude Richards. The "concert" consisted of Monty playing his record albums on his $2,800 phonograph. At one point during the evening, he stopped playing records and asked the men assembled a strange question: "What piece of music would you like to hear if you were going to be executed tomorrow morning?" Despite the macabre question, his friends said he was in good humor when they left his apartment at 2 a.m. to head to a hotel for drinks.

On Friday, September 13 (a bad luck omen if you believed in superstitions), Monty practiced the piano at a music studio and nothing appeared unusual according to the manager, Harry Rosen. He also said Monty appeared to be in good spirits.

Monty returned to his "lavishly appointed" first-floor studio apartment on Wendell Street. The tragic event took place between midnight Friday and midnight Saturday, according to the medical examiner. At some point he locked the front door and doubly secured it by placing a chair under the knob. The police initially wondered if he feared for his life. All the windows were locked. He undressed and folded his clothes and laid them on his neatly made bed and put on his pajamas. He removed a cushion from the couch and placed it on the floor of the kitchenette. On Thursday he had said that he would want Beethoven's Ninth Symphony to be played at his execution, but instead, he played Bruckner's Ninth Symphony on his phonograph before entering the six-by-eight-foot kitchenette, locking the French doors separating it from the rest of the apartment, wrapping himself in a sheet and a blanket, and lying facedown.

On Monday, September 16, the woman Monty hired to clean his apartment discovered his body. It was believed that he had been dead for two or three days.

The police were very interested in speaking to twenty-one-year-old Helen Lambert, a music student who lived in New York City, who was described as "petite honey-haired blonde, very pretty" and very sensitive—Monty's possible friend, paramour, or even his wife; gossip said they were secretly married. She said she was shocked to hear about his death. She agreed to come to Cambridge but failed to arrive for an interview and went into hiding—her uncle argued that she should not be subjected to "nerve-wearing questioning."

There were no signs of a weapon or of violence in the apartment. Monty's friends said "that the neatness and order of the body's disposition was typical of his immaculate orderliness in life." The police captain speculated that if he had taken poison that "violent muscular convulsions would have been likely to disturb the body's position." No poison was discovered, but the police found three glasses, two empty and one half-filled with a brown liquid in a receptacle, after receiving a phone tip from an unnamed person. The police were criticized for missing this possible clue and for not taking fingerprints. But they observed that the gas stove was turned off and that there was no suicide note. The medical examiner could not ascertain a cause of death after completing an autopsy and turned over Monty's vital organs to a toxicologist for the state police to examine.

Eventually, the medical examiner changed his initial findings, concluding that Monty died by suicide by illuminating gas—although the gas meter registered no usage. It failed to show any usage for the month preceding his death too, although a check indicated that the meter was functioning. The conclusion was that he filled the room with illuminating gas, closed the jets, and awaited death. John J. Canney, the chief inspector in Cambridge, concluded that Monty took his life because "he failed to come up to his own standards" in terms of a potential career as a concert pianist.

News coverage was heightened because of Monty's association with Harvard and because his grandfather was the highly decorated Spanish-American War naval hero Admiral Winfield Scott Schley and because his father, Dr. Arthur D. Variell, was a well-known leprosy expert knighted by several European monarchs. Tragically, Dr. Variell preceded Monty in death by a few months. Headlines included, "Mystery Death at Harvard," "Investigate Death of Harvard Student," "Secret Wedding Hinted in Mystery of 'Sealed Room,'" "'Sealed Room' Death of Heir Baffles Police," and "Suicide Verdict Deepens 'Sealed Room' Mystery."

Monty left an estate worth $81,000 comprising two life insurance policies for $56,000 and $25,000, worth approximately $1,826,000 in 2025. The mysterious Helen Lambert was the beneficiary of the $25,000 policy—worth approximately $564,000 in

2025. Monty's funeral and burial took place in Kennebunk, Maine, where he had spent his summers since infancy at the family estate and nearby Kennebunkport. He was buried in Evergreen Cemetery. Reed would receive $11,000 (worth around $250,000 in 2025) from the $81,000 policy and any savings in bank accounts in various New England banks. There was only one catch: the money would not be released to Reed unless he came home to claim it. Finally, his family thought, Reed would see reason and come home. However, once again, Reed refused to leave Arne.

Reed's emotional reaction to the news of Monty's death is unrecorded, but he must've been shattered. Monty had wondered in a previous letter when the two friends would meet again. It would never happen.

Meanwhile, informed that Reed refused to sail on the ship where his passage was booked, the Rosenwald Fund immediately contacted Reed on September 20, 1940. They wrote:

> We are at a loss to understand why you have not taken up this ticket. I am writing to advise you that unless you accept our offer and come back on the first ship available, we will ask the American Export Lines to cancel the ticket and refund our money. Your letter to us indicated that you were in distressed circumstances, and that you were extremely eager to leave for the United States. We therefore do not understand why you have not returned, and why we have not heard from you.
>
> It is our feeling that delay may make it impossible for you to travel should the war spread to Spain and Portugal, and

we cannot state too strongly that we will take no further responsibility in getting you back to America unless you immediately accept our offer of transportation and sail on the first ship on which accommodations can be secured.

The Rosenwald Fund then advised the American Export Lines to contact Reed again, but if he refused to board a ship, they should cancel his ticket. On October 25, 1940, the company said they would refund the money. They attached a copy of the letter Reed sent to their Genoa office. It said:

My situation remains unchanged from what I described in my last letter to you; therefore, I see no possibility of accepting the sailing on October 23rd, in spite of the risks which I incur by a refusal.

You would oblige me if you could somehow inform the purchasers of the ticket, The Rosenwald Foundation . . . , how unrealistic it is of them to demand that I sail at any given date. If it is necessary for the ticket to be refunded, it would be much more human and practical to have the sum made payable to me, inasmuch as I have been for some months living in most frightful economic circumstances which were not at all alleviated by the temporary grant of a ticket and fifty dollars cash payable in Lisbon.

Other people contacted the Rosenwald Fund on Reed's behalf, including Elmer A. Carter of the Unemployment Insurance

Appeal Board in New York City. Carter mentioned that Beryl was also trying to help Reed. An exasperated M. O. Bousfield responded on behalf of George M. Reynolds, their director of fellowship, who was away. Bousfield wrote, "There has been no end of correspondence in here about this young man." He stated that they had done all that they could for Reed. Bousfield wrote again to Carter on October 29, 1940, updating him on Reed's situation and saying, "Refusing transportation in general is really silly." Carter thanked him. But he wrote to Bousfield a couple of weeks later, beginning with, "I hate to bother you about this man Peggram . . ." He said Beryl tried to explain that Reed couldn't get the money unless he went to Lisbon but needed funds to get to Lisbon, and he turned down the ticket not because he didn't want to return but because he couldn't, and Carter hoped that the Rosenwald Fund could help him. Carter wrote, "I don't know whether this information would have any effect on the attitude of the Fund but somehow I am a little distressed and can't get it off my mind that this young fellow of some ability . . . is stranded and destitute in a country at war." Bousfield, more blunt than others at the Rosenwald Fund, replied, "I regret that as far as the Fund is concerned the Peggram matter is closed. Every effort has been made to bring this young man back. We are firmly of the opinion that he really doesn't want to come home." There was more correspondence between the Rosenwald Fund and the American Export Lines—they wanted their money returned.

The November 11, 1940, docket of the trustees' meeting of the Julius Rosenwald Fund noted:

At the close of his fellowship period, Mr. Peggram elected to remain in Europe in spite of the war. He is now in Florence, Italy, and although he claims to be in straitened circumstances, he has recently refused our offer of return transportation.

An administrator from the Harvard Appointment Office wrote to Dean Ferrell on November 22, 1940:

Have you had any recent word from Mr. Peggram? This morning I received a letter from President Randolph of Claflin University stating that he is holding the place there for Mr. Peggram. My cable to Mr. Peggram brought me no positive word as to his plans for returning to this country. His Grandmother, with whom I have just talked, has nothing additional to add. He is not working and she has been supplying him with what money she could, but I imagine it has been hard for her. It is difficult to know what more I can do for Mr. Peggram wrote a very unsatisfactory letter in answer to my cable and gave me no idea when he would return nor if he wanted to. I think I sent you a copy of it. I am sorry to bother you with all this but you wrote to us in the summer about Mr. Peggram's dire need for a job and I thought you would be interested in the results of our efforts in his behalf. If you have any suggestions to make I shall welcome them.

Ferrell replied a week later and said, "Mr. Peggram's behavior is very puzzling to me."

Apparently, the Rosenwald Fund had a change of heart and made one last-ditch effort to support Reed. On December 10, 1940, George M. Reynolds sent a telegram to Reed with a pre-paid reply telegram. Their telegram said, "Will furnish you two hundred dollars for trip Florence Lisbon and ticket home first available sailing. Will you come?"

The Rosenwald Fund also contacted Laura, informing her about how far they were willing to go to bring Reed home. On December 11, 1940, Reynolds wrote:

> I think you will be interested in knowing that we have just cabled your grandson, Reed Peggram, that we would furnish him two hundred dollars for transportation from Florence, Italy, to Lisbon, Portugal, and a ticket home on the first available sailing of one of the ships of the American Export Lines. We made arrangements to prepay a return message, and asked him to say whether or not he would come at this time. This is the second offer that has been made to him, and I hope that he will now be ready and able to take advantage of the provisions we will make. I will let you know what we hear from him.

Reynolds sent a second cable to Reed on December 13, 1940: "Only willing send two hundred dollars for trip Florence Lisbon and provide passage home. Export Lines will arrange with you sailing date. Cable acceptance or rejection." They again prepaid for a reply cable. Reed replied, "CASH NECESSARY ILL."

Laura sent a handwritten note to the Rosenwald Fund and revealed the real reason Reed refused to return:

Dear Sir: Your letter recently received and I cannot express in enough words my gratefulness for your efforts to aid my grandson, Reed Peggram, in getting home from Florence, Italy. I do hope it will be successful this time. His mother also extends her many thanks too.

According to my grandson's letters, he has refused to come without a Danish man who makes it very urgent that Reed remain until he can enter this country. As we understand the situation the fellow says he will die if Reed leaves him and of course, my grandson has

The rest of the letter is missing.

On January 6, 1941, after months of correspondence, the Rosenwald Fund sent Reed a long two-page letter ending with:

It is evident that you are not ready to come and hence you have yourself stopped us from helping you get to the United States. We do not feel that it is at all advisable to attempt to provide you with money to live in Italy.

The Rosenwald Fund offered to arrange transportation for him, but Reed concluded, "But this does not help us very much, because no one has arranged anything for Arne yet."

Reed continued:

I'm sure you think I am quite mad, but you must believe in me. Some day the world is going to appreciate me for what I am really worth. I personally think I'm worth much more than the Rosenwald Fund has already given me. I have examined this problem many many days from all possible angles, and the only solution I can see is to remain here until something happens in our favor.

The Rosenwald Fund sent Laura another letter on January 6, 1941, reminding her of their generous offer to bring Reed home. They informed her of his response:

He has cabled that he wants the entire amount in dollars and will come when he is ready.

We have insisted that he take the first boat possible and have told him it is impossible for us to subsidize his stay in Italy. From his cables to us and the letter which we received a few days ago, we are not assured that he would sail at the earliest possible moment. We are not unmindful of the difficulty in getting a Portuguese visa, but we are advised by the American Express Company that Americans are getting through even though they experience some delays.

I am very sorry that Mr. Peggram has decided that he cannot accept the offers we have made. Frankly, I do not understand the situation.

This second letter surely incensed Laura and Mary—to see that Reed was offered a solution that would bring him safely home and to learn that he had refused!

In desperation, Reed reached out to the Guggenheim Foundation on January 13, 1941. He had applied for a Guggenheim Fellowship while in Copenhagen but was rejected. He contacted them anyway, apprised them about his dire current situation, and asked for a $500 loan. He emphasized that he wanted funds, "NOT a ticket to NY, because while I obviously want to leave Europe, I have no reason to go directly to the U. S." He suggested he could live more cheaply in Central America or in the West Indies.

Reed ended the letter with:

> If this proposal seems outrageous to you, just throw my letter into the waste basket and forget it. The answer doesn't interest me if your reaction is negative. But if you feel at all inclined to respond, I beg of you to do so at once. It would be an act of humanity which would have cultural reverberations. Refusal would undoubtedly mean my death—to say nothing of the death of my intellectual endeavors—but the Foundation is certainly intelligent enough to realize this, unless it believes I am lying.

Henry Allen Moe of the Guggenheim Foundation contacted the secretary of state informing him about Reed's situation while acknowledging that they did not know anything about his circumstances other than the fact that Reed was a Rosenwald Fellow, which meant he was "regarded as a very promising young Negro scholar." Moe also contacted Reynolds at the Rosenwald Fund and was brought up to date about Reed's case, noting that they had been trying to assist him since July 1940 and it was now February 1941. Moe, perhaps embarrassed, contacted the State Department again and apprised them about what Reynolds told him, quoting directly from his letter.

It had been almost a year since Reed and Arne arrived in Italy, and they were without a clear path of leaving together. Overwhelmed by their circumstances, Reed began to decline in mental health, and he became hysterical, laughing and crying at the same time. Arne put him to bed. Although they felt bad about the strain they caused Laura with their numerous telegrams and letters, they had to finally admit that "we are in despair." Despite their desperation, Reed was determined to remain in Italy. They just needed money.

Reed did not give up and contacted Reynolds at the Rosenwald Fund again on May 1, 1941. He said:

Excuse my delay in answering, but one simply can't have postage stamps lying about when one has nothing to buy them with, can one? Is it really possible that the Foundation believes I wish to remain in Italy (which is at war, by the way) because I preferred instead of a ticket to America the equivalent in cash? What a deplorable lack of fantasy.

And he concluded the letter with, "But you will realize your mistake later. So glad you feel morally justified."

One of the last documents in Reed's Rosenwald Fund file was a receipt for the refund of their $419 minus cable and other expenses, for a total of $388.10. The agent added a note: "We hope you will find this in order and we are sorry we were not able to get this passenger over to you." As far as the Rosenwald Fund was concerned, they were done with Reed Peggram.

Concluding that asking for money from the Rosenwald Fund was fruitless, Reed developed a new plan. He would go with Arne to Argentina, which was neutral for most of World War II. He hoped that a Cambridge, Massachusetts, attorney named Theodore Wentworth Sprague, who was managing the distribution of funds from Monty's estate, would be able to send money to a bank in Argentina. Reed had to prove that he could financially support himself while living there in order to get a visa to enter the country. On June 25, 1941, he applied for an exit visa, stating that he had recently contacted an agency in Buenos Aires to reserve a Lisbon–to–Buenos Aires ticket on a ship. He asked the Bank of Italy for authorization from the Italian government for the importation of Argentine pesos so that he could pay his debts in Italy and pay for his airline ticket from Rome to Lisbon.

The Department of the Minister of the Interior assessed his visa request to determine if it was urgent and necessary. Reed gave the following reasons for the request: (1) He had intended to leave throughout the last year. His affairs were now in order since he had received an inheritance. (2) He was a twenty-seven-year-old professional writer who went to Europe to study and travel but now wanted to go to Argentina, believing he had better opportunities there. (3) Because he was of African origin, he suffered a lot in the winters of Europe and North America. He hoped to improve his health in the climate of Argentina. (4) His passport was stamped on June 23, 1941, and was valid until August 11, 1941, for air travel from Rome to Lisbon to Spain where he could travel on a nonbelligerent steamship to Argentina. He had one month left on his passport but could have it extended in Lisbon. And (5), he was informed by the Bank of Italy on June 27, 1941, that he would not get authorization to import Argentine pesos into Italy for his personal expenses without first knowing the response from the Minister of the Interior.

Reed's request to leave Italy was received favorably.

Now he could request that money be sent to Argentina and then transferred to Italy to pay his many personal debts, which included housing and food where he was living in Florence at Pensione Ospizio Evangelico Tedeso, Via dei Serragli 148. These worries contributed to his deteriorating mental health. The Prefecture of Florence noted that Reed also owed his former pensione, Marchetti, 2,800 lire.

In July 1941, Germany told the United States to close all of their consular offices in Nazi-occupied territories, which would include Italy. This made Arne's ability to obtain a visa to enter the United States impossible, and he would no longer be able to petition the US government for assistance in Italy.

Reed's family received an alarming telegram from him on August 21, 1941. Someone translated it from Italian to English for them since he was forbidden to send messages in English: "Dollars Argentina immediately. Inform Sprague situation very urgent. I can't wait any longer. Question of life and death."

Laura received a handwritten letter from Reed on September 7, 1941, tallying his debts to various people and his hope to go to Buenos Aires, but they needed $1,000 in a bank account under both of their names. Reed said, "You have no idea what we have been through this year. . . . We are worn and weary and weak."

Laura showed one of Reed's letters to Mary and she wrote to Reed saying that while she was sympathetic, he should just come home. Now Reed found his mother to be less sympathetic to his plight than Laura.

Somehow, Reed and Arne found the funds to make their way back to Genoa to make arrangements to leave Italy. While in Genoa, they encountered a Danish man from Copenhagen, Mogens Brandt, who had arrived on May 20, 1940, for what he called personal business affairs. He hadn't spoken to his family in over two years. The three men decided to get dinner at a local restaurant on October 2, 1941. They were observed.

Carlo Secillano Favagrossa, the undersecretary for war production for Italy, was having dinner in the same restaurant when he overheard three people with foreign accents sitting near his table. None of the people with him knew who they were. Favagrossa pointed them out to an army patrol and asked them to identify these foreigners. The Carabinieri "invited" the three foreigners to the police station. They established that Reed and Arne were authorized to be in Genoa in order to obtain entry visas to Argentina. Once their identities and reasons for being in Genoa were determined, they were immediately released. This incident was recorded in a report labeled "Supervision of foreigners."

For whatever reasons, perhaps their requests for visas were denied or one person was denied and the other refused to go, but Reed and Arne were still in Italy on December 7, 1941. On that day, the Japanese military attacked the US military base at Pearl

Harbor in Honolulu, Hawaii, shattering the United States' neutrality. The great loss of lives resulted in President Franklin D. Roosevelt declaring war on Japan and the United States entering World War II. A few days later the United States also declared war on Germany and Italy. Reed was now a citizen of a country at war with Italy.

TWELVE

An Overly Intimate Relationship

talian officials were concerned that Reed, suddenly a citizen of an enemy nation, and Arne, a citizen of a German-occupied nation, could potentially report on military movements in a major Italian city such as Florence. The two were sent to live in the town of Montecatini Terme about thirty-seven miles away in the province of Pistoia, still within the Tuscany region. They found accommodations at the Pensione Mariani located at Piazza Cesare Battisti 5. Under different circumstances, during good times, they would've enjoyed being in this town, which was the largest of the spa towns in Italy, where visitors flocked to bathe in the curative waters.

They were not as anonymous in this small town as they had been in Florence. Reed and Arne were once again being observed. The police informed Arne that he had to leave by March

13. He believed that a family member of the landlady, Mariani Alaide, had made a false complaint against them so that she could rent the room they occupied.

The minister of the interior suggested that the relationship between Arne and Reed was morally suspicious. Arne reluctantly moved to Borgo a Buggiano, which was still in the province of Pistoia. The distance between the two towns was just a little more than two miles, but the authorities hoped it would be just far enough away to prevent the two men from interacting.

Arne lived under even more precarious circumstances without funds from Reed. He asked to receive 1,200 lire from his joint bank account in Lisbon, which had been blocked due to the war. If these funds existed, it is not clear how the two accumulated the money in this account. Perhaps it came from Laura.

On May 1, 1942, Reed received clearance to exit Italy by the end of the month. Arrangements were made for him to be in Rome by June 4 in order to board a special train for American returnees that would leave the following day. He received a pass, but if he decided not to leave, he had to send an explicit declaration regarding his refusal to return to the United States. Reed declared his refusal to "return to my homeland." He told the Swiss Legation that they had misinterpreted the content of his recent letters. He did not want to repatriate. He wanted to receive money from his private funds in order to pay his considerable debts (around 10,000 lire) in Italy. He was now penniless despite stating that he had half a million lire in the United States—most likely referring to his inheritance from Monty.

Feeling pressured to leave Italy, Reed reached out to Ezra Pound, a prominent and controversial American writer living in

Italy. Beginning in 1941, Pound regularly delivered antisemitic broadcasts on Italian radio in support of the Fascist government.

Reed wrote to Pound at his address in Rapallo, about one hundred miles away from Reed. The location was called the Italian Riviera because of its coastline. Although Reed must've been aware of Pound's controversial and racist views, he did not address that in his letter.

His June 4, 1942, letter began with a strange introduction:

It is natural that I should have heard of you and that you should not have heard of me, because you publish what you think about and I do not. The first time I had an almost personal, but one-sided, contact with you was when I read your commentary, in 6 type-written pages, upon a bachelor's honors thesis which a Radcliffe girl whom I knew had written about your work.

However, all this is beside the point, and bores me as much as it bores you.

Reed asked:

Has our government the right to blackmail us into leaving Italy? I mean, has it the right to refuse to send us our subsidy because we do not care to return to America? I don't doubt that it will carry out its threat, but I wonder if there exists any constitutional justification for such a procedure (after all, the U.S. is at war to save the world for democracy). Naturally, I am not so naïve that I don't realize that

Mr. Roosevelt can and will do anything he likes at the present time. But I merely want to know to what extent one can rely upon the American constitution to protect the rights of individual U.S. citizens in an enemy country during war.

Reed continued that he was broke: "I personally haven't a soldo in Italy." He said, "I have definitely rejected the repeated proposals of the Swiss Legation to repatriate." Because, he said, his future plans differed from the ones suggested by the US State Department. He ended the missive strangely:

Meanwhile (and this is a fact, by the way, which Buddha and Jesus understood much better than Confucius), I am not at all frightened at what may happen to me, but really terribly annoyed. The reason why I tell you all about it is because there are lots of Americans but very few fellows.

It is unknown if Pound responded to this letter from a stranger, but he retained Reed's missive. This unusually worded letter might have been a sign of Reed's deteriorating mental health. He did not wait for a response from Pound. A few days after sending the letter, on June 8, 1942, Reed contacted the Prefecture of Rome and renounced his repatriation to the United States.

Back in Borgo a Buggiano, Arne was literally starving. He had not eaten in days and the owners of his pensione either refused to offer him any food or could not spare any since he had not been able to pay them. Arne's circumstances were becoming quite desperate. He was asked to leave the Savoia Hotel, but he was still waiting for funds from Lisbon, so he asked for a temporary subsidy that he would repay if necessary so that he could cover his room and board. The money was apparently blocked because the funds were from the United States. The minister of the interior wrote to Arne, "We would like to point out that the difficulties you have encountered so far in releasing and transferring the sum in question depend exclusively on the attitude taken by the United States of America towards our country following recent international events"—an unhelpful justification to Arne, whose basic needs were now caught up in global conflict. Arne had some success with the minister of the interior, who explored settling his housing and restaurant bills, which had come to 2,663 lire. Arne requested permission to join Reed, citing his financial dependence on him. He said he had no interest in returning to Denmark and was willing to renounce the temporary subsidy offered by the minister of the interior if he could be transferred to Montecarlo to be with Reed, who moved there on July 1, 1942. Montecarlo was about eight miles away from Reed's previous location in Montecatini Terme. This commune was located in the province of Lucca in Tuscany, about thirty-one miles west of Florence. Reed lived in places with dazzling views and stunning architecture, but could he even appreciate the beauty given the trying circumstances he was under?

Finally, Arne was allowed to go to Montecarlo in early August, perhaps to relieve the financial burden he was imposing on the places where he lived and dined while leaving various hotel and restaurant bills unpaid in Borgo a Buggiano after resorting to charity and public assistance in order to live. Now reunited, the pair had a new plan: Reed and Arne requested assistance to leave Italy for Switzerland through Lisbon. Reed asked if he could withdraw money from his own funds in the United States to pay his debts to Italian creditors, and the two petitioned the Italian government to be allowed to go to Switzerland, insisting that their departure had to be together, despite their differing nationalities, because of their financial codependency. The last reason was likely unpersuasive but demonstrated their fervent desire to be together. If their artistic and scholarly partnership would not persuade, they clearly hoped that a financial dependency would hold some water.

In August 1942, Reed was informed by the Swiss Legation that his subsidy would terminate in September following new instructions from the American government, who were no longer sending funds to citizens through the Swiss Legation. Once again, Reed and Arne asked for permission to leave Italy as soon as possible. Meanwhile, the police headquarters in Rome wanted to know why Reed had failed to board the special train in June bound for Lisbon when arrangements had been made to assist Americans to leave Europe and return to the United States. They wanted to know why he did not repatriate when he had an opportunity to do so. They wanted an explicit declaration about his refusal to return to his homeland. On September 18, 1942, the Italian government, the ministry, declared there was nothing preventing the granting of an exit visa for Reed to repatriate. It appears that the Swiss Legation now provided funds to Reed since the United States would not or could not send funds. He received 1,200 lire that he had to use to support both himself and Arne. Arne was authorized to exit the Kingdom of Italy in

October 1942 and to return to Denmark. He was told to report to the border police.

A November 27, 1942, letter in Reed's files stated, "After Italy's declaration of war with the United States, Peggram no longer received the monthly allowances mentioned above, but only a subsidy of 1000 lira fixed by the American Government and which was remitted to him through the Swiss Legation." Additionally, another letter on the same date stated:

> The aforementioned foreigners, who had long since begun procedures to leave the Kingdom, obtained the relevant authorization from the Ministry, but found themselves in the absolute impossibility of leaving because they lacked any means, and also because they were detained by the various creditors who demand payment of the numerous debts they contracted.

Because of their dire circumstances, the ministry was considering granting them "a daily subsidy and the accommodation allowance in the amount established for indigent internees" until the Swiss Legation could restore Reed's allowances.

Arne and Reed lived together in Montecarlo for several months until old accusations resurfaced. On February 4, 1943, the minister of the interior informed the chief of police in Rome that no charges were made against Reed and Arne, but in Montecarlo their "overly intimate relationship" was deplored but tolerated by the local authorities. The report noted that two foreigners—Reed was called "half-breed" or "mestizo," depending upon the translation, the only overt mention of his race—were living together in a single room with a single bed. Who knew this information and who reported it? The record was silent on the name of the informer. They were identified as two degenerates engaged in sexual perversion. The minister of the interior proposed to an official, the questore of Lucca, to transfer one of them to another municipality in Lucca.

This time Reed was told to leave. He departed Montecarlo around February 20, 1943, and was sent to Bagni di Lucca, a commune in Tuscany about thirty kilometers away at the foothills of the Apennine Mountains. In May 1943, Italian officials warned Arne not to go to Bagni di Lucca for any reason.

It is unclear what happened between May 1943 and September 1943, but it is likely that Reed and Arne were living apart and that both were in dismal straits financially and mentally. And their situation took a turn for the worse.

On September 8, 1943, Italy surrendered to the Allies following an armistice, but the Germans took over before the Allied forces arrived. Italian soldiers were expected to surrender, but instead many stripped off their uniforms and attempted to blend in, to avoid being sent to German prison camps. Germany now occupied northern Italy where Reed and Arne lived. Southern Italy was behind Allied lines that were steadily moving northward. In the north, Germans and Italian Fascists fought against partisan groups who threw hand grenades and sabotaged their enemies. The Nazis often retaliated by killing large numbers of citizens to avenge the killing of a single German soldier.

During this time, Laura and Mary did not hear from Reed, but they were contacted by the Boston Metropolitan Chapter of the American Red Cross, which wrote to Laura on October 21,

1943. The organization had received an inquiry from Reed through the International Red Cross. The enclosed inquiry was lost but they told Laura:

> If you come to this office we shall be glad to assist you in framing a message, to which you may add your signature in your own handwriting. THIS MUST BE DONE THROUGH OUR OFFICE AS CENSORSHIP RULES ARE VERY STRICT. Red Cross is always glad to serve you.

At least they knew that Reed was alive.

The Germans were now in charge of the section of Italy where Reed and Arne lived separate lives. In December 1944, Reed was interned in a concentration camp in Bagni di Lucca. Italy had established concentration camps after entering the war on June 10, 1940. There were about fifty camps scattered throughout the country. The newly constructed prisons had barbed wire and towers controlled by guards. Because both the Italian Red Cross and the International Committee of the Red Cross monitored them, few prisoners stated that they were mistreated. There was little to no violence. But eventually, the small number of Jewish prisoners were sent to German concentration camps in other parts of Europe, and only a few of them survived.

Despite the lack of violence, living conditions were wretched. The tents provided little shelter from the elements and were often flooded. The prisoners suffered during the cold-weather months and during the heat of the summer. The toilets and showers were filthy, reeking of urine and excrement and sweat.

There was barely food to feed the prisoners, "just enough soup to lead a miserable existence," Reed recalled. The food that they did receive was of poor quality. But he got used to starving.

The memoirs of other prisoners of war in Italy reported similar circumstances. In *Two Men and a Blanket*, Robert Garioch said the days were monotonous in the camp. They lived in tents and waited for Red Cross packages often containing soap, a few cigarettes, potted ham, cheese, hardtack (a dense biscuit or cracker), sugar, salt, dried fruit, oleomargarine, and powdered milk. Sometimes the prisoners ate margarine by itself to stave off hunger pains. Chicory was used as a coffee substitute. The prisoners were irritable because of hunger and the lack of nicotine. The camps were infested with lice. Books were scarce and were frequently swapped—anything to fill the time. Prisoners were often made to stand outside in the cold weather for the check-parade, which was used to make sure all the prisoners were accounted present. The guards would often lose count and had to start all over again. In another memoir, *Wine, Cheese & Bread*, Charles Webster Smith also described the constant hunger and filthy conditions. Additionally, they did not have a change of clothes. Each internee received a very small daily stipend from the Italian government. They could use the funds to buy meals. Foreign newspapers and books were forbidden. While mail was permitted, it was strictly monitored. The whole experience was described as "endlessly boring." For someone who loved to attend concerts, to read, to write, and to dine out, the boredom was almost as unbearable to Reed as the dirtiness of the camps.

At some point, Arne was interned too. A March 20, 1944, letter from the Prefecture of Lucca stated that Arne Gerdahn

Hauptmann was interned in the Colle di Compito concentration camp located about twenty six miles from where Reed was housed. This camp was originally established in 1942 as a prisoner-of-war camp to hold British soldiers. In 1943, when the Germans took over, Colle di Compito housed foreigners, Jewish people, and political prisoners. The camp was essentially a series of tents and the conditions were equally deplorable as the ones at Bagni di Lucca. After all Reed and Arne had gone through to remain together, the greatest agony must have been being separated and not knowing when or if they'd see one another again.

In June 1944, the prisoners in Colle di Compito were moved to the Bagni di Lucca camp after a machine-gun attack by Allied forces. Once again, Reed and Arne were reunited. They must have been shocked and relieved to see each other again after being apart for a little over a year. But they were soon separated and placed in solitary confinement after they were told a Dane should not be friends with a Negro. Reed claimed that the Nazis classified him as Aryan because he was Catholic, and he received better treatment and even apologies from his captors, who explained that they had to keep him and Arne imprisoned because they were prisoners of war.

Reed said, "For months we did not see a single human being. In fact, we saw nothing that was living. Not even bugs. There was no light, no action." To break up the monotony of his existence, Reed used his recently acquired Italian-language skills and previous German-language skills to translate between the prisoners and the prison guards. He lost track of time as each day blended into the next. There was nothing to do "but a great deal of time to think about what was in store for us."

Reed had no way of knowing that possible help was on the way. On a rainy Saturday morning on July 15, 1944, the SS *Mariposa* set sail from Newport News, Virginia, with the Buffalo Soldiers of the 370th Regimental Combat Team on board. They did not know their destination and could not have felt entirely sanguine about going to war. Adding to their anxiety, many had never been on a ship before, and several were seasick. Nine days after embarkation, the ship arrived in Oran, Algeria. The soldiers transferred to the navy ship USS *George C. Squier* and only then were they told that their final destination was Italy.

The troops were accompanied by embedded reporters sent by African American newspapers to provide war coverage. Many of their stories included messages for family and friends in the United States.

As far as we know, Reed did not write any letters to Laura and Mary while he was detained. Perhaps he was too depressed to write, or he did not have anything to write with or on or funds to purchase paper, envelopes, and postage stamps. Maybe he was ashamed about his predicament. After all, they had pleaded with him to come home and now he was in a most undesirable position. He could have been back in the United States, in Boston, years earlier when the war seemed imminent. They could not and would not know why he risked his life refusing to return. Reed spent his thirtieth birthday, July 26, 1944, in a concentration camp in Italy. But a few days later, things would take a dramatic turn.

There are differing accounts about how Reed and Arne escaped. In one version, the Italian government said Reed "lived in various concentration camps and prisons until July 31, 1944, when he was freed as a result of prisoner exchange with partisans, with whom he remained for a long time, until he returned to Florence on December 19, 1944." Did the Germans really negotiate with the Italian partisans? Given their usual violent reprisal tactics, why would they? And why would the Germans exchange an American and a Dane for German prisoners? And, if true, why didn't the United States take Reed into custody instead of letting him wander the countryside for months?

In a more probable account, suddenly Allied bombs fell near the Bagni di Lucca camp. The Allies had slowly but determinedly made their way up from southern Italy, capturing towns and pushing the Germans north. The attack was a surprise to the prisoners, cut off from the news, who took cover as guns strafed the ground. They choked on the smoke and shuddered when the earth shook. The prison guards left their posts unattended to fight the enemy. Reed had trouble seeing through the smoke, but he could hear the planes flying overhead. He looked for Arne. They had been separated in the camp, held in different tents.

Reed's ears rang, deafened by the sounds of machine guns and bombs. But occasionally there were breaks in the smoke. During the ensuing chaos, many prisoners attempted escape. Amid the smoke and the explosions, Reed found Arne. They did not have much time to gather their few belongings before they made their way into the mountains, fleeing for their lives. They escaped with just the clothes on their backs. But now what?

THIRTEEN

"Two Men with Strange Story Walk Through Battle Lines"

Reed and Arne swam across lakes and hiked through the bitter cold, rain, and the snow-covered Apennines, eating chestnuts to stave off hunger. They had escaped but they were not safe. They were still behind German lines without resources or their passports or any identification. They did not know whether they would survive. Perhaps Reed's patron, Saint Bernard, the patron saint of hikers and mountain climbers, was watching over him.

During the day they hid in the hills and, if lucky, in the homes of friendly partisans who offered them food, blankets, clothes, and sometimes boots, although those were often impossible to obtain, and a safe, warm place to stay. They had to rely on their instincts to determine who they could trust. Reed recalled, "We can't explain just how we did it, but soon as we figured that something was fishy, we moved on. So far, our guesses have been right."

The consequences for the partisans could be brutal if they were caught helping the escaped. Once, when thirty Nazi soldiers were killed, the Germans retaliated by killing over three hundred people—ten people for each Nazi. The soldiers had lost count. The Cervi family saw all seven of their sons executed for participation in the partisan resistance movement. Reed remembered, "We learned how to spot our friends on sight." They experienced hunger for such a long time that at some point it stopped hurting.

At night, they hid in barns, in the woods, and slept near the water, hoping that the Allied forces were near. They discussed where they would live after the war, fantasizing about their future, which they'd always envisioned together. Reed wanted to bring Arne to Boston or to New York City. His focus was now on his writing, and he seemed to give up his dream of teaching. Or maybe he would work as a translator given his facility with languages.

The biggest commodity desired by escaped prisoners was information. What were the safest routes? How close were the Allies? Were they coming to rescue them? Other escaped prisoners from Italian camps chronicled their experiences in *Wine, Cheese & Bread*: Once they bolted from the camps, they often had no idea where they were because they did not have any maps. They only knew that they were in the Apennines. They took cover during the day and walked at night. They often hid in caves in the bitter cold. The countryside was filled with escapees. Their clothing, including socks and shoes, was becoming threadbare, infested with fleas and lice. They even ate raw eggs given to them by a farmer because they were too hungry to worry about getting sick. All the time they wondered if the Allied forces would arrive. The months of fighting the cold, hunger, and abject living conditions and the fear of being found and killed took their toll both mentally and physically.

After months of wandering and hiding, finally, there was a miracle. In December 1944, near collapse from exhaustion and hunger, their clothes dirty, tattered, and torn, Reed and Arne encountered an advance patrol led by Lieutenant James Young of the all–African American 370th Regiment of the 92nd Division near a town on the Fifth Army front. It was pure happenstance. Reed must have thought he was experiencing an illusion. Not only were these American soldiers, but specifically African American soldiers, who surely would help him.

The soldiers provided them with clothes, soap (the first that they'd seen in a long while) for bathing and shaving, and food and cigarettes. They "appeared to be as happy as two kids talking about what Santa Claus had brought them." Afterward, Lieutenant Young introduced Reed and Arne to the embedded reporters. Reed was a curious sight—another Black man, slim with an erect carriage, who claimed he was an American even though he sounded British, identifying himself as a Phi Beta Kappa graduate of Harvard's Class of 1935 and now a doctoral student in comparative literature at Harvard studying in Paris. The troops and reporters were curious about him and clambered to take a photograph with him. *Stars and Stripes*, the American military daily newspaper, carried a picture and caption with Reed meeting another African American man, Sergeant Steve David Jr. of Greenville, Mississippi, towering over him.

Reed took a drag of his cigarette and told the reporters about his capture and his eventual escape. The story, riddled with factual inaccuracies and some exaggerations, still told a harrowing tale that was unbelievable. Yet it might also be true. Reed told many tales that the papers reported with a straight face—everything about the two men and the scene when they encountered them must have seemed bizarre, and their narrative was the one reporters had to go on. They claimed that while in the concentration camp they were both sentenced to death by firing squad, and were saved when the partisans raided Bagni di Lucca and they escaped.

The datelines of the subsequent articles were purposefully vague in order to not reveal the movements of the troops. One article simply said: "SOMEWHERE IN ITALY."

Reporter Max Johnson covered the Mediterranean in 1943 and 1944 for various African American newspapers, including the Baltimore *Afro-American*, which had a circulation of about 170,000 in the 1940s; the Cleveland *Call and Post*; and the New York *Amsterdam News*. Johnson arrived around August 1944 and covered the 92nd Division and 370th Regiment.

In one photograph, Johnson wears an army jacket, hat, pants, and combat boots and is writing in a notebook while Arne looks at him with his hands stuffed in the pockets of a long coat. He's wearing a suit jacket, pants, and a long scarf draped around his neck. Both men have footwear caked in mud. Reed does not have on a coat but is also wearing a suit jacket, a shirt and tie, cuffed pants, and a scarf wrapped around his neck, and it appears that a handkerchief is jutting out of a breast pocket. He is cradling a cigarette between two fingers while observing Johnson writing.

His other hand is stuffed in his pocket. With their casual body language, if you didn't know better, you would think they were at a cocktail party. This image appeared in the *Afro-American* under the headline "A Modern Damon and Pythias Talk for the AFRO." Johnson declared Reed and Arne's "bonds of friendship so strong that even the Nazis were unable to break them." The caption underneath the photograph said that they "have been inseparable since 1938 when they met while studying in Paris."

In another photograph the two men are intensely focused on something not captured in the photograph—perhaps Johnson. Behind and between the two men a firearm leans against a wall under a window. Reed acknowledged that he turned down opportunities to return home when he received an $11,000 inheritance from Monty but refused to leave Arne behind.

When Johnson asked Reed about his future plans, he said he was not concerned about returning to the United States. His main objective was to remain with Arne so they could work together in peace. He hoped that their racial differences would not be a problem, Reed said. "Racial differences are so silly," he said, "because our first desire is friendship and collaboration. We are in agreement on so many things: literature, music, ideas, and religion." But if they encountered what Reed called racial difficulties, they would go to France or Switzerland.

Reporter John Quincy Jordan was known as "the Rover" from his popular column "The Rambling Rover" in the *Journal and Guide* based in Norfolk, Virginia, with a circulation of approximately eighty thousand. Jordan became the paper's overseas war correspondent, going to Italy in June 1944 and spending time on the Gothic Line with the 92nd Division.

Jordan, wearing military fatigues and a helmet, was photographed with Reed and Arne. He called their tale "an amazing story of hunger and hardships in the custody of Fascists and Germans." He described the duo as an "odd, exciting pair" and recalled, "The sight of this Negro in civilian clothes and his blond Danish friend caused a mild sensation among our front-line troops as they marched in from the enemy lines." Additionally, "Peggram's flawless English and perfect elocution caused many a lifted eyebrow."

Douglass Hall was a reporter and on the editorial staff of the Baltimore *Afro-American*, usually covering news in the Washington, D.C., area. He was assigned to cover the 370th Infantry, 92nd Division, in Italy, where he was enlisted. The tale that he recorded was wildly different than the previous reports. Reed and Arne said they tried to escape to France but were captured by the Germans and spent time imprisoned in Italy, France, and Germany and for a time in a concentration camp. In this version, the Germans would allow Reed, an American, to leave but said that Arne had to stay and fight for Germany as a citizen from a German-occupied nation. They refused and were imprisoned in solitary and sentenced to death. What was likely true was Reed lamenting, "One of my greatest losses was my diploma from Harvard. They don't issue duplicates. But I still have my Phi Beta Kappa key." Their interview was suddenly interrupted by shells falling outside, which unnerved them and made them jump, giving them flashbacks, Reed said. "For a moment we thought we were back behind enemy lines." People began running for shelter and the three men lowered their voices even though they were miles from the fighting. They continued talking to Hall and said that they both had suffered nervous break-downs during the past six weeks. But Reed wanted his family in Dorchester (he gave the street—Sumner Court) to know that he was still alive, "although I can't explain just why or how." He clearly wanted Laura to read about him in the newspapers. They were too tired to think about what would happen when they went to the United States—Reed was still hopeful that Arne could obtain a visa—they just wanted to get some rest.

After their interviews, Lieutenant Young took Reed and Arne to be questioned by authorities at headquarters, likely to establish their identities since they were without their papers.

The reporters submitted their articles in the African American newspapers with purposefully provocative headlines: "Negro Escapes German Camp in Italy," "Two Scholars Flee Concentration Camp," "Two Men with Strange Story Walk Through Battle Lines," and "Boy Friends Scorn Bombs, Come Out OK." Was the last headline filled with innuendo? Had the reporters figured out the nature of the relationship between the two men?

Reed was finally able to write a letter to his family to let them know he was alive. They had not heard from each other in several years, since 1941. The letter was dated December 27, 1944, and written from Via della Pergola in Florence. As usual, it was written to his grandmother. He joked, as was his way with uncomfortable information, that he was back in Florence after three years of an exciting adventure. He thanked Laura for everything she had done for him when he'd first arrived in Italy in 1940 and 1941 and for loving him, trusting him, and believing in him. It was unusual for Reed to be so openly sentimental, but then the war had changed him. In some ways, for the worse.

As far as he knew, his widowed mother was now in Boston. And while he must have worried about her worrying about him—after his desperate pleas for money followed by such a prolonged silence—it was probably unimaginable to Reed that his beloved Laura would ever leave him. While his family feared that Reed had died during the war, he had no way of knowing that his grandmother was dead. The one person who always stood by his side was gone.

A month before Reed was rescued, Laura Reed died, on November 13, 1944, of stomach cancer at the age of seventy-five. She died before learning the fate of her firstborn grandchild. She was buried on November 16 at Mount Hope Cemetery in Boston. A woman of limited education and means, she had become a homeowner and provider, making sure that her daughter received a high school education and seeing her first grandchild attend some of the most elite schools in the United States and abroad.

On May 2, 1945, the Germans surrendered to the Allied forces in Italy.

It is unknown what happened to Reed and Arne after their rescue in December 1944, but at some point Reed was hospitalized in an American military hospital as his mental health deteriorated. Arne wrote to Reed's mother on June 17, 1945. He explained he was writing to her because Reed "has lost interest in everything for the moment."

Referring to Reed by his middle name, Edwin, he wrote:

I hasten to assure you that although your son has suffered a nervous break-down and is at present staying in a hospital, I do not think that his illness is serious. I have very good reasons to believe that he will be as well as ever within a month or two.

Perhaps Arne was being overly optimistic, or perhaps he was trying to allay Mary's fears with the contents of the brief, one-page letter. He assured Mary that "there is no cause for worries—he will be all right." He concluded that they were trying to get him transferred to an Italian hospital for a more radical cure, and "the american Consul at Florence has informed me that no repatriation of civilians will be possible for at least three months, so Edwin was forced to give up the idea of going to the States for his cure."

The war in Europe was over, but their predicament had not eased. After everything they'd been through, after how hard they'd fought to stay together for nearly five years in Italy, Arne went back to Denmark. Reed had no choice but to return to the United States and to an uncertain future.

FOURTEEN

Medfield State Hospital

Reed boarded the hospital ship USAHS *Algonquin* in Naples, Italy. These ships were easily identified and distinguished from military ships because they were painted white. They also flew their nation's flag beside the Red Cross flag, and were used to repatriate citizens such as Reed. It was a far cry from the send-off Reed received in the United States before he boarded the luxurious SS *Veendam* that he took to Europe.

No doubt Reed was proud that he had published two academic articles in *Modern Language Review* and the essay on André Gide in *Twice a Year* during his time abroad. But he had not completed the academic work on his doctoral dissertation that brought him to Paris in the first place. He was no longer mentally capable of returning to his studies at Harvard to finish his doctorate. He did not have a faculty position waiting for him, and besides, he was not capable of teaching at this time. Most important, he had to leave the love of his life behind in Europe.

Upon his arrival to the United States, he was hospitalized to continue the treatment begun in Italy. Did Reed fear that he would spend the rest of his life in mental institutions like his father? When he was in Copenhagen, he had written to his grandmother assuring her, "But you needn't think, dear, just because I am the same age my father was when the last war broke out that I am going to go mad too." And yet it appeared that he was repeating this tragedy.

Reed arrived in the United States two weeks after leaving Italy, landing in Charleston, South Carolina, on August 14, 1945. During his voyage, the United States dropped nuclear bombs on the Japanese cities of Hiroshima, on August 6, and Nagasaki, on August 9. Despite the mass destruction, Japan would not surrender until several weeks after Reed's return—on September 2, 1945—finally bringing World War II to an end.

Just twenty-four years old when he arrived in Paris, ready for a grand adventure in the City of Light, he returned to the United States as a thirty-one-year-old. Although he finally confessed that he did not intend to leave after his scheduled year, he had no idea that he would remain in Europe for seven years—most of them in distress with anxiety about his finances, food, and safety. He had spent nearly the entire war in Europe.

Reed became a patient at the Roper Hospital in Charleston. The superintendent of the hospital, F. O. Bates, wrote to his mother, Mary, on September 3, 1945. He told her that her August 31 letter was forwarded to the doctor in charge of Reed's case, and she could expect to hear soon about Reed's condition.

Two days later, J. R. Ridlen, the medical director of the US Public Health Service in Charleston, informed Mary that Reed was being sent to the US Public Health Service Hospital in Lexington, Kentucky, on September 5, "where he will be treated for a mental disorder. Please be assured that he will receive the best of care & medical attention that this organization can render."

Mary wrote to this institution on September 17. How worried she must've been. Her son was finally back on domestic soil, seven years since she last saw him, and he was still not in Boston. She was told by James V. Lowry, senior surgeon and clinical director, that Reed was admitted on September 7. Lowry explained:

At the time of admission your son was pleasant and coherent although he manifested some confusion as to the past together with some apprehension. During the short while he has been in the hospital there has been no essential change and it is felt that a definite prognosis may be given only after an extended period of observation. He is in good physical condition and appears to be quite content in his present surroundings.

He closed by stating, "We shall be glad to give you any information concerning changes which may occur in his condition from time to time."

Finally, Reed wrote to her on October 1. He began by telling her about his journey from Charleston to Lexington, where he had been for three weeks. He was still trying to figure out the requirements to get Arne to the United States. He said that "we both tried working in Italy after the arrival of American authorities, in order to show our willingness to cooperate with democratic freedom." Much of the letter, though, did not make sense, and reflected the drastic change in Reed's mental health. He continued, "I perhaps bother the consul a lot . . . but we were both cordially received and congratulated on our escape from danger since my friend was often mistaken for a German." And:

> I never suspected that immigration questions would be as ponderous, but I suppose grandmother would have been able to live longer even if I had been an axe murderer. The war of nerves is very agitating and sometimes makes me speak very harshly, but I do think there will probably be less racial discrimination over here now that the problem has been studied so exhaustively.

He signed off, "Affectionately, Reed."

During wartime, Mary lost her mother and worried about her son in war-torn Europe. The stress and sorrow must have been unimaginable. Reed did not seem to register or much care about his own illness; instead he focused much of the letter on Arne and getting him to the United States—which must have infuriated her.

Dr. Lowry contacted Mary again on November 15 with troubling news. He wrote:

> Since the time of admission, your son has shown confusion, withdrawal and expressed many peculiar ideas of unreality.

In the past few weeks his mental condition has deteriorated, and it is felt that electric shock or insulin therapy would be most beneficial in facilitating an early recovery from his mental illness. Widespread use of the treatment has proven that little danger is attendant to such procedures. Please sign and return the form in duplicate.

A self-addressed, stamped envelope was included for her convenience. He finished the letter with, "We wish to assure you that everything is being done for the welfare of your son."

It is unknown if Reed received insulin therapy, also known as insulin shock therapy. This was used to treat schizophrenia in the United States in the 1940s and 1950s. The therapy consisted of injecting patients with large doses of insulin to induce a coma. Treatment often was daily over several weeks. The theory was that it would shock the patient out of their symptoms—give them a jump start when they awakened. Ultimately, this method of treatment was discontinued because there was no scientific evidence that it worked.

Reed did receive electric shock treatment, introduced in the 1930s and commonly used to treat depression and other mental illnesses, including suicidal ideation and schizophrenia, by using an electric current to trigger a brief seizure in the brain that would hopefully rewire the brain and quickly treat the symptoms. It was thought then to be a safe and effective treatment.

Reed was transferred to Medfield State Hospital in Medfield, Massachusetts, which was closer to his family—approximately forty miles away, about an hour's drive. The hospital opened in

1896. The grounds, spreading across fifty-eight buildings on 166 acres of land, was called a campus, as if it was a university. The same Charles River that Reed saw flow by Harvard University streamed past this institution.

During his hospitalization at Medfield in the 1940s, there were approximately twenty-three hundred patients, double the planned capacity, to the chagrin of both staff and patients, whose safety suffered. There were reports of murders due to lack of adequate staff observations, and of staff killing patients by beatings or leaving them in scalding tubs of water.

The racial backgrounds of the patients were not recorded in the annual reports, but it was notable that Reed, unlike his father, was not treated in a segregated institution. Reed was an outlier in one area. He was thirty-one years old when he entered Medfield, at a time when 41 percent of the admissions were over the age of sixty and 22 percent were over the age of seventy.

A 1947 report showed an institution struggling but committed to the treatment of the patients. Lack of funds and staff shortages were a constant problem, as was a scarcity of building materials due to the war: patients' toilet and bathing facilities were antiquated and in need of upgrades; the male bath suites were discontinued due to lack of staff, and the female bath suites were only opened part-time. Reed loved to take baths and would have been deeply disappointed by the closure of the male bath suites. A major concern was the lack of spaces to isolate patients with tuberculosis. The wards were overcrowded and the need to construct separate buildings for isolation and treatment was deemed essential. Efforts to recruit more staff were unsuccessful and the vacancies put pressure on the existing staff to work overtime and to cover areas outside their scope of employment. Some patients, depending on the status of their illness, also helped to run the institution. Pay was low and the hospital struggled greatly to hire and retain doctors, nurses, and other staff. To make things worse, the rate of admissions for new patients did not decrease but remained the same. Many of the newly hired employees lacked experience in similar settings. The hospital once had a nursing school to train new employees, but that closed during the war.

If Reed continued practicing religion, he would have been able to attend Catholic services on Sundays and to go to confession. For recreation and entertainment, patients could watch picture shows, attend dances, and enjoy parties for Halloween, New Year's, and Post-Lenten. The hospital no longer had its own baseball team, but the Medfield Town Team played on the hospital grounds—it's unclear if the patients just watched or also competed. No doubt, Reed was unlikely to have participated, given his lack of interest in sports, but perhaps he watched the games only to break up the monotony of his days.

Medfield had its own farm and dairy, which provided enough milk to serve the patients. The chickens in the poultry plant provided eggs. However, the piggery was closed during the war and remained closed.

Reed continued receiving electric shock therapy for the next two years. On June 20, 1947, the superintendent of Medfield State Hospital contacted Mary with very disturbing news and a suggestion:

As you know, your son, Edwin Reed Peggram, has received several courses of electric shock treatments and these have had only a very temporary effect. Since he has shown no great improvement I am writing to you to suggest that you consider the advisability of having him studied for a brain operation known as pre-frontal lobotomy.

He recently was transferred from Ward D-3 to C2 as it appeared that he mad [*sic*] made an attempt at suicide by tightening his tie about his throat. In his case there is no [*sic*] only the danger of suicide but there is also danger of him doing harm to others because of his deep-set delusions. It is with this in mind that I am writing to you concerning the consideration for brain operation.

The superintendent explained that a lobotomy was an "operation [that] consists of making a small opening through the skull and cutting certain nerve fibers leading from the upper to the lower part of the brain."
He continued:

At the present time this work is being done at the *Boston Psychopathic Hospital.* This would not incur any additional expense for his care. It would be necessary to transfer him to the Boston Psychopathic Hospital for study for consideration for this operation. I am therefore enclosing a form requesting the operation and transfer to the Boston Psychopathic Hospital in case you decide you wish to have this considered. If you wish to speak to his physician here at the hospital or with your own family physician before deciding this would be perfectly agreeable to us.

The superintendent told Mary that there was a long waiting list and there were no guarantees that Reed would be accepted for the study. But if Mary had the financial means to have the procedure done privately, Reed could get the treatment sooner. Lobotomies were commonly used to treat schizophrenia and suicidal depression and delusions, anxiety, and hallucinations.

The Boston Psychopathic Hospital, founded in 1912, was approximately eighteen miles from Medfield State Hospital. According to the 1947 annual report from Medfield, "Thirty patients were transferred to the Boston Psychopathic Hospital for lobotomy operation." And, "The experience of this hospital's treatment by prefrontal lobotomy operation has been generally favorable and would seem to indicate that this procedure is a valid method of treatment." The report stated, "Serious complications among our cases referred for operation have been rare and in a few instances one or more epileptic convulsions have occurred and in three instances convulsions have continued to occur occasionally." It continued, "There has been a measurable degree of improvement in the mental condition of all of the lobotomized patients with one possible exception where no benefit has been evident after several months post-operative observation." And:

In a few, extremely severe cases with very gloomy prognosis, a spectacular improvement followed the operation. Sufficient time has not yet elapsed to allow a final appraisal to be made of the permanency of these results but, in general, the trend has seemed to suggest that gradual improvement continues to occur even many months after the operation is performed.

There's no official confirmation that Reed had a lobotomy, but his nephew Tarik thought he did, and his niece Debra recalled "seeing faint markings on the side of his head" like those commonly associated with where lobotomy instruments are placed. Reed had epilepsy, which was often a side effect of this treatment. However, despite his hospitalization, Debra said, "It's a miracle that his intellect survived."

Back home, in Dorchester, Reed's family suffered another loss. His younger brother Phillip Farrar Jr. died on March 24, 1946, of "lidel cell disease" at the age of twenty. Lidel cell disease was possibly related to sickle cell disease. He was buried in the same plot in Mount Hope Cemetery as Laura, who had died two years earlier. Reed's two brothers were approximately thirteen and twelve years younger than him. Besides his briefly living with them in Bayonne, New Jersey, they had not really grown up together. Reed rarely mentioned one without the other, often referring to them collectively as "the boys" in his letters. But no doubt he must've been sad to hear about the death of his young brother.

During this time, back in Denmark, Arne married Irmelin Agnete Marie Luise von Killinger Smidt, who went by Tota, in Copenhagen on September 3, 1948. Her maternal uncle was a notorious Nazi, Manfred von Killinger. Arne's occupation was listed as a writer on their marriage certificate and Tota's occupation was recorded as a painter. They resided at Sankt Annæ Gade 4B in the Christianshavn neighborhood of Copenhagen with the writer and poet Jens August Schade. Perhaps they were part of an artists' collective.

As Arne settled into a domestic life in Copenhagen, Reed was discharged from Medfield State Hospital after four years of treatment, the same amount of time he spent at Harvard as an undergraduate. He went to live with his mother in Dorchester in her two-family home.

FIFTEEN

Dorchester Redux

Harvard College Class of 1935
Fifteenth Anniversary Report, 1950

After the Second World War, which I saw from Denmark and Italy, I passed through four years of hospitalization for a nervous breakdown. It appeared that I had been using seven languages more fluently than I was capable of doing.

Reed was unusually frank in his update by sharing his mental health diagnosis. Examples of more typical entries preceded and succeeded Reed's entry: Roy Messer Pearson Jr. gave the name of his wife and the names and birthdates of his daughter and son, listing his additional degree and places of employment and hobbies. Everett Hall Perkins listed his wife and the date of their marriage and the name and birthdate of his stepson, his postgraduate degree, and his employment in various schools and service in the air force. What did Reed's fellow former classmates think of his unusual entry that mentioned a taboo subject like his mental health?

After his discharge from Medfield, Reed lived upstairs at 1 Sumner Court in Dorchester, sharing the apartment with Mary. In order to support herself and her eldest child, Mary, now fifty-nine years old, worked in an office a few hours a week. If Laura had survived, she would've been pleased to see Mary working in an office instead of cleaning homes. Mary was now Reed's legal guardian, much to his chagrin. He felt that only his grandmother had ever really cared for him and had once told Laura that he considered her to be his mother, and he viewed Mary as more like a sister.

Reed's occupation, according to the census, was "unable to work." Although he wanted to work, Mary thought he was not capable, or perhaps she was following the advice of the medical professionals, who recommended that patients who had received electric shock therapy and a lobotomy resist doing work that was too taxing. So Reed occasionally did some translations for pay and lived off unknown money—perhaps the inheritance from Monty. Maybe he still dreamed of publishing his children's book about the adventures of Pusé the cat, or the translated poems of Jens Peter Jacobsen that he worked on with Arne in Copenhagen, but those manuscripts were either lost or buried in Italy. Reed surrounded himself with books, chain-smoked cigarettes, and listened to the classical music records he got at the main branch of the Boston Public Library in Copley Square. He visited the library often. But perhaps he went there for an alternative purpose. In 1978, the police set up a sting operation in the Copley Square library, Reed's favorite branch, after numerous complaints from male patrons, who were either propositioned or saw sexual encounters in the bathrooms in the library's basement. Nearly one hundred men were arrested in a ten-day sweep, including a college professor, business executives, schoolteachers, students, and graduate students. Luckily, Reed was not there during that time, although it is unknown if he ever used the library for that purpose.

Books in his personal library reflected his interest in understanding his sexuality. Titles included an 1886 book, *Psychopathia Sexualis, with Especial Reference to the Antipathic Sexual Instinct, a Medico-Forensic Study* by Dr. R. v. Krafft-Ebing, described as one of the earliest books to discuss homosexuality. Originally published in German, it was translated into many languages, including English. Another book in Reed's library was the 1908 publication *The Sexual Life of Our Time: In Its Relations to Modern Civilization* by Iwan Bloch, M.D., that discussed sexuality and sexual behavior, including sexual pathology.

Reed's brother Vincent lived downstairs and worked as a waiter for the railroad. His wife, Martha, was a homemaker. They lived with their daughter, Patricia, and Martha's mother, Martha Holliday. Two additional children later joined the household: a son, Vincent (who eventually went by Tarik), and a daughter, Debra, who was called Deb.

Back in Copenhagen, Arne's first son, Morten Michael von Killinger Hauptmann, was born in 1950. But by the time their second son, Marc, was born on December 6, 1952, the couple had already divorced, on March 6, 1952. Tota married for a second time in 1956, in Vridsløselille Statsfængsel, a prison west of Copenhagen, by the prison vicar. Her new husband, Preben

Frode Kurt Andersen, was incarcerated. It was another short-lived marriage; Preben died in Bispebjerg Hospital on October 17, 1957. Tota married for a third and final time to John Fussinger in 1958 a few months after their daughter, Helle, was born. Arne's two sons would use John's surname.

In 1950, Reed's father, Harvey, remained a patient at the Veterans Administration hospital in Alabama. The language involving people in mental institutions had evolved. Instead of being called an inmate like in the previous census records, Harvey was now listed as a patient. He died on August 16, 1956, of pulmonary edema, or fluid in his lungs, associated with his arteriosclerotic heart disease. He was sixty-four years old and had spent thirty-six years in mental institutions. Harvey's survivors included his brother and official next of kin Oscar E. Pegram, sister Ella Pegram, niece Ella Mae Wiggins, nephew David Pegram, and other relatives Richard and Gilbert Peggram. Reed was not listed in obituaries as a pallbearer, an attendee at the funeral, or even as a survivor. It is unknown if Reed knew that his father was dead.

Like Reed, Harvey had a life that began with much promise. He dreamed of being an entertainer and a poet. He traveled and performed in various states before the Great War took him to France, and, like his son, he returned to the United States mentally disabled. Despite his dreams and migrating to the North, Harvey was buried in Poplar Grove National Cemetery, a military cemetery in Petersburg, Virginia, in Dinwiddie County, the same place where his life had begun.

A year later, on July 16, 1957, Harvey's seventy-year-old sister Ella died. She was a patient at Central State Hospital where

Harvey was initially hospitalized in Petersburg. Did mental illness run in the family? Was Harvey's and Reed's mental illness inherited, caused by genetics, instead of the trauma of two different wars? Ella was a patient for five years and five months before she died. Her cause of death was listed as arteriosclerotic heart disease with meningovascular syphilis and acute glaucoma.

Harvard Class of 1935
Twenty-Fifth Anniversary Report, 1960

My own postgraduate history is no particular triumph. . . . Either I am too lazy or too comfortable (scarcely the latter) to function as a professional translator. . . . All of which reduces my current occupation to singing in Episcopal Church choirs and cultivating enough courage to offer my antique, revised, unpublished doctoral dissertation to a publisher.

He concluded with:

My congratulations, meanwhile, to whatever more ambitious colleague has been recognized as V.I.P.

Additionally, Reed wrote:

Eccentrically, I prefer association with college students to the companionship of my contemporaries who finished twenty-five years ago. The aspirations of these young idealists may indeed soar to unattainable heights, but they are uncolored by cynical emphasis upon subjective disillusions.

The report contained two photographs of Reed, a younger one from around the time of his graduation and a current photograph with his hair receding in the front and at the temples.

In comparison, his classmate Everett Hall Perkins, who followed alphabetically, was now the head of the Modern Language Department at the Columbus Academy in Ohio. He was still married and now had a daughter along with his stepson.

During the 1960s and the early part of the 1970s, to keep himself occupied, Reed sang in a church choir in Beacon Hill every Sunday after converting to High Episcopalianism. He had ill-fated love affairs with several, often-closeted, white men, including a five-year affair with a man named Michael, who was married and twenty years his junior, until Michael eventually abandoned him. Another man, David, visited Reed regularly. Reed also dated Joe, an Italian American man, whose father urged Reed's mother to make Reed leave his son. No man would ever live up to what Arne had been for Reed and the life they'd shared before circumstances cleaved them forever apart.

Harvard College Class of 1935
Fortieth Anniversary Report, 1975

On this preview of our Fiftieth Reunion we have all surely experienced far greater personality (and physical) changes than we exhibited at our Twenty-fifth.

Nevertheless, there manage to persevere inexplicable qualities absorbed as Harvard undergraduates which enable any alumnus to recognize another almost immediately, without identification. My own associations are more varied than specific, gratifying in a quiet way, where there is no hint of glamour.

Reed's occupation was listed as translator, although it is not clear how much work he actually conducted. He now lived on 30 Vesta Road in Dorchester, Massachusetts, with his mother. His classmate Everett Hall Perkins was now retired and divorced and had taken up photography as a hobby.

Harvard College Class of 1935
Forty-Fifth Anniversary Report, 1980

In retirement, I have lately been learning instead of teaching linguistics, specifically Ancient Greek, the weakest of the seven or eight Indo-European languages which I already know.

Former classmate Roy Messer Pearson Jr.'s entry stood in stark contrast to Reed's. Pearson wrote a more traditional update stating that he was now retired as the seminary president at the Andover Newton Theological School. He was still married and now had four grandchildren. He hoped "to have a little more time for reading, writing, and chopping wood." If Reed had been white and heterosexual, would his life have been like his classmates'? If the world around him had been different, would Reed have become a professor? Perhaps at Harvard as the chair of the French Department?

Mary died on December 8, 1980, at ninety years old. Her life had not been easy. She grew up fatherless. She later wed an artist, which must have been exciting until he was drafted to serve in World War I and returned home completely mentally disabled, leaving her as a single mother to raise a five-year-old son with assistance from her mother. Although her mother had hoped that Mary would escape having to do domestic work, Mary briefly did just that until she remarried. Was it a practical marriage? Her second husband could not have been more different from her first. He was much older than her, and although he was a hard worker, he had limited education. Her relationship with her son, Reed, had not been the one that she had hoped for, and was not helped by her second husband, who drove a wedge between them. Widowed at age fifty, she was left alone to raise two teenage sons. While worried about Reed in war-torn Europe and not hearing from him for years, she lost her mother. When her firstborn returned, he was hospitalized in a mental institution for years. And her son Phillip died at age twenty. She spent the last years of her life taking care of Reed.

Mary was survived by her sons Reed and Vincent and her daughter-in-law, Martha, three grandchildren, three great-grandchildren, and other relatives. Instead of flowers, mourners were asked to donate in her memory to the United Negro College Fund—demonstrating how important she thought education was for African Americans even though she never had the opportunity to study for a college degree.

Reed's later years were spent with occasional dinners with

friends and family gatherings and barbecues. Although he took phenobarbital for his epilepsy and was warned against consuming alcohol, he would still drink red wine. During these times, he would frequently talk to his nephew Tarik about his relationships with Laura and Mary, reminiscing about things in the past, and his feelings—particularly after imbibing. Reed also talked about academic things with his nephew, including topics related to language and literature, the loves that never left him.

A lifelong heavy smoker, Reed developed emphysema, eventually needing to use oxygen tanks, and struggled to walk. When family members refused to purchase his desired Pall Mall cigarettes, he resorted to hoarding tobacco.

Harvard Class of 1935
Fiftieth Anniversary Report, 1985

Reed Edwin Peggram died on April 20, 1982, at Dorchester, Massachusetts.

Reed died of a myocardial infarction due to coronary artery disease. He'd had a massive heart attack and was found dead in his study surrounded by his books. At age sixty-seven, after traveling all over Europe, dreaming of a life abroad filled with music and intellectual pursuits, his life ended where it had begun in Dorchester. He never saw Arne again.

Endings

During World War II, back in Paris, Sylvia Beach, the proprietor of the Shakespeare and Company bookstore and lending library where Reed was a member, was forced to close after the occupation of Paris in 1941 when she refused to sell a book to a Nazi. She was interned for six months before being released. She never reopened her bookstore. The current Shakespeare and Company bookstore, which draws large lines, is in a different location with an unrelated owner. Beach died in 1962.

Cyril and Olgy, a.k.a. "the kittens," both professors at Georgetown, continued living together as "cousins." They co-published a book, *The Order of Malta and the Russian Empire*, in 1969. On September 29, 1969, Olgy died at the age of seventy-three. He was buried in Mount Olivet Cemetery in Washington, D.C. Despite a love affair that began in the 1930s and lasted for decades, no mention was made of Cyril, the most significant person in Olgy's life, in tributes or in an obituary. In despair, Cyril retired from Georgetown University the following year at age fifty-six and moved to Rome.

Composer Howard Swanson, the other Rosenwald Fellow in Paris, left France when the Nazis invaded. Upon his return to the United States in 1941 he took an unusual job at the Internal Revenue Service as a file clerk for two years before returning to his passion—music composition. He had success getting his songs performed, but he reached a new level of accomplishment when Marian Anderson sang his version of a Langston Hughes poem, "The Negro Speaks of Rivers," at Carnegie Hall. Later that year, Howard's "Short Symphony" was performed by the New York Philharmonic. That symphony won the 1951 Music Critics' Award as the best new orchestral work. As a result of these successes, his work was played in many venues in 1951. He continued to win awards and other honors in 1952, including a Guggenheim. He used the funds to return to Europe, where he lived in Paris and Vienna from 1952 until 1965. He lived the life that Reed desired. While in Paris, Howard was part of the writer James Baldwin's social circle. Swanson eventually returned to the United States in 1965 and died in New York City on November 12, 1978, at the age of seventy-one.

At the end of 1979, Reed lost a dear friend. It is unknown if they stayed in touch after their adventures in Europe, but Newton Arnold was dead at age sixty-three in New York City after being hit by a car. He was working as a comptroller for Hansley Industry Inc. Newton left behind a widow, Irene, and two sisters. Had they lost touch? Newton returned to the United States in 1939 after completing his year abroad in Switzerland. He was drafted and served as a captain in the army during World War II, receiving the Legion of Merit "for exceptionally meritorious conduct in the performance of outstanding services as Staff Specialist, Consultant and Research Specialist on Germany" between July 1, 1944, and May 8, 1945. Given that he was beaten in Germany for not showing Adolf Hitler respect after a speech, this must've been quite satisfying. Newton eventually finished his thesis, "A Swiss Resurrection Play of the Sixteenth Century," at Columbia University in 1949. Reed was originally scheduled to leave Europe with Newton in 1939 after studying in Paris. How would his life have been different if he had left, never fallen in love with Arne, and returned to finish his doctoral degree at Harvard?

Bertie, Reed's friend in Copenhagen, who so generously let him live in his attic when World War II began, survived Denmark's Nazi occupation, which ended on May 5, 1945. His brother, Erik Budtz-Christensen, had joined the Danish resistance. Bertie died on December 12, 1983, at the age of seventy-four. He shared an apartment in Copenhagen with Peder Lauridsen for twenty-one years, until his death. Peder was listed as a good friend in Bertie's funeral notice. This was most likely another long-term queer relationship lost to history.

Reed's former editor Dorothy Norman, from *Twice a Year*, continued her involvement in liberal causes in the United States and abroad after World War II. She died in 1997 at the age of ninety-two.

Nearly thirty years after Olgy's death, Cyril died on February 15, 1997, at age eighty-three. He was buried across the ocean from his true love, in the chapel of the Knights of Malta. A several-page-long *In Memoriam* dedicated to Cyril in the *Journal of the Society for Armenian Studies* did not mention his relationship with Olgy. Their decades-long relationship was buried in historical records.

Arne entered the Bispebjerg Hospital in Copenhagen on September 16, 1988. He remained hospitalized for almost three months before succumbing to an unknown illness on December 3, 1988. Arne Gerdahn Hauptmann was seventy-four years old. A notice in the newspaper suggested that relatives contact the quartermaster at the hospital's chapel as soon as possible. This might have been routine, but it suggested an estrangement from his family and the need for someone to collect his body. When his sons were informed that their father had died, they first thought it was their estranged stepfather—they did not grow up in a happy home. Dutifully, they had Arne cremated, and his urn is buried in Bispebjerg Cemetery in Copenhagen in the section called the grave of the unknowns.

Arne's sons had been forbidden to have any contact with him by their stepfather. Despite that, Marc met Arne approximately three or four times in his life. The last time he saw his father he was either twelve or thirteen in 1964 or 1965, when he also met Arne's brother, Sven Hauptmann, a painter who lived in France. Marc's mother said very little about Arne, just bits and pieces. Marc knew Arne was interned in Italy during the war and was told that Arne's experience made it very difficult for him to participate in society upon his return. He viewed Arne's postwar lived experience as similar to being in the military and living from day to day without being able to make plans other than trying to survive. Tota told Marc that "it was impossible to make agreements" with Arne. Initially Arne worked as a tour guide after the war because he was fluent in many languages like Reed. Marc knew his father was bisexual, but had never heard of Reed Peggram.

Marc was aware of the book of poems, *Declaration*, that Arne published in English with a Danish publisher in 1971. The collection contained a poem, "Ante," that appeared to reference his relationship with Reed. It began:

> I remember once—
> we were walking together,
> perhaps in a year or two, you said,
> and we made plans, and discussed
> whether it should be in New York
> —in Paris—or maybe
> somewhere in China.
> We did not know then—
> although perhaps we did suspect it—
> that the apples would not ripen
> on the trees
> that year
> or the next
> or ever.

Epilogue

After I met Reed's great-niece Teju in the fall of 2016, she wrote an article, "Urban Up Close: My History Matters, Even in Copenhagen." Teju said:

To be sitting in Copenhagen hearing the phenomenal unwritten story of my great uncle told by someone who does not know him or me is a feeling I have not found the words to describe. I'm still wondering how I even ended up in Copenhagen, so to see my family history continue to unfold in a place so far from any of my known ancestry is amazing. I am listening to this keynote, completely undone—and at the same time realizing how important Uncle Reed is to the history of Blacks abroad. I myself am Black and abroad and some people believe that we become our ancestors. There's much more that needs to be said about Uncle Reed, but I will leave it for another time.

Although Uncle Reed died long before I was born, he exists in stories from my father and grandfather. I never met him, but I'm reminded of his presence as my sister and I live out our lives and own paths in Europe.

During the ensuing years, I stayed in touch with Teju, interviewed her father, and received copies of approximately two hundred letters that Reed wrote to his grandmother and mother in the 1930s and 1940s from New York City, Paris, Copenhagen, and Florence. I felt like I got to know parts of Reed's family. In 2021, I was sad to hear about the sudden death of Deb's daughter Virginia-Jeni Akila Parkman at age thirty. She was a talented scientist.

In January 2023, I took the Amtrak train from Newark, New Jersey, where I was visiting my family, to Boston. My hotel was in the Back Bay section—an ideal location that Deb recommended in order for me to travel to the sites that were important in Reed's life. My first stop was across the Charles River to Cambridge to see Harvard Yard and Widener Library where I imagined Reed spent many evenings studying and researching for his classes and theses. I walked around the magnificent Boston Public Library at Copley Square and understood why Reed liked to spend so much time in this ornate building. I took a taxi to the Dorchester Historical Society, the former home of Frank L. Clapp, where Laura toiled and where Reed met and impressed Clapp. I tried to imagine both Reed and Laura in this home.

That afternoon, Reed's niece Deb picked me up at my hotel. I had several bouquets of flowers to place on the graves—not knowing that several family members were buried in the same plot under one headstone.

Our first stop was at Mount Hope Cemetery. It began as a private cemetery in 1852. In 1857, the city of Boston purchased its eighty-five acres. Currently, it covers 125 acres. A cemetery worker led us to the final resting place of Reed's grandmother and brother. The marker read:

Mother
LAURA REED
1869–1944

Her Grandson
PHILLIP H FARRAR
1925–1946

We drove a relatively short distance, less than three miles, to our next destination—the Forest Hills Cemetery. This appeared to be a much fancier cemetery, with stunning statues and a body of water called Lake Hibiscus in the middle. Founded in 1848, it now covers 275 acres and is part of the National Register of Historic Places. It offers a variety of walking and self-guided tours of the beautiful grounds. Famous people buried there include poets E. E. Cummings and Anne Sexton, playwright Eugene O'Neill, and abolitionist William Lloyd Garrison.

The stone said:

FARRAR

1927 **MARTHA VIRGINIA** 1990

1890 **MARY R.** 1980

1915 **REED E. PEGGRAM** 1982

FOREVER IN OUR HEARTS

Deb immediately acknowledged that Reed's birth year was incorrect; it should've read 1914. Additionally, Reed would have been unhappy to be buried under the name FARRAR so prominently displayed, given his feelings about his stepfather. He would've preferred to be buried with his dearly loved grandmother, according to a relative. I placed a bouquet of flowers by the headstone. Later, I read that another biographer left a pen on his subject's grave because he was a writer. Reed would've loved the pricey Cross pen I purchased as a souvenir from the gift shop at the main branch of the Boston Public Library.

An astonishing sixty-six years after graduating from the Boston Latin School, Charles Piper, a fellow Class of 1931 alumnus, wrote a letter to the *Los Angeles Times* about an affirmative action lawsuit brought against Boston Latin School. Reed evidently made a strong impression on this classmate, who misguidedly used Reed's academic success as an argument against affirmative action. He was responding to Michael McLaughlin's lawsuit against Boston Latin School for failing to admit his daughter, who scored higher than approximately one hundred Black and Latino students. In a letter published on February 2, 1997, under the title "Quality, Not Race, Should Count," Piper of Rancho Palos Verdes, California, said:

> I attended Boston Latin with the class of 1931. The brightest student in my homeroom was Reed Edwin Peggram, the first black person I had ever known. Racial quotas and set-asides had not been invented. Peggram and everyone else at Boston

Latin was academically qualified. Reed Peggram lived in the black neighborhood of Dorchester, and his mother washed people's clothes to support them. Reed ultimately graduated from the Sorbonne. I thought you might like to know how it was before quotas and set-asides.

Judge Arthur Garrity Jr. ruled that Boston Latin School could not use racial quotas and ordered them to admit Julia McLaughlin. Ironically, Judge Garrity was the same judge who ordered Boston schools to desegregate in the 1970s. The resulting ugly outcry from many white citizens has never been forgotten.

In 2021, in order to increase the socioeconomic diversity of students at Boston Latin School, the institution wanted its admissions committee to admit students from eight distinct neighborhoods in Boston, guaranteeing admissions to students from the entire city. This new system was designed to replace the old system that focused solely on grades and test scores. White and Asian students were disproportionately represented in the current student body. In 2022, parents filed a lawsuit to prevent this new policy. During this time, there was another lawsuit against new affirmative action admissions policies at Reed's other alma mater, Harvard University. In 2023, the majority-conservative US Supreme Court rejected Harvard's race-conscious admissions policies. But in 2024, the Supreme Court refused to hear challenges to the proposed changes in the admissions policies at elite public schools in Boston.

Despite the constant legal cases that sought to limit access to higher education for African Americans and others, Reed's family thrived. Tarik's daughter Shola lived in Paris for several years while pursuing an acting and singing career. And his other daughter, Teju, studied abroad in Denmark, Ireland, Spain, and Austria. Reed's relatives would come to inhabit Reed's former spaces and beyond, their resolve no doubt bolstered by the knowledge of all that Reed had done.

On September 22, 2023, Reed's younger brother Vincent died at the age of ninety-six after a long battle with dementia. Because of his illness, I did not speak with him about his brother. He was buried in Forest Hills Cemetery, joining other family members, including Reed.

In June 2024, I met Marc Fussinger, Arne's youngest son, in a café in Copenhagen along with his wife of nearly twenty years, Carmen, a Brazilian woman of African descent. We chatted and took pictures after Marc filled me in on some family history. They invited me to dinner at a Lebanese restaurant back in their Copenhagen neighborhood called Nordvest. Marc shared a rare picture he had of his father as an older man. Marc looked eerily like Arne.

I invited Reed's niece Deb to stay with me in the two-bedroom, two-bath apartment I rented in Copenhagen for two months during the summer of 2024. I was living in the Christianshavn section of the city just blocks from where Arne lived when he got married. We visited places where Reed went, including a train trip to Kronborg Castle, which Reed once went to see with Bertie, as well as where Reed lived with Bertie at the start of World War II and the location in Vesterbro where Arne and Reed lived in the Central Hotel. A friend suggested that they might have socialized at Café Intime, a still-existing gay bar founded in the 1920s. We spent a fun evening listening to live jazz in this tiny café in Frederiksberg, a small municipality surrounded by Copenhagen.

REED HAD OVERCOME BEING QUEER, Black, and poor in a bigoted world that sought to thwart his advancement at every turn. He went on to attend some of the most prestigious institutions in the world, graduating Phi Beta Kappa, magna cum laude, and earning prestigious scholarships. Reed embodied the hope his grandmother, fleeing the South, had passed down to him. He had exceeded his ancestors' wildest dreams. But just when he had found happiness, world events thwarted his ambitions and his ability to experience joy with the man who was undoubtedly the love of his life.

In the end the thing that broke Reed Edwin Peggram was not the racists or the homophobes or even the Nazis, but the toll that all those forces took on his mental health. And yet, as sad as the end of his life may have been, there is still triumph in his tale.

Reed did not know whether he would survive World War II, but if he did, he told Mary that he planned to write a book about his life and his journeys. He lived, for a brief moment, an exciting life in Boston, New York City, Paris, Copenhagen, and Florence, filled with art, music, and love. While he was never able to write that book, his story was not lost. This is that book.

When I think of Reed, I will always picture him heading out

of Boston to New York City, standing on the deck of the ship even though the rest of the passengers were hiding below from the storm. I picture his eyes shining and his lips curling up at their edges as he looked up, fearless and ready, at the massive bolts of lightning that danced across the sky.

Acknowledgments

I would like to thank Reed's late grandmother and mother for keeping the letters he sent from New York City, Paris, Copenhagen, and Florence. I would like to especially thank his niece Debra "Deb" Farrar-Parkman for preserving the letters after his death. These letters were crucial for telling Reed's story. I also want to thank Deb for giving me a tour around Boston to see places where Reed lived, went to school, and his final resting place. Reed's nephew Dr. Tarik Farrar generously shared his memories of his uncle. I'll cherish the serendipitous encounter in Copenhagen with Teju Adisa-Farrar, Reed's great-niece, who told me about the existence of Reed's letters.

My agent, Jennifer Herrera at the David Black Agency, immediately recognized the potential of turning my article, "The Gay Black American Who Stared Down Nazis in the Name of Love," edited by William Akers at *Narratively*, into a book and guided me in the process.

Emily Wunderlich, an excellent and supportive editor at Viking, helped to make this process both informative and enjoyable. I couldn't have asked for a better editor. Her editorial assistant, Carlos Zayas-Pons, was a joy to work with. I am grateful for their positive energy. And I am thankful for all the people at Penguin Random House who worked behind the scenes.

Archivists and librarians are essential to the work of biographers. Several helped me along the way including: Edward Copenhagen, reference archivist, Harvard University Archives; Valerie Uber of the Boston Latin School Archives; Meghan Capone, archivist for reference and outreach, City of Boston Archives; Diona E. Layden and Connor Joseph, special collections librarians at the John Hope and Aurelia E. Franklin Library at Fisk University; Lisa C. Moore, head of research services, Amistad Research Center at Tulane University; Micaela Sullivan-Fowler, distinguished academic librarian, University of Wisconsin–Madison; Mark Eden Horowitz, senior music specialist, Music Division, Library of Congress, Leonard Bernstein Collection; and Spencer Bowman, reference and archivist librarian at Tacoma Public Library, who introduced me to David F. Martin, curator and author, who included the portrait of Reed by Thomas Handforth in an exhibition at the Cascadia Art Museum and in his book *The Lavender Palette: Gay Culture and the Art of Washington State.*

To Deyane Moses, director, programs and partnerships, Afro Charities, for supplying the photographs from the pages of the Baltimore *Afro-American* of Reed and Arne in Italy.

Presentations at the Collegium for African American Research (CAAR) conference in Berlin; the National Nordic Museum in Seattle; and the Society for the Advancement of Scandinavian Study (SASS) conference provided wonderful feedback.

I published a second article, "Unpacking Reed Peggram's Library," in the special issues of *Modernism/modernity* and *The Jour-*

nal of Cultural Analytics about the World of Shakespeare and Company, co-edited by Joshua Kotin and Rebecca Sutton Koeser.

I honed my writing skills by taking Meghan O'Gieblyn's class "Writing the Personal Essay" through *Creative Nonfiction* and Mayuhk Sen's "How to Write Profiles and Biographies" course through *Off Assignment.*

Genealogist Shari Jensen sifted through Danish records to find critical information about Reed's friend Bertie and about what happened to Arne after World War II. She provided contact information for his son Marc Fussinger. I met Marc and his wife, Carmen, in Copenhagen, where he filled me in on family history and treated me to dinner.

Thank you to Anders Larsen for interviewing me for his podcast episode, "Why Isn't This a Movie? The Story of Reed Edwin Peggram."

Artists residencies at Hedgebrook, Ucross, the Virginia Center for the Creative Arts, and Yaddo provided fantastic writing retreats and nourishment.

This research was part of a larger project about African Americans in twentieth-century Denmark that received funding from the American-Scandinavian Foundation, the Lois Roth Foundation, and the Fulbright Program.

My institution, the University of Wisconsin–Madison, provided funding and fellowship for this project through the Office of the Vice Chancellor for Research and Graduate Education, the Graduate School, and the Institute for Research in the Humanities' Race, Ethnicity, and Indigeneity Faculty Fellowship. My colleagues in the Department of African American Studies writing group: Christy Clark-Pujara, Thulani Davis, Christina

Greene, Brenda Gayle Plummer, and April Haynes (History) critiqued early writings about Reed Peggram. I also want to thank staff in my department including Veneta Kovacs for processing my reimbursements, and Hope Kelham for taking the author's photo.

I am grateful for friends who listened and discussed with me the process of making this book: Raquel Von Cogell, Sandra Adell, Anne Lucke, Furaha Norton, Tochukwu Okafor, Karen Redfield, Cherene Sherrard-Johnson, and Tamara Walker.

Finally, I would like to thank my immediate family: my mother, Valerie Whitmire, sister Denise Whitmire O'Shea and Neal and Milo, and my brother Darren Whitmire for their support.

Notes

PROLOGUE

1 **On Saturday, August 20, 1938:** Stadsarchief Rotterdam, Archieven van de Holland Amerika Lijn (HAL): Passage A, https://stadsarchief.rotterdam.nl /zoek-en-ontdek/.

2 **"comparable to a native born Frenchman":** "Wins Coveted Phi Beta Kappa Key at Harvard," *Pittsburgh Courier*, December 8, 1934, 2.

3 **But Reed ignored this call:** Reed Edwin Peggram, "A Comparison of the Personal Element in *Madame Bovary* and *L'Éducation sentimentale*" (bachelor's thesis, Harvard University, 1935).

3 **Seventy-eight years after:** "Denmark and African American Culture," University of Copenhagen, accessed June 18, 2025, https://humanities.ku.dk /calendar/2016/9/ctas-symposium/.

6 **I saw his library card:** "Reed Peggram," Shakespeare and Company Project accessed on June 18, 2025, https://shakespeareandco.princeton.edu/members /peggram/cards/.

8 **The headlines about Reed:** Max Johnson, "Two Scholars Flee Concentration Camp: Modern Damon and Pythias Story Revealed as Men Reach 92nd Lines," *Afro-American*, December 30, 1944, 1; Max Johnson, "Boy Friends Scorn Bombs, Come Out OK: Pal Scorns Money, Freedom to Stick," *Amsterdam News*, February 3, 1945, 1; Max Johnson, "Negro Escapes German Camp in Italy: Harvard Grad Shunned $11,000 in America," *Call and Post*, December 30, 1944, 2.

8 **War correspondent Max Johnson:** Johnson, "Two Scholars Flee Concentration Camp," 1.

10 **"my trip to Europe":** Reed Peggram to Mary Farrar, September 4, 1939, private collection.

CHAPTER 1. "AN UNUSUALLY FINE REPRESENTATIVE OF HIS RACE"

11 **Although many of the 1890 census:** Ancestry.com, "Virginia, U.S., Select Marriages, 1785–1940" (online database online). Original data: Family Search, "Virginia, Marriages, 1785–1940."

13 **A few years later:** United States of America, Bureau of the Census, *Twelfth Census of the United States, 1900* (Washington, D.C.: National Archives and Records Administration, 1900), microfilm publication T623, 1,854 rolls.

13 **By 1910, when Mary:** United States of America, Bureau of the Census, *Thirteenth Census of the United States, 1910* (Washington, D.C.: National Archives and Records Administration, 1910), microfilm publication T624, 1,178 rolls.

14 **It is not known how:** New England Historic Genealogical Society, Boston, MA, Massachusetts Vital Records, 1911–1915, Volume: 1914/MV1.

15 **At the time of their marriage:** National Archives in Washington, D.C.; Record Group: Records of the Bureau of the Census; Record Group Number: 29; Series Number: M432; Residence Date: 1850; Home in 1850: Norfolk, Norfolk (Independent City), Virginia; Roll: 964; Page: 76a.

15 **Mary's new family:** Boston Public Library, "Boston Lists of Residents," https://guides.bpl.org/c.php?g=496866&p=3400777, accessed May 2023.

16 **"The professor showed great ability":** "West Side News Notes," *Pittston Gazette*, May 18, 1917, 7.

16 **Other evidence of Harvey's striving:** National Negro Business League, *Official Souvenir Program (Illustrated): Sixteenth Convention of the National Negro Business League . . . August 18th, 19th, 20th, 1915: With a Brief History of Negro Business and Professional Men of Boston from 1846 to 1915, and Other Facts of the Race* (Boston: Boston Negro Business League, 1915), No. 1.

17 **He boldly declared on his draft card:** United States, Selective Service System, *World War I Selective Service System Draft Registration Cards, 1917–1918* (Washington, D.C.: National Archives and Records Administration), M1509, 4,582 rolls.

18 **"Who is that man who's very straight":** Harvey Thomas Peggram, "'Who Is That Man?' or 'The Lieutenant,'" *Richmond Planet*, March 9, 1918, 8.

20 **Justice H. A. Maurice listened:** "Justice Maurice Discharged Colored Trooper," *Richmond Planet*, March 16, 1918, 2.

21 **After he completed training:** National Archives at College Park, MD, Record Group Title: *Records of the Office of the Quartermaster General, 1774–1985*; Record Group Number: *92*; Roll or Box Number: *584*.

21 **Harvey was eventually diagnosed:** King E. Davis, email message to author, May 16, 2024.

21 **Mary filed for divorce:** Guardianship of Reed E. Peggram, #241304 filed in Suffolk County Probate and Family Court in 1929.

24 **His eyes twinkled:** Boston Public Schools Office Record Student Records Collection.

25 **He studied German:** *Latin School Register* 50, no. 7 (1931). Class Day issue.

25 **After Reed had lived:** Guardianship of Reed E. Peggram.

26 **Reed applied to college:** Harvard University, Faculty of Arts and Sciences, Undergraduate Student Records, Student folder of Reed Edwin Peggram, AB 1935 (UAIII 15.88.10 1890–1968, Box 3816), Harvard University Archives.

27 **Laura's home at 1 Sumner Court:** Boston Public Library, "Boston Lists of Residents," https://guides.bpl.org/c.php?g=496866&p=3400777; United States of America, Bureau of the Census, *Fifteenth Census of the United States, 1930* (Washington, D.C.: National Archives and Records Administration, 1930), microfilm publication T626, 2,667 rolls.

27 **As would be evident:** Harvard University, Faculty of Arts and Sciences, Undergraduate Student Records, Student folder of Reed Edwin Peggram.

CHAPTER 2. HARVARD UNIVERSITY

29 **Reed was one of a thousand:** "Class of 1935, 296th to Enter, Takes Possession of Yard Today," *Harvard Crimson*, September 25, 1931, https://www.thecrimson.com/article/1931/9/25/class-of-1935-296th-to-enter/.

30 **remarks from President A. Lawrence Lowell:** "Class of 1935, 296th to Enter, Takes Possession of Yard Today."

30 **Cyril's brother enlisted:** William Wright, *Harvard's Secret Court: The Savage 1920 Purge of Campus Homosexuals* (New York: St. Martin's Press, 2005).

31 **The other five banned students:** Nell Painter, "Jim Crow at Harvard: 1923," *New England Quarterly* 44, no. 4 (1971): 627–34.

32 **Founded in 1636:** Morton Keller and Phyllis Keller, *Making Harvard Modern: The Rise of America's University* (New York: Oxford University Press, 2001), 285.

33 **"a white man's education":** Katherine Chaddock Reynolds, *Uncompromising Activist: Richard Greener, First Black Graduate of Harvard College* (Baltimore: Johns Hopkins University Press, 2017), 34.

34 **"in Harvard, but not of it":** W. E. B. Du Bois, "A Negro Student at Harvard at the End of the Nineteenth Century," in *Blacks at Harvard: A Documentary History of African-American Experience at Harvard and Radcliffe,* edited by Werner Sollors, Caldwell Titcomb, and Thomas A. Underwood (New York: New York University Press, 1993), 76.

34 **"never regarded in absence":** Randall Kennedy, "Introduction: Blacks and the Race Question at Harvard," in *Blacks at Harvard,* xxx.

34 **Locke was "icily distant":** Jeffrey C. Stewart, *The New Negro: The Life of Alain Locke* (New York: Oxford University Press, 2018), 54.

37 **The course met on Tuesdays:** *Official Register of Harvard University*, Vol. XXVIII, September 24, 1931, No. 45, *Announcement of the Courses of Instruction offered by Faculty of Arts and Sciences, 1931–32*, Published by the University, Cambridge, Massachusetts, 86.

37 **However, his arrogance:** Harvard University, Faculty of Arts and Sciences, Undergraduate Student Records, Student folder of Cyril Toumanoff, Class of 1935 (UAIII 15.88.10 1890–1960, Box 5035), Harvard University Archives.

38 **Cyril's recommender noted:** Student folder of Cyril Toumanoff.

38 **Another letter writer remarked:** Student folder of Cyril Toumanoff.

39 **"His chief weakness":** Student folder of Cyril Toumanoff.

39 **"suffers from a rather":** Student folder of Cyril Toumanoff.

39 **"Isolation from actual life":** Student folder of Cyril Toumanoff.

40 **Cyril encountered difficulties:** Student folder of Cyril Toumanoff.

41 **His assessment from his high school:** Harvard University, Faculty of Arts and Sciences, Undergraduate Student Records, Student folder of Montfort Schley Variell (UAIII15.88.10 1890–1968, Box 5126), Harvard University Archives.

41 **His astronomy professor:** Student folder of Montfort Schley Variell.

42 **But there is another reason:** Student folder of Montfort Schley Variell.

42 *The Chicago Defender* **reported:** "Federal Home for Soldiers Finished," *Chicago Defender*, August 27, 1932, 3.

43 **"My father was disabled":** Harvard University, Faculty of Arts and Sciences, Undergraduate Student Records, Student folder of Reed Edwin Peggram, AB 1935 (UAIII 15.88.10 1890–1968, Box 3816), Harvard University Archives.

43 **But he argued:** Student folder of Reed Edwin Peggram.

44 **"He is one of the highest":** Student folder of Reed Edwin Peggram.

45 **Finally, Hanford wrote:** Student folder of Reed Edwin Peggram.

45 **"I should like to thank you":** Student folder of Reed Edwin Peggram.

45 **The letter informing Reed:** Student folder of Reed Edwin Peggram.

46 **Psychology professor Gordon Allport:** Student folder of Reed Edwin Peggram.

46 **Interestingly, Zipf concluded:** Student folder of Reed Edwin Peggram.

47 **"He is facile":** Student folder of Reed Edwin Peggram.

47 **Professor A. F. Whittem:** Student folder of Reed Edwin Peggram.

47 **He completed a fifty-eight-page thesis:** Reed Edwin Peggram, "A Comparison of the Personal Element in *Madame Bovary* and *L'Éducation sentimentale*" (bachelor's thesis, Harvard University, 1935).

48 **Commencement took place:** "Commencement Week Program Announced," *Harvard Crimson*, April 17, 1935, https://www.thecrimson.com/article/1935/4/17/commencement-week-program-announced-pbright-college/.

50 **"I had extensive contact":** John Hope Franklin, "A Life of Learning," in *Blacks at Harvard: A Documentary History of African-American Experience at Harvard and Radcliffe*, edited by Werner Sollors, Caldwell Titcomb, and Thomas A. Underwood (New York: New York University Press, 1993), 291.

50 **"[A] day, and often an hour":** John Hope Franklin, *Mirror to America: The Autobiography of John Hope Franklin* (New York: Farrar, Straus and Giroux, 2005), 61.

CHAPTER 3. COLUMBIA UNIVERSITY

54 **On his first day:** Reed Peggram to Laura Reed, Monday, private collection.

54 **He mentioned dropping his glasses:** Reed Peggram to Laura Reed, October 13, 1936, private collection.

55 **He told her not to worry:** Reed Peggram to Laura Reed, Monday.

56 **"People here look":** Reed Peggram to Laura Reed, Monday.

56 **"People here are not":** Reed Peggram to Laura Reed, February 3, 1937, private collection.

58 **The delighted audience:** "Marian Anderson 'Delights' New York Audience," *Atlanta Daily World*, April 12, 1937, 2; Noel Straus, "Marian Anderson Delights Vast Audience: New York Concert Is Great Triumph," *Pittsburgh Courier*, April 10, 1937, 9.

58 **"She had been abroad":** Reed Peggram to Laura Reed, April 3, 1937, private collection.

59 **"Perhaps we shall have":** Reed Peggram to Laura Reed, April 28, 1937, private collection.

59 **"I am prejudiced":** Reed Peggram to Laura Reed, April 3, 1937.

60 **She introduced herself as Jan Gay:** Reed Peggram to Laura Reed, April 21, 1937, private collection.

61 **"I would rather go there":** Reed Peggram to Laura Reed, May 28, 1937, private collection.

62 **She said it was a nice place:** Reed Peggram to Laura Reed, June 2, 1937, private collection.

62 **"I must confess":** Reed Peggram to Laura Reed, June 2, 1937.

62 **"Colored people in France":** Reed Peggram to Laura Reed, May 6, 1937, private collection.

63 **"Certainly, a colored gentleman":** Reed Peggram to Laura Reed, May 6.

63 **Despite his displeasure:** Reed Peggram to Laura Reed, April 17, 1937, private collection.

64 **Meanwhile, his classes finished:** Reed Peggram to Laura Reed, April 28, 1937.

64 **Reed preferred this dining experience:** Reed Peggram to Laura Reed, June 2, 1937.

65 **He knew he was being bold:** Reed Peggram to Laura Reed, May 14, 1937, private collection.

65 **Reed was wistful:** Reed Peggram to Laura Reed, June 2, 1937.

CHAPTER 4. HARVARD REDUX: "THIS REGRETTABLE INCIDENT"

67 **"ecstasy and agony at once":** Reed Peggram to Leonard Bernstein, October 20, 1937, Box 60I, folder 13, Leonard Bernstein Collection, Music Division, Library of Congress, Washington, D.C.

68 **letters "Devotedly, Reed":** Reed Peggram to Leonard Bernstein, October 19, 1937, Box 60I, folder 13, Leonard Bernstein Collection, Music Division, Library of Congress, Washington, D.C.

68 **"To Leonard in deepest affection":** Reed Peggram to Leonard Bernstein, October 20, 1937.

68 **He began one letter with:** Reed Peggram to Leonard Bernstein, October 19, 1937.

68 **He opened another letter with:** Reed Peggram to Leonard Bernstein, October 20, 1937.

69 **"Thank you for letting me know":** Reed Peggram to Leonard Bernstein, October 21, 1937, Box 60I, folder 13, Leonard Bernstein Collection, Music Division, Library of Congress, Washington, D.C.

70 **Crushed, Reed asked Leonard:** Reed Peggram to Leonard Bernstein, October 23, 1937, Box 60I, folder 13, Leonard Bernstein Collection, Music Division, Library of Congress, Washington, D.C.

72 **"I have a short story":** Reed Peggram to John Lehmann, n.d., box 73, folder 2, John Lehmann Collection (Manuscript Collection MS-02436), Harry Ransom Center, University of Texas at Austin.

73 **"I have written this story":** Reed Peggram to John Lehmann, October 14, 1937, box 73, folder 2, John Lehmann Collection (Manuscript Collection MS-02436), Harry Ransom Center, University of Texas at Austin.

74 **In November 1937:** Reed Peggram to Julius Rosenwald Fund, November 7, 1937, Box 440, Folder 7, Fisk University, John Hope and Aurelia E. Franklin Library, Special Collections, Rosenwald Fund.

75 **"to see what were the aims":** Statement of Plan of Work, Box 440, Folder 7, Fisk University, John Hope and Aurelia E. Franklin Library, Special Collections, Rosenwald Fund.

75 **"This young man has great":** Letters of Reference, Fernand Baldensperger, Box 440, Folder 7, Fisk University, John Hope and Aurelia E. Franklin Library, Special Collections, Rosenwald Fund.

76 **He also stated:** Letters of Reference, Lawrence S. Mayo, Box 440, Folder 7, Fisk University, John Hope and Aurelia E. Franklin Library, Special Collections, Rosenwald Fund.

76 **Although Reed mentioned:** Statement of Plan of Work, Box 440, Folder 7, Fisk University, John Hope and Aurelia E. Franklin Library, Special Collections, Rosenwald Fund.

76 **"I wonder would you":** Reed Peggram to John Lehmann, January 5, 1938, box 73, folder 2, John Lehmann Collection (Manuscript Collection MS-02436), Harry Ransom Center, University of Texas at Austin.

77 **"Of course I would like":** Dorothy Norman to Reed Peggram, January 18, 1938, MSS 792, box 77, Dorothy Norman Papers, Yale Collection of American Literature, Beinecke Rare Book and Manuscript Library.

77 **She politely replied:** Dorothy Norman to Reed Peggram, August 5, 1938, MSS 792, box 77, Dorothy Norman Papers, Yale Collection of American Literature, Beinecke Rare Book and Manuscript Library.

CHAPTER 5. BON VOYAGE

79 **He fearlessly recalled:** Reed Peggram to Laura Reed, August 18, 1938, private collection.

79 **Reed said cryptically:** Reed Peggram to Laura Reed, August 18, 1938, private collection.

80 **They had a madcap last night:** Reed Peggram to Mary Farrar, December 2, 1939, private collection.

81 **"gaudy, and not at all":** Reed Peggram to Laura Reed, August 18, 1938.

82 **"I had just a little fear":** Booker T. Washington, *Up from Slavery: An Autobiography*, of Cambridge Library Collection—Slavery and Abolition (Cambridge: Cambridge University Press, 2014), 275.

82 **"I only wish":** Reed Peggram to Laura Reed, n.d., private collection.

CHAPTER 6. A DISTINGUISHED SCHOLAR IN PARIS

85 **He was dismayed, though:** Reed Peggram to Laura Reed, September 17, 1938, private collection.

86 **"I personally prefer":** Reed Peggram to Laura Reed, September 28, 1938, private collection.

87 **"I don't mean what you think":** Reed Peggram to Laura Reed, November 18, 1938, private collection.

88 **"I have already impressed them":** Reed Peggram to Laura Reed, October 17, 1938, private collection.

90 **"eloquent, humorous, ironic":** "Antoni Graf Sobański (1898–1941)," Porta Polonica, accessed June 18, 2025, https://www.porta-polonica.de/en/atlas-of -remembrance-places/antoni-graf-sobanski-1898-1941.

91 **Toni, who knew them:** Reed Peggram to Laura Reed, September 18, 1938, private collection.

91 **"while there is still some left":** Reed Peggram to Laura Reed, September 18, 1938.

91 **Foresythe, born in London:** Bob Stanley, "They Got Rhythm: The Interwar British Dance Bands Who Pointed Towards Pop," *Guardian*, May 4, 2022, https://www.theguardian.com/music/2022/may/04/they-got-rhythm-the -interwar-british-dance-bands-who-pointed-towards-pop.

92 **"it creates to be an American":** Reed Peggram to Laura Reed, September 28, 1938.

93 **Rudolph Dunbar, the London correspondent:** "European Comments," *The Call*, September 9, 1938, 17.

93 **Reed crowed to Laura:** Reed Peggram to Laura Reed, October 3, 1938, private collection.

93 **"I shall stick it out":** Reed Peggram to Laura Reed, September 28, 1938.

93 **"In Paris they were actually":** Reed Peggram to Laura Reed, October 3, 1938.

94 **the mood in Paris in 1938:** Janet Flanner, *Paris Was Yesterday, 1925–1939* (New York: Penguin, 1979), 191.

94 **"For their protection":** Flanner, *Paris Was Yesterday*, 192.

95 **"I guess we will have peace":** Reed Peggram to Laura Reed, October 3, 1938.

95 **He hoped to meet them:** Reed Peggram to Laura Reed, September 18, 1938.

95 **"But I must say":** Reed Peggram to Laura Reed, October 3, 1938.

96 **He marveled at the low cost:** Reed Peggram to Laura Reed, September 28, 1938.

96 **"But perhaps they could afford":** Reed Peggram to Laura Reed, October 17, 1938.

97 **"I really hate to take":** Reed Peggram to Laura Reed, February 3, 1939, private collection.

98 **Howard told Reed:** Reed Peggram to Laura Reed, February 3, 1939.

98 **"I have created":** Reed Peggram to Laura Reed, May 12, 1939, private collection.

98 **He got lots of letters:** Reed Peggram to Laura Reed, July 11, 1939, private collection.

100 **According to the author Edmund White:** Edmund White, *The Loves of My Life: A Sex Memoir* (New York: Bloomsbury, 2025), 204.

101 **The Rosenwald Fund's director of fellowship:** George M. Reynolds to Reed Edwin Peggram, November 7, 1938, Box 440, Folder 7, Fisk University, John Hope and Aurelia E. Franklin Library, Special Collections, Rosenwald Fund Collection.

102 **Next to "Part of the country preferred":** Harvard University Appointment Office Registration Blank, Harvard University, Faculty of Arts and Sciences, Undergraduate Student Records, Student folder of Reed Edwin Peggram, AB 1935 (UAIII 15.88.10 1890–1968, Box 3816), Harvard University Archives.

103 **"determined to do all that":** Reed Peggram to Laura Reed, October 3, 1938.

103 **"I am becoming a real scholar":** Reed Peggram to Laura Reed, December 8, 1938, private collection.

103 **"I am wild about it here":** Reed Peggram to Laura Reed, November 18, 1938.

104 **"The Editor of NEW WRITING has":** Norman MacLeod to Reed Peggram, n.d., box 36, folder 9, John Lehmann Collection (Manuscript Collection MS-02436), Harry Ransom Center, University of Texas at Austin.

104 **"Incidentally, I have spoken":** Reed Peggram to Dorothy Norman, March 19, 1939, MSS 792, Box 77, Dorothy Norman Papers, Yale Collection of American Literature, Beinecke Rare Book and Manuscript Library.

104 **"Undoubtedly Monsieur Jean Giraudoux":** Reed E. Peggram, "A Neglected Dutch 'Amphitryon' of 1679," *Modern Language Review* 36, no. 1 (1941): 112–15.

105 **"An investigation of the editions":** Reed Edwin Peggram, "The First French and English Translations of Sir Thomas More's 'Utopia,'" *Modern Language Review* 35, no. 3 (1940): 330–40.

106 **"he produced something":** Reed Peggram to Mary Farrar, November 10, 1938, private collection.

106 **"It seems a shame":** Reed Peggram to Laura Reed, November 10, 1938, private collection.

107 **"He likes colored people":** Reed Peggram to Laura Reed, January 26, 1939, private collection.

107 **"It is funny, really":** Reed Peggram to Laura Reed, January 27, 1939, private collection.

107 **"I don't know what you":** Reed Peggram to Laura Reed, January 27, 1939.

108 **They shared an interest in "music":** Reed Peggram to Mary Farrar, November 10, 1938.

109 **"I do think I shall be":** Reed Peggram to Laura Reed, November 28, 1938, private collection.

109 **"But you know I have never":** Reed Peggram to Laura Reed, November 18, 1938.

110 **The reviewer called:** Peter Monro Jack, "Papers D. H. Lawrence Wrote," *New York Times*, November 29, 1936, 29.

110 **"I am quite flattered":** Reed Peggram to Laura Reed, January 15, 1939, private collection.

111 **"When I found the house":** Reed Peggram to Laura Reed, n.d. (first page missing), private collection.

111 **The butler returned:** Reed Peggram to Laura Reed, n.d. (first page missing).

112 **"This is a point":** Reed Peggram to Laura Reed, June 27, 1939, private collection.

CHAPTER 7. ARNE

113 **"It was such fun":** Reed Peggram to Laura Reed, April 24, 1939, private collection.

114 **He described Arne:** Reed Peggram to Laura Reed, May 19, 1939, private collection.

114 **Arne was born on March 11, 1916:** Shari Jensen, email message to author, January 14, 2023.

115 **Reed was aware that war:** Reed Peggram to Laura Reed, July 3, 1939, private collection.

115 **"would the Committee":** Reed Peggram to George M. Reynolds, May 2, 1939, Box 440, Folder 7, Fisk University, John Hope and Aurelia E. Franklin Library, Special Collections, Rosenwald Fund Collection.

115 **"In short, it takes":** Reed Peggram to Laura Reed, May 12, 1939, private collection.

116 **"I feel that I am worth":** Reed Peggram to Laura Reed, May 2, 1939, private collection.

116 **He felt that the Rosenwald Fund:** Reed Peggram to Laura Reed, June 27, 1939, private collection.

117 **Laura celebrated her seventieth:** Reed Peggram to Laura Reed, July 25, 1939, private collection.

117 **Reed had to hand over:** Reed Peggram to Laura Reed, July 24, 1939, private collection.

118 **He thought they should give him:** Reed Peggram to Laura Reed, July 25, 1939.

120 **"If things turn out":** Reed Peggram to Laura Reed, July 11, 1939, private collection.

120 **"Particularly because they":** Reed Peggram to Laura Reed, August 1, 1939, private collection.

120 **"Dear Mother, I know that":** Reed Peggram to Mary Farrar, August 10, 1939, private collection.

121 **"Dear Nana, Courage, darling":** Reed Peggram to Laura Reed, August 10, 1939, private collection.

122 **During the nights:** Janet Flanner, *Paris Was Yesterday, 1925–1939* (New York: Penguin, 1979), 223.

CHAPTER 8. "LIFE IS VERY PEACEFUL HERE IN DENMARK (SO FAR)"

123 **"Anyway, you see":** Reed Peggram to Mary Farrar, September 4, 1939, private collection.

124 **"I must say things":** Reed Peggram to Laura Reed, August 31, 1939, private collection.

124 **"recent European events":** Reed Peggram to Dorothy Norman, September 4, 1939, MSS 792, box 77, Dorothy Norman Papers, Yale Collection of American Literature, Beinecke Rare Book and Manuscript Library.

124 **A little before 4 p.m.:** Special Cable to *The New York Times*, "Bombs Drop on Neutral Denmark, but 'Raid' Is Held Unintentional: At Least Two Esbjerg Residents Are Killed—Small Countries are Anxious—Fleet of Unknown Planes Violate Netherlands," *New York Times*, September 5, 1939, 2.

125 **"Virtually all of the exiles":** Tyler Edward Stovall, *Paris Noir: African Americans in the City of Light* (Boston: Houghton Mifflin, 1996), 84.

125 **"I still think it's funny":** Reed Peggram to Mary Farrar, December 2, 1939, private collection.

125 **"I wish I knew Danish better":** Reed Peggram to Laura Reed, September 20, 1939, private collection.

126 **"a lovely street":** Roy De Coverley, "Beauty, Beer and Beechwoods," *Challenge: A Literary Quarterly* 1, no. 3 (May 1935): 42.

126 **"My typewriter is being repaired":** Reed Peggram to Mary Farrar, October 13, 1939, private collection.

127 **"Of course, I don't see him":** Reed Peggram to Laura Reed, September 20, 1939.

127 **"I still have plenty":** Reed Peggram to Laura Reed, September 20, 1939.

127 **"After all, I have":** Reed Peggram to Laura Reed, September 20, 1939.

127 **"I don't feel in any danger":** Reed Peggram to Laura Reed, September 30, 1939, private collection.

128 **He called it "a silly old war":** Reed Peggram to Mary Farrar, January 28, 1940, private collection.

128 **he compared his plight:** Reed Peggram to Laura Reed, September 16, 1939, private collection.

129 **"I always carry":** Reed Peggram to Laura Reed, October 6, 1939, private collection.

129 **"Oh, I lost that":** Reed Peggram to Laura Reed, October 6, 1939.

130 **Unlike his friends in France:** Reed Peggram to Mary Farrar, October 13, 1939.

130 **"elegant and charming":** Reed Peggram to Mary Farrar, October 13, 1939.

130 **"People here love pastry":** Reed Peggram to Laura Reed, September 20, 1939, private collection.

130 **"a very charming apartment":** Reed Peggram to Laura Reed, September 20, 1939.

130 **"I've never been":** Reed Peggram to Laura Reed, October 27, 1939, private collection.

131 **She was often compared favorably:** Giovanni Russonello, "Valaida Snow: The Charismatic 'Queen of the Trumpet' Was a Sensation Who Helped Bring Black Music from the Vaudeville Stage into the Audiovisual Age," *New York Times*, February 24, 2020, 1.

132 **"We filled her up":** Reed Peggram to Laura Reed, November 11, 1939, private collection.

132 **"I wrote Mother":** Reed Peggram to Laura Reed, October 16, 1939, private collection.

134 **He didn't feel safe crossing:** Reed Peggram to Laura Reed, November 18, 1939, private collection.

134 **"This has been":** Reed Peggram to Laura Reed, November 18, 1939.

134 **While grateful for the free housing:** Reed Peggram to Mary Farrar, October 13, 1939.

134 **"Bertie is quite willing":** Reed Peggram to Laura Reed, October 24, 1939, private collection.

CHAPTER 9. THE CENTRAL HOTEL

138 **"pick up and leave":** Reed Peggram to Laura Reed, November 11, 1939, private collection.

138 **"writing more now":** Reed Peggram to Laura Reed, September 30, 1939, private collection.

138 **"I like Bent better":** Reed Peggram to Laura Reed, October 21, 1939, private collection.

139 **Arne and Reed continued writing:** Reed Peggram to Dorothy Norman, April 8, 1940, MSS 792, box 77, Dorothy Norman Papers, Yale Collection of American Literature, Beinecke Rare Book and Manuscript Library.

140 **"life is very peaceful":** Reed Peggram to Mary Farrar, December 2, 1939, private collection.

141 **"At the present moment":** Box 440, Folder 7, Fisk University, John Hope and Aurelia E. Franklin Library, Special Collections, Rosenwald Fund Collection.

143 **"Christmas is a big festival":** Reed Peggram to Laura Reed, December 28, 1939, private collection.

144 **"until the food":** Reed Peggram to Laura Reed, December 28, 1939.

145 **Ola and Eddie explained:** Ola and Eddie Alston, "Defender Scribe Gets News from War Torn Europe: Tells How American Performers Are Hit Ola and Eddie Write from Copenhagen, Denmark," *Chicago Defender*, January 27, 1940, 21.

145 **Since they could not get work:** Ola and Eddie Alston, "Ola and Eddie on Way Back to U.S.A.: American Dance Team Tell of Conditions in Europe," *Chicago Defender*, February 17, 1940, 20.

145 **The US government urged:** Reed Peggram to Mary Farrar, January 28, 1940, private collection.

147 **While little is known:** Peter Edelberg, "The Queer Road to Frisind: Copenhagen 1945–2012," in *Queer Cities, Queer Cultures: Europe Since 1945*, edited by Matt Cook and Jennifer V. Evans (New York: Bloomsbury Academic 2014), 55–74; Wilhelm von Rosen, "Denmark 1866–1976: From Sodomy to Modernity," in *Criminally Queer: Homosexuality and Criminal Law in Scandinavia*,

1842–1999, edited by Jens Rydström and Kati Mustola (Amsterdam: Aksant 2007), 61–90.

147 **Reed did not discuss:** Anders Hagerup Larsen, "Café Intime and All That Jazz," in *111 Places in Copenhagen That You Shouldn't Miss*, edited by Jan Gralle, Vibe Skytte, and Anders Hagerup Larsen (Frydenlund, 2021).

148 **"And even that is no Paradise":** Reed Peggram to Mary Farrar, January 28, 1940.

148 **"These have been a two year":** Reed Peggram to Mary Farrar, February 16, 1940, private collection.

148 **"Of all things!":** Reed Peggram to Mary Farrar, January 28, 1940.

149 **"a flustered morning":** Reed Peggram to Laura Reed, February 20, 1940, private collection.

149 **"Needless to say":** Reed Peggram to Laura Reed, February 20, 1940.

150 **"When I was in Germany":** Reed Peggram to Mary Farrar, February 16, 1940.

150 **He hoped to do a little sightseeing:** Reed Peggram to Mary Farrar, January 28, 1940.

151 **"Italy is sure to be":** Reed Peggram to Laura Reed, February 22, 1940, private collection.

151 **"parents are quite willing":** Reed Peggram to Laura Reed, March 11, 1940, private collection.

151 **"Now don't worry":** Reed Peggram to Mary Farrar, February 26, 1940, private collection.

151 **"I'm really not depressed":** Reed Peggram to Mary Farrar, February 16, 1940.

152 **"STOP! As one says":** Reed Peggram to Mary Farrar, February 26, 1940.

152 **her "wandering boy":** Reed Peggram to Mary Farrar, February 26, 1940.

152 **"I would be very happy":** Reed Peggram to Edwin R. Embree, March 2, 1940, Box 440, Folder 7, Fisk University, John Hope and Aurelia E. Franklin Library, Special Collections, Rosenwald Fund Collection.

153 **The cost of the plane ticket:** Reed Peggram to Laura Reed, March 11, 1940.

153 **"Between you and me":** Reed Peggram to Laura Reed, March 11, 1940.

154 **ran around with their suitcases:** Reed Peggram to Laura Reed, March 30, 1940, private collection.

155 **Reed hoped to persuade Howard:** Reed Peggram to Laura Reed, March 30, 1940.

155 **This time they boarded:** Reed Peggram to Laura Reed, March 11, 1940.

CHAPTER 10. "ITALY AS A WHOLE IS VERY PEACEFUL"

157 **"the increasingly oppressive atmosphere"**: Iris Origo, *A Chill in the Air: An Italian War Diary, 1939–1940* (London: Pushkin Press, 2017), 182.

159 **"Florence is the most beautiful"**: Reed Peggram to Laura Reed, March 30, 1930, private collection.

159 **"wild about its beauty"**: Reed Peggram to Laura Reed, April 26, 1940, private collection.

159 **In fact, to be a male homosexual:** Lorenzo Benadusi, "Chapter 7. Fascism, War and Homosexuality," in *Queer in Europe During the Second World War*, ed. Régis Schlagdenhauffen (Strasbourg: Council of Europe Publishing, 2018); Lorenzo Benadusi, *The Enemy of the New Man: Homosexuality in Fascist Italy* (Madison: University of Wisconsin Press, 2012); Michael R. Ebner, "Chapter 9. The Persecution of Homosexual Men Under Fascism," in *Gender, Family and Sexuality: The Private Sphere in Italy, 1860–1945*, ed. Perry Wilson (New York: Palgrave Macmillan, 2004).

160 **There were quotas and complicated requirements:** "What Did Refugees Need to Obtain a US Visa in the 1930s?," United States Holocaust Memorial Museum, accessed June 18, 2025, https://exhibitions.ushmm.org/americans -and-the-holocaust/what-did-refugees-need-to-obtain-a-us-visa-in-the-1930s; "Documents Required to Obtain a Visa," Holocaust Encyclopedia, accessed June 18, 2025, https://encyclopedia.ushmm.org/content/en/article/documents -required-to-obtain-a-visa.

161 **"The uncle is very rich"**: Reed Peggram to Laura Reed, May 23, 1940, private collection.

162 **"You can also understand"**: Reed Peggram to Laura Reed, June 25, 1940, private collection.

162 **"I hope now the letter"**: Arne Hauptmann to Laura Reed, June 29, 1940, private collection.

163 **"Why in the hell doesn't he"**: Reed Peggram to Laura Reed, June 20, 1940, private collection.

164 **"It pained me like hell"**: Reed Peggram to Laura Reed, April 2, 1940, private collection.

164 **"rescued me from"**: Reed Peggram to Dorothy Norman, April 2, 1940, MSS 792, box 77, Dorothy Norman Papers, Yale Collection of American Literature, Beinecke Rare Book and Manuscript Library.

164 **he called "cumbersome"**: Reed Peggram to Dorothy Norman, April 8, 1940, MSS 792, box 77, Dorothy Norman Papers, Yale Collection of American Literature, Beinecke Rare Book and Manuscript Library.

164 **"Firenze is very pleasant"**: Reed Peggram to Dorothy Norman, April 2, 1940.

165 **"André Gide is a man":** Reed Edwin Peggram, "André Gide—Novelist," *Twice a Year*, issue 5/6 (1940/41): 270.

165 **She wrote, "By the way":** Dorothy Norman to Reed Peggram, May 16, 1940, MSS 792, box 77, Dorothy Norman Papers, Yale Collection of American Literature, Beinecke Rare Book and Manuscript Library.

165 **"It is my eleventh month":** Reed Peggram to Dorothy Norman, January 16, 1941, MSS 792, box 77, Dorothy Norman Papers, Yale Collection of American Literature, Beinecke Rare Book and Manuscript Library.

168 **"Just how long it will take":** Reed Peggram to Dorothy Norman, April 9, 1941, MSS 792, box 77, Dorothy Norman Papers, Yale Collection of American Literature, Beinecke Rare Book and Manuscript Library.

168 **"You will also remember":** Reed Peggram to Dorothy Norman, November 22, 1940, MSS 792, box 77, Dorothy Norman Papers, Yale Collection of American Literature, Beinecke Rare Book and Manuscript Library.

169 **"extraordinarily little real information":** Origo, *A Chill in the Air*, 113.

169 **"While the Norwegians":** Clarence Lusane, *Hitler's Black Victims: The Historical Experiences of Afro-Germans, European Blacks, Africans, and African Americans in the Nazi Era* (New York: Routledge, 2002), 169.

169 **"We got out":** Reed Peggram to Laura Reed, April 21, 1940, private collection.

170 **They took the opportunity:** Reed Peggram to Laura Reed, April 21, 1940.

170 **"I go up to Florence":** Origo, *A Chill in the Air*, 129.

170 **"In Florence the atmosphere":** Origo, *A Chill in the Air*, 129.

171 **"Everything is like a game":** Reed Peggram to Montfort S. Variell, May 20, 1940, MI DGPS Foreign Internees and Espionage Peggram Reed Edwin, Ministry of Culture, Italy.

171 **A "strictly confidential" document:** MI DGPS Foreign Internees and Espionage Peggram Reed Edwin, Ministry of Culture, Italy.

172 **"I can't leave until":** Reed Peggram to Laura Reed, May 10, 1940, private collection.

173 **Iris Origo's May 28 and May 29:** Origo, *A Chill in the Air*, 140.

174 **"By now my chief emotion":** Origo, *A Chill in the Air*, 146.

CHAPTER 11. "WE ARE WORN AND WEARY AND WEAK"

175 **They were in dire straits:** Reed Peggram to Laura Reed, June 17, 1940, private collection.

175 **"It only put us on a better footing":** Reed Peggram to Laura Reed, June 22, 1940, private collection.

176 **"Please let me know"**: Mary Farrar and Laura Reed to Dear Sir, July 8, 1940, private collection.

176 **"I am writing to you because"**: Arne Hauptmann to Laura Reed, July 30, 1940, private collection.

177 **Reed added a note**: Reed Peggram to Laura Reed, July 30, 1940.

177 **Reed admitted that he**: Reed Peggram to Mary Farrar, July 31, 1940, private collection.

178 **"With the spread of hostilities"**: Geo. L. Brandt to Mary Farrar, August 2, 1940, private collection.

180 **"I have been obliged"**: Reed Peggram to Bill Pratt, June 29, 1940, Harvard University, Faculty of Arts and Sciences, Undergraduate Student Records, Student folder of Reed Edwin Peggram, AB 1935 (UAIII 15.88.10 1890–1968, Box 3816), Harvard University Archives.

181 **"I can't understand why"**: Reed Peggram to Edwin R. Embree, July 5, 1940, Box 440, Folder 7, Fisk University, John Hope and Aurelia E. Franklin Library, Special Collections, Rosenwald Fund.

182 **"Under normal conditions"**: Edwin R. Embree to Harrison H. Farrell, July 19, 1940, Box 440, Folder 7, Fisk University, John Hope and Aurelia E. Franklin Library, Special Collections, Rosenwald Fund.

182 **"Details of our conversation"**: Harrison H. Ferrell to Edwin R. Embree, July 13, 1940, Box 440, Folder 7, Fisk University, John Hope and Aurelia E. Franklin Library, Special Collections, Rosenwald Fund.

182 **"But seriously, Mother"**: Reed Peggram to Mary Farrar, August 16, 1940, private collection.

183 **"In his last letter to me"**: Beryl Orris to Laura Reed, September 5, 1940, private collection.

185 **"I regret that I"**: Reed Peggram to Gentleman, September 21, 1940, Harvard University, Faculty of Arts and Sciences, Undergraduate Student Records, Student folder of Reed Edwin Peggram, AB 1935 (UAIII 15.88.10 1890–1968, Box 3816), Harvard University Archives.

186 **At one point during the evening**: David Charnay, "'Sealed Room' Mystery Solution Is Cop's Secret," *Daily News*, September 19, 1940, 444.

186 **Monty returned to his**: David Charnay, "'Sealed Room' Death of Heir Baffles Police," *Daily News*, September 18, 1940, 204.

187 **The police were very interested**: Charnay, "'Sealed Room' Mystery Solution Is Cop's Secret," 444.

187 **She agreed to come**: David Charnay, "Secret Wedding Hinted in Mystery of 'Sealed Room,'" *Daily News*, September 19, 1940, 648.

187 **Monty's friends said:** Charnay, "'Sealed Room' Death of Heir Baffles Police," 204.

188 **Headlines included, "Mystery":** "Mystery Death at Harvard," *Lowell Sun*, September 17, 1940, 1; "Investigate Death of Harvard Student," *Ludington Daily News*, September 18, 1940, 1; Charnay, "Secret Wedding Hinted in Mystery of 'Sealed Room,'" 648; Charnay, "'Sealed Room' Death of Heir Baffles Police," 204.

189 **"We are at a loss":** George M. Reynold to Reed Peggram, September 20, 1940, Box 440, Folder 7, Fisk University, John Hope and Aurelia E. Franklin Library, Special Collections, Rosenwald Fund.

190 **"My situation remains unchanged":** Reed Peggram to American Export Line, n.d., Box 440, Folder 7, Fisk University, John Hope and Aurelia E. Franklin Library, Special Collections, Rosenwald Fund.

191 **"There has been no end":** M. O. Bousfield to Elmer A. Carter, October 11, 1940, Box 440, Folder 7, Fisk University, John Hope and Aurelia E. Franklin Library, Special Collections, Rosenwald Fund.

191 **"Refusing transportation in general":** M. O. Bousfield to Elmer A. Carter, October 29, 1940, Box 440, Folder 7, Fisk University, John Hope and Aurelia E. Franklin Library, Special Collections, Rosenwald Fund.

191 **"I hate to bother you":** Elmer A. Carter to M. O. Bousfield, November 16, 1940, Box 440, Folder 7, Fisk University, John Hope and Aurelia E. Franklin Library, Special Collections, Rosenwald Fund.

191 **"I regret that as far":** M. O. Bousfield to Elmer A. Carter, November 20, 1940, Box 440, Folder 7, Fisk University, John Hope and Aurelia E. Franklin Library, Special Collections, Rosenwald Fund.

192 **"Have you had any recent word":** Unknown to Harrison H. Ferrell, November 22, 1940, Harvard University, Faculty of Arts and Sciences, Undergraduate Student Records, Student folder of Reed Edwin Peggram, AB 1935 (UAIII 15.88.10 1890–1968, Box 3816), Harvard University Archives.

192 **"Mr. Peggram's behavior":** Harrison H. Ferrell to Florence K. Leetch, November 30, 1940, Harvard University, Faculty of Arts and Sciences, Undergraduate Student Records, Student folder of Reed Edwin Peggram, AB 1935 (UAIII 15.88.10 1890–1968, Box 3816), Harvard University Archives.

193 **"I think you will be interested":** George M. Reynolds to Laura Reed, December 11, 1940, Box 440, Folder 7, Fisk University, John Hope and Aurelia E. Franklin Library, Special Collections, Rosenwald Fund.

194 **"Dear Sir: Your letter":** Laura Reed to Dear Sir, December 16, 1940, Box 440, Folder 7, Fisk University, John Hope and Aurelia E. Franklin Library, Special Collections, Rosenwald Fund.

194 **"It is evident that you are"**: George M. Reynolds to Reed Peggram, January 6, 1941, Box 440, Folder 7, Fisk University, John Hope and Aurelia E. Franklin Library, Special Collections, Rosenwald Fund.

194 **The Rosenwald Fund offered:** Reed Peggram to Laura Reed, July 25, 1940, private collection.

194 **"I'm sure you think"**: Reed Peggram to Mary Farrar, August 16, 1940, private collection.

195 **"He has cabled that"**: George M. Reynolds to Laura Reed, January 6, 1941, private collection.

196 **"NOT a ticket to NY"**: Reed Peggram to Gentlemen, January 13, 1941, Box 440, Folder 7, Fisk University, John Hope and Aurelia E. Franklin Library, Special Collections, Rosenwald Fund.

196 **Henry Allen Moe:** Henry Allen Moe to Secretary of State, February 6, 1941, Box 440, Folder 7, Fisk University, John Hope and Aurelia E. Franklin Library, Special Collections, Rosenwald Fund.

197 **Although they felt bad:** Reed Peggram to Laura Reed, June 17, 1940.

197 **"Excuse my delay"**: Reed Peggram to George M. Reynolds, May 1, 1941, Box 440, Folder 7, Fisk University, John Hope and Aurelia E. Franklin Library, Special Collections, Rosenwald Fund.

197 **The agent added a note:** R. E. Good to George M. Reynolds, March 6, 1941, Box 440, Folder 7, Fisk University, John Hope and Aurelia E. Franklin Library, Special Collections, Rosenwald Fund.

200 **"You have no idea"**: Reed Peggram to Laura Reed, September 7, 1941, private collection.

CHAPTER 12. AN OVERLY INTIMATE RELATIONSHIP

205 **"It is natural that I"**: Reed Peggram to Ezra Pound, June 4, 1942, MSS 43, Box 40, Folder 1686, Ezra Pound Papers, Yale Collection of American Literature, Beinecke Rare Book and Manuscript Library.

207 **"We would like to point out"**: MI DGPS A4bis Foreign Internees and Espionage Hauptmann Arne Gerdahn, Ministry of Culture, Italy.

209 **A November 27, 1942, letter:** MI DGPS Foreign Internees and Espionage Peggram Reed Edwin, Ministry of Culture, Italy.

209 **On February 4, 1943:** MI DGPS Foreign Internees and Espionage Peggram Reed Edwin, Ministry of Culture, Italy.

211 **"If you come to this office"**: Jessie Goldsmith to Laura Reed, October 21, 1943, private collection.

212 **There was barely food:** Douglass Hall, "How Boston Lad Studying in Denmark Escaped Nazis: Rosenwald Student at University of Copenhagen, Reed Peggram Tells How He Found Safety and Protection with the 92nd Division in Italy," *Afro-American*, March 17, 1945, 5.

212 **The memoirs of other prisoners:** Robert Garioch, *Two Men and a Blanket: Memoirs of Captivity* (Edinburgh: Southside, 1975).

212 **described as "endlessly boring":** Ruby Simon Smith, as told by Charles Webster Smith, *Wine, Cheese & Bread: A POW's Story of Survival in Italy* (Austin, TX: Woodburner Press, 1998).

213 **"For months we did not see":** Hall, "How Boston Lad Studying in Denmark Escaped Nazis."

214 **On a rainy Saturday morning:** Michael E. Lynch, *Edward M. Almond and the U.S. Army: From the 92nd Infantry Division to the X Corps* (Lexington: University Press of Kentucky, 2019).

214 **There are differing accounts:** MI DGPS A16 Stranieri Peggram Reed Edwin, Ministry of Culture, Italy.

CHAPTER 13. "TWO MEN WITH STRANGE STORY WALK THROUGH BATTLE LINES"

217 **"We can't explain":** Douglass Hall, "How Boston Lad Studying in Denmark Escaped Nazis: Rosenwald Student at University of Copenhagen, Reed Peggram Tells How He found Safety and Protection with the 92nd Division in Italy," *Afro-American*, March 17, 1945, 5.

218 **"We learned how to spot":** Hall, "How Boston Lad Studying in Denmark Escaped Nazis."

218 **The biggest commodity desired:** Ruby Simon Smith, as told by Charles Webster Smith, *Wine, Cheese & Bread: A POW's Story of Survival in Italy* (Austin, TX: Woodburner Press, 1998).

219 **The soldiers provided them:** Max Johnson, "Boy Friends Scorn Bombs, Come Out OK: Pal Scorns Money, Freedom to Stick," *Amsterdam News*, February 3, 1945, 1.

219 **The troops and reporters were curious:** "Aided by Partisans," *Rome Stars and Stripes*, December 21, 1944, 5.

220 **The datelines of the subsequent:** Hall, "How Boston Lad Studying in Denmark Escaped Nazis."

221 **This image appeared in:** Johnson, "Boy Friends Scorn Bombs."

221 **Johnson declared Reed and Arne's:** Max Johnson, "Two Scholars Flee Concentration Camp: Modern Damon and Pythias Story Revealed as Men Reach 92nd Lines," *Afro-American*, December 30, 1944, 1.

221 **The caption underneath the photograph:** "A Modern Damon and Pythias Talk for the AFRO," *Afro-American*, December 30, 1944, 2.

221 **He hoped that their racial differences:** John Jordan, "Two Men with Strange Story Walk Through Battle Lines," *New Journal and Guide*, December 23, 1944, 2.

222 **He called their tale:** Jordan, "Two Men with Strange Story Walk Through Battle Lines."

222 **What was likely true:** Hall, "How Boston Lad Studying in Denmark Escaped Nazis."

222 **giving them flashbacks:** Hall, "How Boston Lad Studying in Denmark Escaped Nazis."

223 **But Reed wanted his family:** Hall, "How Boston Lad Studying in Denmark Escaped Nazis."

224 **A month before Reed was rescued:** Record of Laura Reed at Mount Hope Cemetery in Boston, Massachusetts, interment no. 71226.

224 **"I hasten to assure you":** Arne Hauptmann to Mary Reed, June 17, 1945, private collection.

CHAPTER 14. MEDFIELD STATE HOSPITAL

227 **Reed boarded the hospital ship:** Ancestry.com, U.S., "Atlantic Ports Arriving and Departing Passenger and Crew Lists, 1820–1959" (online database). Original data: Records from Record Group 287, Publications of the U.S. Government, Record Group 85, Records of the Immigration and Naturalization Service [INS] and Record Group 36, Records of the United States Customs Service, National Archives, Washington, D.C.

228 **When he was in Copenhagen:** Reed Peggram to Laura Reed, 16 September 1939, private collection.

228 **The superintendent of the hospital:** F. O. Bates to Mary R. Farrar, September 3, 1945, private collection.

229 **Two days later:** J. R. Ridlen to Mrs. Mary Farrar, September 5, 1945, private collection.

229 **"At the time of admission":** James V. Lowry to Mrs. Mary R. Farrar, September 20, 1945, private collection.

229 **Finally, Reed wrote to her:** Reed Peggram to Mary Farrar, October 1, 1945, private collection.

230 **"Since the time of admission":** James V. Lowry to Mrs. Farrar, November 15, 1945, private collection.

232 **During his hospitalization:** *Annual Report of the Board of Trustees of Medfield State Hospital*, 1947, HathiTrust.org.

233 **"As you know, your son"**: Earl K. Holt to Mrs. Mary Farrar, June 20, 1947, private collection.

236 **"It's a miracle"**: Debra Farrar-Parkman to author, private communication.

236 **His younger brother Phillip Farrar Jr.**: Record of Phillip Farrar at Mount Hope Cemetery in Boston, Massachusetts, interment no. 72961.

CHAPTER 15. DORCHESTER REDUX

240 **"unable to work"**: Population Schedule for Boston, Suffolk, Massachusetts, roll 4702, page 16, ED 15-759, Seventeenth Census of the United States, 1950, Records of the Bureau of the Census, RG 29, National Archives, Washington, D.C.

240 **In 1978, the police:** "90 Men Seized in Boston Library for Solicitation as Homosexuals," *New York Times*, March 25, 1978, 8.

242 **The language involving people:** *Population Schedules for the 1950 Census.*

242 **He died on August 16, 1956:** Certificate of Death for Harvey Peggram, Alabama Center for Health Statistics, State of Alabama.

242 **Harvey's survivors included:** "Harvey T. Pegram," *Progress-Index* (Petersburg, VA), August 17, 1956, 18.

242 **Harvey was buried:** Ancestry.com, "Petersburg, Virginia, U.S., Poplar Grove National Cemetery, 1866–1973" (online database).

242 **A year later:** "Virginia, Deaths, 1912–2014," Virginia Department of Health, Richmond.

246 **Mary died on:** "Death Notices," *Boston Globe*, December 10, 1980, 46.

246 **Reed's later years:** Tarik Farrar, email message to author, July 24, 2022.

247 **Reed died of a:** Commonwealth of Massachusetts, Department of Public Health, Registry of Vital Records and Statistics.

ENDINGS

249 **back in Paris, Sylvia Beach:** Sylvia Beach, *Shakespeare and Company* (New York: Harcourt, Brace, 1959); Mary McAuliffe, *Paris on the Brink: The 1930s Paris of Jean Renoir, Salvador Dalí, Simone de Beauvoir, André Gide, Sylvia Beach, Léon Blum, and Their Friends* (Lanham, MD: Rowman & Littlefield, 2018).

249 **He was buried in Mount Olivet Cemetery:** "Olgerd P De Sherbowitz-Wetzor," Find a Grave, accessed June 18, 2025, https://www.findagrave.com/memorial/186991374/olgerd_p-de_sherbowitz-wetzor.

250 **Composer Howard Swanson:** Marsha J. Reisser, "Howard Swanson: Distinguished Composer," *The Black Perspective in Music* 17, no. 1/2 (1989): 5–26.

250 **At the end of 1979:** Obituary in the *Wichita Beacon*, December 20, 1979.

251 **He was drafted and served:** War Department, Adjutant General's Office, Washington, D.C., Officer Selected to Present Decoration.

251 **Reed's former editor:** Roberta Smith, "Dorothy Norman, 92, Writer Who Sought Social Change," *New York Times*, April 14, 1989, 38.

251 **Nearly thirty years after Olgy's death:** "In Memoriam. Cyril Toumanoff," *Journal of the Society for Armenian Studies* (1997): 355–60.

252 **Arne's sons had been forbidden:** Marc Fussinger, email message to author, January 23, 2023.

253 **Marc was aware of the book of poems:** Gerdh Hauptmann, *Declaration* (Copenhagen: Strube, 1971).

EPILOGUE

255 **"To be sitting in Copenhagen":** Teju Adisa-Farrar, "Urban Up Close: My History Matters, Even in Copenhagen," *Medium*, September 27, 2016, https://medium.com/world-unwrapped/urban-up-close-my-history-matters-even-in-copenhagen-975efb6b3175.

258 **"I attended Boston Latin":** Charles Piper, "Quality, Not Race, Should Count," *Los Angeles Times*, February 2, 1997, E2.

259 **In 2021, in order to increase:** Ellen Barry, "Boston Overhauls Admissions to Exclusive Exam Schools," *New York Times*, July 15, 2021.

259 **In 2022, parents filed a lawsuit:** Marie Szaniszlo, "Group of White and Asian Parents Sue BPS over Exam School Admissions Policy," *Boston Herald*, June 8, 2022.

259 **In 2023, the majority-conservative:** Adam Liptak, "Supreme Court Rejects Affirmative Action Programs at Harvard and U.N.C.," *New York Times*, June 29, 2023.

259 **But in 2024, the Supreme Court:** Chris Benson, "Supreme Court Refuses to Hear Challenge to Admission Policy in Boston Schools," UPI, December 9, 2024.

Credits

Images of Reed's mother and grandmother: Courtesy of Debra Farrar-Parkman.

Reed Peggram elementary school photo: Edward Everett District. Student records, Collection 0420.001. Courtesy of the City of Boston Archives.

Boston Latin School club photographs: Photographs provided courtesy of Boston Latin School.

Photographs of Cyril Toumanoff and Phi Beta Kappa class: Courtesy of the Harvard University Archives.

Photograph of Montfort Schley Variell: Courtesy of the Harvard University Archives.

Reed Peggram graduation photo: Fisk University, John Hope and Aurelia E. Franklin Library, Special Collections, Julius Rosenwald Database. http://rosen wald.fisk.edu/.

Reed Peggram portrait: Thomas Handforth (1897–1948), *Untitled*, Paris 1938, Conté crayon and ink, 24 x 18 ¼ in. Collection of the Tacoma Public Library.

Photographs of Reed Peggram and Arne Hauptmann in Italy and with Max Johnson: Courtesy of the AFRO American Newspapers Archives.

Index